Leadership
Series

The
Leadership
Series

Rayola Kelley

authorHOUSE®

AuthorHouse™
1663 Liberty Drive
Bloomington, IN 47403
www.authorhouse.com
Phone: 1-800-839-8640

Published by AuthorHouse   05/07/2013

ISBN: 978-1-4817-4626-7 (sc)
ISBN: 978-1-4817-4627-4 (e)

Library of Congress Control Number: 2013907421

Any people depicted in stock imagery provided by Thinkstock are models, and such images are being used for illustrative purposes only.
Certain stock imagery © Thinkstock.

This book is printed on acid-free paper.

Because of the dynamic nature of the Internet, any web addresses or links contained in this book may have changed since publication and may no longer be valid. The views expressed in this work are solely those of the author and do not necessarily reflect the views of the publisher, and the publisher hereby disclaims any responsibility for them.

Cover artwork © by Jeannette Haley

The painting of Moses on Mount Sinai receiving the Law on the front cover of this book is one of 14 murals painted by the artist, Jeannette Haley. These murals depict the life of Jesus and are displayed at the Chapel of the Resurrection in Bothell, Washington.

This material is part of the series of information being offered byGentle Shepherd Ministries for the purpose of the edification of the Body of Christ.

Except where otherwise indicated, all Scripture quotations in this book are taken from the King James Version of the Bible.

Dedication:

To Wanda Hiebert
For your friendship, courage, and inspiration.
You are truly a soldier of the cross.

CONTENTS

BOOK ONE: OVERCOMING

BOOK TWO: A MATTER OF AUTHORITY AND POWER

BOOK THREE: THE DYNAMICS OF TRUE LEADERSHIP

OVERCOMING

✝

Book One

INTRODUCTION

In my studies of Scripture, I found myself coming face-to-face with a certain reality that always challenged any fanciful or nominal Christian attitude or lifestyle that I was adopting. This particular reality had to do with overcoming. In my fanciful notions about the Christian life, I could hide behind the concept of God's love and grace. After all, in my mind God loved me enough to overlook my blatant inconsistencies and desired to show me grace during times of personal failures and struggles. I would console myself at such times that the deviations in my character and the prevailing selfish moods that were being expressed in my attitude would be glossed over as long as I showed some attempts to control and subdue them. However, when I came to the matter of overcoming, I could not ignore that such deviation of character and attitude would never be deemed tolerable or acceptable to God.

Scripture clearly points out that overcoming is not an option. It has always been the product of those who truly live the Christian life. Such a life is marked by the authority and power that ensures a truthful reality. It was not a matter of if one could overcome; rather, he or she must overcome if he or she is going to be in line with what the Bible has clearly presented as inspired by the Holy Spirit and established on the truth of God's Word.

It has taken me years to get my hands around the concept of what it means to overcome. The particular book you hold in your hands reveals what I have discovered about this subject. It is my prayer that the concept of "overcoming" ceases to be a vague or distant notion to the reader, but becomes a reality that clearly outlines that the Christian life is indeed a victorious overcoming life that is possible to obtain even in this present age in which we live.

1

Duty Calls

As Christians, we need to realize that we are at war. In the religious environment of our churches, it is easy to sit in our pews, sing upbeat songs about victory, and swing emotionally from one sentimental branch to another about the blessings attached to the Christian life. However, this life clearly entails a fierce battle that must be won outside of the sentimental hype that seems to be attached to the activities surrounding most modern churches.

As believers, we are called to be good soldiers.[1] Granted, if Christians have never been exposed to the concept of the military, it can prove hard to connect the seriousness and urgency attached to such a call. But, the reality is that the Bible is clear that we are being called to military duty. The Apostle Paul tells us that we must endure hardship as good soldiers who are no longer entangled in the affairs of the world.

To be a "good" soldier means we must be soldiers that benefit the kingdom of heaven. What does it take to be "good" at being a soldier of the cross? Can we as believers afford to take such a position lightly? Can we expect to be effective soldiers if we hold to unrealistic notions about the Christian life? Can we expect to survive if we fail to take seriously the call to active duty as soldiers of the kingdom of God, as well as being prepared to go into battle? To reiterate my point, the Apostle Paul tells us that we must endure as good soldiers who no longer become entangled in the affairs of the world. Clearly, the apostle made it clear that we are in a war.

The Apostle Paul was also clear about his declaration at the end of his life that he had indeed fought a good fight. He was quite aware of the battle that had to be fought and won on the battlefields of the world. He himself fought a good fight, a fight that proved beneficial to the kingdom he represented. He knew at the end of his earthly life that he had succeeded in putting up a "good" fight. He was ready to be offered up on the altars of the world without regret. He had, after all, finished

---

[1]   2 Timothy 2:3-4

the course and kept the faith. Now he looked forward to receiving a crown of righteousness.[2]

As I pondered Paul's declaration, I had to examine my own life. Would I be able to look back without regret and be able to declare that I had fought a good fight as a soldier? If I failed to recognize my calling in this area, how could I ever look back without such regret, yet it appeared that there are very few in the Christian realm that stress that we are in such a conflict. Even if the call to duty is not being done from our pulpits, it is clear that the Word of God has stipulated that we as believers have been entrusted with such a responsibility. Clearly, there will be no excuse when people stand before God as to why they failed to adhere to this particular call.

Perhaps it does help to have a military background to understand the call to duty. However, many may have never been exposed to such a background, but it still does not negate that our Christian responsibility in this matter has been made clear in Scripture. The Apostle Paul was never in the military, but the days in which he lived presented a clear picture of the soldier's life and duty.

The Roman Army was an army that was not only quite visible during the Apostle Paul's day, but it was active in the affairs of the matters that affected the empire. For those who were part of this army, it usually meant a lifetime of commitment that took the soldier to every part of the known world, as well as demanded excellent, sacrificial service. For many who said "goodbye" to their families, it would be the last they would see of them and their homes. These soldiers understood the commitment of being "good" soldiers for the empire. It was not just some career they embarked on, it was a sacrificial way of life that would most likely end in death.

Soldiers have other responsibilities. We can see this in regard to our army of brave men and women who risk their lives on the different battlefields of the world. They may have a family, other jobs, and various activities. But, in the back of their minds they, as soldiers, know that they are on call at all times. Being a soldier is their preeminent duty regardless of their other responsibilities. It will take center stage when there is a war. As soldiers, these individuals know that they do not have any say over their lives. They must be prepared and ready to go into battle at anytime,

---

[2] 2 Timothy 4:6-8

regardless of their other responsibilities. They must be prepared to take up arms at a minute's notice. There are no romantic or sentimental notions about the positions they hold in the army. It is a sobering reality that is meant to keep them grounded and realistic as to their duty.

"Good" soldiers are also trained to be soldiers, often seasoned by battles and always being prepared at all times to fight the good fight. They know how to stand when confronted with facing the enemy, withstand when the war becomes intense, and are prepared to stand when all seems lost and impossible. However, they had to be trained before they could stand, experience battles before they could withstand, and count the cost in order to remain standing.

This brings us to the real crux of the problem for most Christians. They have never been trained to be soldiers by the various pastors or churches of America. They have never been truly discipled to learn the disciplines of being a good soldier. They have never been seasoned by any battle because many have avoided the battles. Granted, they may have sung about such battles, waved their flags as if they have been victorious in some unseen battle, and marched around the confines of the church's sanctuary as if they have truly marched through the battle line and survived the onslaught of the enemies' firing. But, such activities are all show and pretense. These individuals have never been in the battle nor do they have any real consensus that there is a battle raging outside of their controlled environments. They have been hiding in some surreal environment that affords them the luxury or appearance of putting on the show of being "good" soldiers without tasting the harsh reality of what it takes to be an "excellent" soldier.

The sad reality about this scenario is that there have been battles raging in people's lives. Some are tasting defeat in their personal lives because they are not prepared to be soldiers. For others their homes could be falling apart because they are not fighting a good fight. As for the many members who make up local bodies, the battle may be raging outside the door of their churches as they sing their songs and march through the aisles, but they have no real consensus as to the battle that is before them. These attitudes reveal that many in the church do not understand the gravity of being soldiers. They have failed to heed the call to duty, thereby, they have never been trained to endure hardship as "good" soldiers. They are unprepared to face the real battles, untrained as to the disciplines of being a soldier, and unseasoned in fighting in a war that is real—a war where the enemies of our souls are playing for real.

One of the main reasons many Christians, who are being called to active duty as soldiers, are not prepared to heed their calling is because they have failed to develop a soldier's mentality. The purpose of boot camp is to get a hold of the mind of a civilian and transform it into a military mind. It is all about changing the attitude.[3]

It is for this reason that the main strongholds that keep people from realizing victory are found in the mind. Regardless of the best intentions, if a person's carnal attitude is not changed, he or she will never become a good soldier of the cross. Such a person will never be able to consecrate his or her body for the type of sacrificial service that will be required to win the war. Without thoughts, actions, and activities being tempered through the various disciplines of training, a person on the battlefield will prove to be counterproductive to those who may be in the thick of the battle.

As long as a person thinks as a civilian, he or she will never be a good soldier. The civilian mindset is one of independence. For the Christian, the civilian mindset is represented by the carnal mind.

A carnal mind is the opposite of the mind that has been transformed by the Spirit of God.[4] It has no intention of giving way to the mindset a soldier must develop. It wants to call the shots and determine when and how it is going to do something. However, a soldier is trained to listen for orders, prepared to obey such orders without question, and see a matter through regardless of the circumstances or obstacles that may loom before him or her.

Sadly, many Christians have not experienced boot camp. Jesus made reference to the radical change that must occur for the Christian to be a true soldier of the cross. He called His followers to be His disciples.

In such a disciplined life a true follower of Jesus will learn His voice, be ready to respond in obedience, and follow Him wherever He may lead. Such a life will not let half-hearted disciples slide by in a state of nominal commitment; rather, it will call them to a higher

---

[3] If you would like to know more about the discipline and ways of a soldier, see the book, *Godly Discipline*, in the third volume of the foundational series.

[4] Romans 8:5-11

and more excellent way. It will not allow them to be untrustworthy with obligations, but will require them to be responsible in taking their rightful position in this army. Since some Christians do not understand the disciplines in the Christian life, they can pretend to be soldiers, without ever becoming one.

For this reason many Christians are becoming casualties. They are not trained to recognize their real enemies nor are they equipped to fight them on whatever terrain they may encounter them. Many have not been trained to properly use their weapon, the Word of God, and as a result, such inexperienced soldiers mishandle their weapon. Subsequently, some Christians have become victims to what we refer to as "friendly fire." This occurs when there is confusion as to the enemy and the target. It speaks of an inexperienced soldier that is not clear about the orders. In such confusion and uncertainty, many Christians have been wounded by those who claim to be part of the army of God. They have been rendered ineffective because of the friendly firing taking place within their own Church body through gossip and maliciousness. Those who are mishandling their place in this army clearly do not understand the various aspects of the battle or the weapon they have been entrusted with. No doubt they still maintain and hold to their "civilian" mentality. They are unable to be part of an army that must learn to march together, fight together, and stand together no matter how fierce the battle may prove to be.

Once again, we are reminded that we, as soldiers of the cross, are being called to be more than those who slide by in their lives. We are being challenged to be good or beneficial to the whole of God's kingdom. If we are honest about our calling, we will have to admit that our Lord does not deserve nominal service; rather, He deserves the highest quality of service from each one of us. But, we must be sure that we develop a right attitude towards our call as soldiers of His great army.

"Good" soldiers will do what they have to do to prove beneficial to Jesus, His kingdom, and His army. It is for this reason that Christians must quit playing at being a soldier and become one. They must quit running around on the outskirts, giving the impression that they are part of this great army, and they must soberly find their place in it. They must quit waving flags of victory and actually pick up their weapons to secure victory. It is time for the army of God to get rid of the foolishness of their carnal, civilian ways that seem to be evident in their attitudes. They must prepare to go into a battle that will ultimately determine the eternal destination of that which is weighing in the balance.

As soldiers of the cross, we have been provided with a powerful weapon. We must not only know how to effectively use it, but we must maintain its effectiveness. We must understand the target or objective in order to be prepared to enter into any conflict. We also must understand the uniform and armor we have been issued.

Uniforms entail distinction and identification. As believers, we must realize what our uniform as soldiers of the cross consists of in order to best represent the kingdom of God. For Christians, there is only one uniform that will clearly distinguish them and that is humility.[5] Without the uniform of humility, the armor will not properly fit.

As addressed later in this book, armor is designed to nicely cover the body, but if we are wearing the wrong garb, it will prove to be ineffective. The one attitude that distinguishes a seasoned soldier from an immature, unrealistic, and zealous soldier in God's kingdom is humility. If humility is missing, the armor that has been issued to us as soldiers will not be effective in protecting us in battle.

Duty is calling each of us to take our place in God's army. As a believer, are you merely playing army or are you taking your position as a soldier? We each must realize that the war we are in is not a make-believe war. We also must recognize that our enemies are capable foes that are able to take us captive and destroy us on the battlefields of the world.

---

[5]   1 Peter 5:5

2

COMING TO TERMS WITH OUR WEAPON

Christians are in an incredible life and death war. We are called to be soldiers, and we must remember that no war is won unless battles are fought. In battles one side can win, while the other side appears defeated. However, the battles do not cease until the leader of one kingdom concedes complete surrender to the other side. Until then, there cannot be any declaration as to who is the winner.

For the winning side, there can appear to be various defeats along the way, but once again such defeats do not indicate the winner. Winning a war does not come down to how many battles have been won; rather, it comes down to how the war as a whole has been fought. Battles are to prove or test the resolve and character of those involved. All great wars have tried men's souls, defined the vision of the people, and established character that was seasoned and tempered by embracing that which was greater and worthy of consideration and sacrifice.

The war that must be fought and won in relationship to our spiritual lives is one that carries the necessary criteria. As believers, we already know the Victor. However, we must fight the good fight to endure and see this war through to the end. Whether we prove to be beneficial to the fight will not be determined by how many battles we win or lose, for the truth is Satan will win many battles along the way. After all, this is his world, his territory, and he is a powerful foe.

It is for this reason we must recognize that as soldiers of the cross, we will taste defeat and the bitterness of loss along the way. However, it will always come back to what we learned in each battle. What did the battle reveal about our character and about the enemy?

We can always feel infallible, self-sufficient, and even cocky when we perceive ourselves to be on the winning side. But, as soldiers, we cannot learn what it means to overcome unless we know the bitter taste of defeat. What will defeat reveal about us? It is out of defeat that the real cowards and heroes emerge. People can be quite zealous over a cause that creates a deceptive wave of infallibility and excitement, but let that wave crash against the shoreline of defeat, leaving people battered, bleeding, and uncertain, and then you will see those emerge who have counted the cost in their hearts.

Such times will reveal that these individuals' character and foresight goes beyond mere personal patriotism and sentimental zeal to something that is much greater. That which is greater, worthy, or more excellent than the individual will not necessarily benefit the person; rather, it will call the individual to avail him or herself to become part of that which would prove to be beneficial to a greater cause.

It is from the perspective of greatness that stout individuals are able to deem such acts or deeds as necessary, reasonable, and righteous. From this premise they are willing to count the cost to obtain that which is worthy of consideration and sacrifice. As the saying goes, "When times get tough, the tough get going." Obviously, those who are flying high off of zeal and sentiment will slide off into the shadows of obscurity, while those who have caught the fire of vision will become more resolved in their being to see it through to the end, regardless of personal cost.

As true soldiers of the cross, there is no retirement plan as long as we are stationed on the foreign fields of this present age. We will always walk toward our demise until we are finally called home from the battle front. Even though we may become weary, we must not be deterred from carrying out the mission. Our duty as soldiers will not be over until death opens the door to our final homecoming, or the enemy completely surrenders to the King of kings and Lord of lords.

By way of a reminder: the battles can occur at three fronts: the flesh, the world, and the devil. The greatest target is our faith.[1] Each enemy wants to rob us of it, undermine it in some way, or discredit it as being foolish, to insufficient to confront the times we live in, or a crutch that will fail us. Jude 3 is clear that we must contend for the faith that was first delivered to the saints. We are not trying to take new territory, but maintain the territory already committed to the kingdom of God with unfeigned faith towards our Lord, knowing that it alone will please Him.[2]

All battles must be initially won in the mind. We can easily faint in our minds; therefore, we need our minds to be transformed by the renewing of the Spirit. As soldiers, we need to stop being carnal in our

---

[1]   Jude 3

[2]   Hebrews 11:6

thinking, fleshly in practice, and worldly in attitude. It is for this reason that as soldiers of the cross we must not become entangled in the affairs of the world.[3] We must cease to think as civilians influenced by the age we live in, and began to think as soldiers of a superior kingdom. Our attitude and conduct will reveal that we have been changed in our way of thinking, tempered in our responses, disciplined in our conduct, and set apart by a high calling of excellence in service and purpose.

This brings us back to the fact that every great army is prepared to fight. This means that such armies not only are trained, but are provided with the uniform, armor, and weaponry. This brings us to the weapon. The uniform may set us apart and the armor may protect us, but it is the weapon that gives us the offensive advantage in the battles that must be fought.

When I was preparing to present the material in regards to overcoming, the Lord laid upon my heart the urgency to express the importance of the weapon He has given us to overcome. Sadly, the weapon that God has given us has been rendered useless or regarded as being obsolete, especially in the quasi religious atmosphere that presently exists. In many ways the effectiveness of this weapon has been stripped of its authority to have an impact on people's lives, even though our Lord and Savior used it effectively when confronted by the enemy. Clearly, people take liberty with how they choose to use this weapon by adding their own elements to it, or by taking away from its authority so as to use it to make some type of impression.

"Quasi" points to something that resembles something else, but is not the real thing. It is simply a poor, unrealistic substitute for what is real. For example, in Revelation 2:1-5, we read about the church of Ephesus. From all appearances this body of believers would be considered an acceptable church, but Jesus made it quite clear that something was missing. What was missing was that there was no real passion for Him. This body had left its first works of loving God, ultimately accepting a quasi environment. How do we, as believers, leave our first works, thereby losing passion for what must be considered important to us?

The passion we have towards Jesus is often inspired by the attitude we adopt towards our weapon. Every soldier is issued a weapon. Being part of the army of God is no different. The Lord has provided us

---

[3]   Romans 8:5-10; 2 Timothy 2:3-4; Hebrews 12:3

with a very effective weapon—His Word. The Apostle Paul reaffirmed this in Ephesians 6:17. The Apostle John in his first epistle tells us that the young men had overcome the wicked one because the Word of God abided in them.[4] We are also told in Hebrews 4:12 that it is a double-edge sword. It will not only cut through, it will dissect. Either way it will effectively hit its target.

When we consider that the largest chapter in the Bible, Psalm 119, is about the Word, we should realize how significant it is to our spiritual survival. It is considered our milk and meat.[5] We must learn how to partake of it to ensure our spiritual growth and maintain our strength in God.

Jesus brings out the significance of this weapon in His temptation in Matthew 4:1-11. He stated that we are to live by every word that has proceeded out of the mouth of God. We know the Bible is God's diary to us, His infallible Word that is to be considered law, irrefutable, and immovable. It is to be considered His testimony or record as to what is true and acceptable. It contains His precepts or pure doctrines, His judgments that are wise, His statutes or ordinances that contain shadows of what will be, and His commandments that must be adhered to in Spirit and truth.

Jesus used it to silence the tempter at each point of temptation. However, to overcome with the Word of God, we as soldiers, must believe it to stand against attacks, and we must obey it to withstand. It is not enough to know about this weapon, we must understand how it works and how to effectively use it. We must not wield it lightly at the enemy without understanding its authority, or pick it up to use against others until we have first learned to tremble before it in dread of misusing it in any counterproductive way. It is the mishandling of the Word of God that has ended up becoming "friendly fire" to other Christians who found themselves on the receiving end of the weapon. Left wounded, these individuals often crawl to the sideline in disillusionment, only to walk away scarred by unbelief.

Jesus instructed the poor in spirit, encouraged the seeking heart, challenged the self-righteous, and healed the wounded by the Word of God. He never used it as a weapon on people, but only on the enemies of God. When He did use it in confrontations, it was to lift up the truth

---

[4]   1 John 2:14

[5]   Hebrews 5:12-14; 1 Peter 2:2

as a light so that it could penetrate into the darkness of men's souls to awaken them to their real plight. Such handling of the Word allowed the Spirit of God to take the weapon and use it as a means to impact sin-laden souls with conviction, while the real example of righteousness was being upheld. Such righteous intent was to allow those seeking individuals to recognize the judgment that would be eventually unveiled, and hopefully flee into the loving arms of God, seeking His mercy.

It is for this reason that the Word has admonished us to study it so we can rightly divide it. We are warned that if we do mishandle it in unrighteousness that the wrath of God abides upon us. We have also been given examples of those who foolishly showed contempt for it like King Saul. To show contempt for it simply means that the individual has disobeyed God's simple instructions.[6]

It has taken me years to understand how to effectively use this weapon. I am not saying that I am an expert at using it now. However, through the years I have become more sober, wise, and experienced in handling it. Much of what I understand about using this weapon has been based on the destruction or chaos that has followed when I have misused it. I would swing it in relationship to doctrine so others could be impressed with how much I knew about it. I would raise it up as a means to harshly judge those who did not see it my way. I would console myself that I had some religious clout because it was apparent that I was reading and studying it. What I failed to realize is knowledge of the Word is a good platform in which to puff up oneself; but, it will never impart in me the one distinguishing fruit of a Christian, and that is *love*.

Jesus said of His Word that it is Spirit and life. In other words, if the Holy Spirit does not bring life to it, it will simply remain dead-letter facts and doctrines that will never have any life. The life in God's Word is the life of Jesus, and without His life being imparted in each of us by His Spirit, His words will have no meaning and purpose.

I discovered that when I abided in lifeless words, I was never able to possess the love of God. It is the love of God in me, being shed abroad in my heart that enables me to love God in the proper way and love others in a humble and meek way.[7] Occasionally, I still shake in my shoes as I realize that in the past I have mishandled the Word of God, often using

---

[6]   1 Samuel 15:22-23; Romans 1:18; 2 Timothy 2:15

[7]   John 6:63; Romans 5:5; 7:6; 2 Corinthians 3:6

it to judge God and others according to my foolish, immature, and self-righteous arrogance and notions.

As my attitude changed towards the Word of God, I discovered that it also changed towards the One who brought it forth. The more I grew to love God's Word, the more I fell in love with the Lord. The more I allowed the Holy Spirit to impact my life with its truths, the more I was able to impact the lives of others.

It is at this point that I would like to say this to religious leaders: You are responsible to teach the Word, not the popular philosophies of the world. Do not deceive yourselves, you will be held accountable for your attitude towards the Word and how you handled it. If you do not live by the Word and according to the Word, I have this statement to make to you. "Shame on you! Shame on you for serving as hireling shepherds who do not feed on the Word of God for wisdom as a means to properly and effectively lead Jesus' sheep! Shame on you for failing to seek its instruction in righteousness, submit to its work of spiritual sanctification, and receive its ongoing revelation of the great redemption that awaits God's sheep! You will give an account and on the day of reckoning, and you will have a greater indictment brought against you."

Today I am zealous about the Word. My excitement towards it abounds as I discover its many treasures, witness the unfolding of the wisdom that can be found in its mysteries, and experience the depth of its life in its revelations. At times I stand awed by it, unable to describe its unfolding wonderment, while at other times I feel overwhelmed, undone, and totally exposed by its ever penetrating light.

In my zeal towards the Word of God I want to impart the same depth to others. In my excitement I so desire Christians to catch the same passion for it as I have for it. In my new discoveries, I want to shout them from the roof tops to create the same type of liberation or joy that often floods my soul. I want the powerful change it has brought to my life to be a reality in those who suffer from leanness in their souls, caused by the various detours and rabbit trails of the world.

I have a love for the Word of God. However, the truth of the matter is I cannot impart such zeal, excitement, joy, change, and love for it in other people. The reason I cannot accomplish such a feat is because I cannot obey it for other people. The Word remains surface and insignificant to some Christians because it has not been engrafted into their souls. To engraft the Word into one's soul, a person must be a doer of it and not simply a hearer.[8]

In order to obey the Word, a person has to approach it with the intent to believe it. "Believing" it means "amen, so be it, for it is so." In other words, the Word is truth; therefore, it will be upheld for it is what it is. It will never change no matter the debate that may ensue. It will never be demeaned regardless of unbelief. It will never lose its power regardless of how much it is outlawed or scoffed at by the despots of the world. It is what it is—God's eternal, unchangeable Word. By faith we approach it to believe it, and in good faith we embrace it as truth, and because of faith we obey it.

Faith comes by hearing, and hearing by the Word of God. The Word can only profit us when faith is applied to it. We clearly have to put feet to our faith by obeying the Word to inherit the promises of God.[9] This is why unfeigned faith is under attack. If faith is absent when we approach the Word of God, it will never become our powerful weapon that will enable us to stand and withstand in the battles that we will find ourselves embroiled in. We will be void of the mirror that will enable us to discern where we are in our spiritual life, and gain our spiritual bearings when the forces of hell rage against us.

What kind of attitude do you possess towards the Word of God? Do you consider it your weapon against the enemies of your soul? It is important as a soldier of the cross you understand how to properly use the weapon that God has provided for you.

---

[8]   James 1:21-22

[9]   Romans 10:17; 2 Corinthians 5:7; Hebrews 4:2: 6:12; James 2:26

3

BARREN WASTELAND

It has always amazed me that Jesus was led out to the wilderness by the Holy Spirit to be tested by Satan. The wilderness represents a barren wasteland. However, it is a stark reminder of what temptation often reveals about man. It reveals that spiritually, his soul is a barren wasteland. Granted, there is potential for life to express itself in a fruitful way from the arenas of his soul, but when it comes to the ways of man, these ways lead to a barren wasteland. This wasteland is often expressed by parched terrain that appears lifeless and resonates with that which speaks of death in some way. Such a terrain reveals man's true spiritual state. This state shows him to be incapable of surviving the harsh elements surrounding him without the necessary intervention of someone who will actually save him and lead him to a place of life and purpose.

Temptation is forever revealing the spiritually poverty-stricken state of man. Such a barren place strips man of all pretences. He may be able to live in the wilderness, but his life will prove to be difficult, the way he travels hard and challenging, and his end marked by sorrow and death.

This brings us to the first enemy that we must confront as soldiers of the cross. The first enemy is what has rendered man to be a spiritually barren wasteland before God. It is the flesh.

People struggle with the concept of the flesh. It points to the body, but it also points to our appetites that can rule our lives. Our appetites insist on, or determine, what we partake of with the intent to experience what we consider to be the essence of our lives. The body is how we interact with the environment around us. It is within the fleshly tabernacle that we express our person. Without the physical body we could not function in the world we live in. For this reason our various activities in the body appear harmless when we partake of the things of the world. Clearly, our bodies have needs and cannot help that they are quite dependent on the surrounding environment. However, what is natural to the flesh can be a source of perversion to the Lord that results in personal oppression and possession of our souls.

The real challenge of the flesh has to do with its appetites. These appetites can quickly turn into lust. In turn, lust becomes subject to the spirit operating in this world, causing a person to run amuck.[1] Although appetites are natural to the functions of the flesh, when they become obsessive, demanding, commanding, and addictive, they will make people enemies of the cross of Christ. The Apostle Paul brings this out in Philippians 3:17-19,

> Brethren, be followers together of me, and mark them which walk so as ye have us for an ensample. (For many walk, of whom I have told you often, and now tell you even weeping, that they are the enemies of the cross of Christ; Whose end is destruction, whose God is their belly, and whose glory is in their shame, who mind earthy things.)

We know that the battle of the flesh takes place within our souls. Even though you would think the battle is a fleshly battle, it entails a spiritual conflict. Obviously, we need to take responsibility for our fleshly appetites and discipline them. The Apostle Paul brings this out in 1 Corinthians 9:27, "But I keep under my body, and bring it into subjection; lest that by any means, when I have preached to others, I myself should be a castaway."

It is vital that we understand in what way the flesh works because this is where the real problem lies. In Galatians 5:19-21, we are told what works of the flesh will manifest in our lives. The list can easily make us cringe. By being honest about what each of these works constitutes, we have to agree with the Apostle Paul's evaluation about the flesh when he stated that there is no good or beneficial thing in it.[2] The flesh is clearly perverted, tainted, treacherous, and unacceptable in light of a holy God. Perhaps we can take small comfort in the fact that we might not be guilty of manifesting all of these works, but the harsh reality is that if we possess such works in our lives, the Bible is very clear that we will not inherit the kingdom of God.

When we study the temptation of Jesus in the wilderness, we must note what Satan tempts first. It was the flesh. What was the real

---

[1] Ephesians 2:2

[2] Romans 7:18

temptation of the flesh? Clearly, after not eating forty days and nights, no one would have begrudged Jesus for eating the bread. It would have been understandable for Him to bow down to the appetites of the flesh. Preserving the physical part of the body is the means by which each of us sustains life on this earth.

However, the real test for Jesus was not simply partaking of the bread of the world to sustain Himself, the real test was whether He would see the physical bread as that which sustained life itself. It is at this point that you must consider what constitutes life and what sustains such a life.

When it comes to the flesh, the life that is often promoted by the flesh has nothing to do with life, but a lifestyle. Granted, we need to eat to live in this world, but the bread that feeds our flesh cannot give us life. At best it will simply sustain us in our present existence. To think that life is tied into the physical realm is to look to that which is temporary.

The physical world can only sustain a form of life or existence that has no real substance behind it. Jesus put it best when He stated that most people followed Him in pursuit of physical bread and not the spiritual bread of heaven that possessed eternal life. The tragedy is that a man will bow down to his fleshly appetites and sell his soul in order to partake of physical bread that is only capable of sustaining him on a temporary basis. It is for this reason that Jesus emphatically stated that we do not live by the bread (of this world) alone, but rather we live by every word that proceeds out of the mouth of God.[3]

This brings us to the real crux of the battle with the flesh. What makes the battle spiritual in regard to the physical aspect of our lives is that the flesh wars against the Spirit of God. Man does not simply represent a physical life that is housed in a body. He is also spirit and soul. As Jesus pointed out, to feed that which is unseen requires that which is eternal.[4] We know that His Word is eternal. Therefore, much of this battle is not fought or won on a physical plane. Rather, it is a spiritual battle due to the unseen cancer of the soul: sin. Sin is not a matter of simply trespassing the Law of God, but it also has to do with who we are, who we become due to who or what we serve, and who we allow ourselves to become based on what or who influences us.

---

3   Matthew 4:4; John 6:26-27, 35
4   Galatians 5:17; 1 Thessalonians 5:23; 1 Peter 1:24-25

We have already made reference to the appetites or lust of the flesh that can end up driving the flesh into extreme, insane, and destructive ways. Such lusts will become gods that demand we bow down to them in order to satisfy them on a continual basis. However, there is another aspect of the flesh that greatly affects it besides its appetites, and that is the self-life that it is governed by.

The self-life points to our selfish, fallen disposition. What governs the self-life is another product of the flesh—pride. Pride sits on the throne of the self-life and declares that the flesh has every right to partake of the things of the world to experience life such as happiness, satisfaction, and contentment. Like the world, the happiness that is experienced in the flesh is temporary, while satisfaction proves to be fleeting and contentment fickle. Scripture tells us in the Beatitudes found in Matthew 5:1-12 that happiness is a matter of having a right attitude. God's Word also goes on to reveal that lasting satisfaction is associated with righteousness, while contentment is something learned within the confines of godly living.[5]

There are people who try to personally put down the works of the flesh, but if they have not learned to recognize pride and avoid giving it any real audience or consideration, it will eventually convince them through logic and debate that the flesh has every right to feed its lusts. After all, the person has worked hard and earned the right to experience certain pleasures in this world. On the other hand, if things do get out of hand and failure and consequences are incurred, pride will turn around and unmercifully judge the moral deviation and destructive fruits of the flesh.

It is for this reason that Jesus' second temptation in the wilderness was directed at what is considered the pride of life. Satan was daring Him to prove that He was who He was. Jesus did not have to prove who He was because Satan full well knew His true identity. The enemy of our souls is not interested in the truth, he simply wanted Jesus to give way to fleshly pride and lower Himself to do that which would prove foolish, vain, and useless.

All battles must be initially won in the flesh before a person can be victorious in any other battles or on any other frontline. The flesh is what serves as the platform upon which the influences of the world will take

---

[5]   Matthew 5:6; Philippians 4:11; 1 Timothy 6:3-11

center stage. It is the inroad in which Satan gains access into a person's way of thinking and being. If the flesh was not in operation, there would be no real personal terrain that could be taken captive and oppressed by this enemy of God.

It is for this reason that as soldiers of the cross, the flesh must be the first enemy we overcome. Since it is natural for us to give way to the flesh, we must understand how weak or vulnerable it is in temptation. Jesus said it best when He stated that the spirit is willing but the flesh is weak.[6]

The flesh is fiercely independent and will refuse to submit to authority if a matter does not serve its desires or purpose. It wants the right and freedom to do as it pleases in order to satisfy its whims or appetites when it feels like it. The flesh is moody, unpredictable, fickle, and silly. It considers how a matter will make it feel according to its appetites and how it will make it look according to its pride. It rides high on vain imaginations as it recklessly heads for the shorelines of destruction.

The fickle ways of the flesh are often what determines the prevailing mood that is emitted from our person via our attitude. Such moods reveal much about a person's inward disposition or environment. When pride is reigning and the flesh is declaring its right to partake of whatever it desires, a person can prove to be mean-spirited, rude, obnoxious, and crude.

This brings us back to the battle that rages in our souls between the flesh and the Spirit of God. The Spirit of God convicts us of sin, but the flesh fights against such conviction. The Holy Spirit is the one who reproves us of sin by bringing to the light the righteous examples and teachings of Jesus, but the flesh will downplay such a contrast with false humility, self-righteous piousness, or self-justification.[7]

The Holy Ghost will ultimately warn of judgment that is upon all who will not flee to receive God's provision. Such people already stand condemned outside of Christ's work of redemption. Granted, pride might comply outwardly to some righteous standard by putting on some religious cloak or cry foul because the way seems too narrow, hard, outdated, or unrealistic. But, in people's attempts to scoff at, show dishonor towards, demote, downplay, or do away with standards of

---

6   Matthew 26:41

7   John 16:7-13

righteousness, they will bring judgment on themselves. Ultimately, such attitudes will show contempt towards God's Word.

Why do people have such contempt towards God's Word? It is because its truths will never adjust to what is dishonorable and profane. These people's pride will end up raging against all righteousness, and scoffing at that which is excellent and eternal, while refusing to compromise or bow down to its arrogant and foolish ways.

The flesh is totally contrary to the Holy Spirit. For this reason it is unable to know anything that is of the Spirit of God. Flesh can do nothing more than to walk according to its own understanding. For this reason the Apostle Paul stated that if we walk in the Spirit, we will not fulfill the lust of the flesh, and if we are led by the Spirit, we will not be under the Law of God that calls for judgment upon all unrighteousness. Instead of reaping the corruption of the flesh, we will reap life everlasting. In fact, we will display the fruit of the Spirit, which no law can bring any claims of wrong doing or accusation against those who walk in such a manner.[8]

What can we learn from the Scriptures regarding the flesh? The flesh can play all the games it will, but it still remains under a death sentence. It can put on all the cloaks of personal "goodness" it desires to cover up its wicked ways, preferences, and false pretenses, but it is an imposter when it comes to the things of God. The flesh can give an appearance of loving and pleasing God, while secretly resenting Him. It can cleverly hide contempt towards His truths and ways, but in the end all of its acts will be brought to the light and judged by the righteous Judge. It can mock righteousness, but in the end it will die in its sins and never inherit the kingdom of God.

The truth is the physical body will go back to being dust in the ground of the earth, but for those who live by the flesh, their spirit and soul will enter eternity as a lifeless, lost soul that will be used up in the tormenting bowels of hell as these individuals experience utter, complete spiritual ruin.

It is clear that we must overcome this enemy of our souls. We cannot be casual about being victorious. The battle with the flesh will prove to be a daily battle, but it is one that we, as soldiers of the cross, must effectively wage and win.

---

[8] 1 Corinthians 2:10-14; Galatians 5:16, 18, 22-23; 6:7-9

23

4

CONFRONTING THE FLESH

We have been considering the barren wasteland of the flesh. It is a barren wasteland because there is no life in it. Due to sin, the works that originate with it are considered to be filthy and perverted before God, resonating with the seeds of death and destruction. Since it operates within an earthly plane from the premise of a worldly understanding, it opposes that which is unseen, heavenly, and eternal.

As soldiers of the cross, we must overcome the flesh or we will in some way succumb to it. If we do not overcome the flesh, we will never finish the course that leads us to a heavenly inheritance. As already stipulated, overcoming is not an option. We have been given all that we have need of to overcome. However, we cannot overcome in our own strength. Overcoming has to do with enduring to the end when one's character is being tested and refined in the fiery ovens of the world.

When it comes to overcoming, soldiers of the cross will experience many personal defeats. They will know the anguish of defeat, the despair of failure, the fires of adversity, the dark night of the soul, and the bitterness of hopelessness. At such times the soldier of the cross must remember that he or she cannot overcome in his or her personal strength. It requires the active participation of the Holy Spirit. As stated in Zechariah 4:6, nothing is done with strength or might alone, but everything is done by the Spirit of God. It is the Spirit of God who must temper strength, channel power, and discipline our steps to endure each battle. After all, overcoming has to do with enduring to the end.

Endurance clearly points to character being tested and refined in spite of the gentle temperance, channeling, and disciplining of the Holy Spirit. As soldiers we must be battle ready, while remaining pliable under the leading of the Spirit. We must be sensitive to hear the voice of our commander and ready to stand when confronted by our enemies.

The problem with most Christians is that they can pride themselves in overcoming that which poses no temptation or inward battle. They can judge what they deem to be personal victories as to their spiritual condition when they feel on top of a matter. But, the real test or battle does not come in areas that pose no real threat or challenge. The test of character has to do with going against the grain of that which is not comfortable, pleasant, or could end in utter defeat. It means doing that which is contrary to what is considered normal, acceptable, or reasonable by the world.

Once again, we must be reminded of our enemies. We must overcome three different foes: the flesh, the world, and Satan. In order to effectively overcome these enemies, we must understand how each one affects us. This requires us to understand the nature of our enemies and the type of terrain that each enemy is after, as well as the target.

Scripture is clear about the target of each enemy. It is simple, they are after our faith. These enemies are not after any "old faith" for there are many so-called "pseudo", "heretical" presentations of faith. These enemies are after the one true faith that was first delivered to the saints. For this reason Jude 3 tells us that we must wrestle or contend for the faith.

One might wonder why faith is the target. It comes down to what or who people put their reliance on, their trust in, or give way to in light of service and devotion.

In the previous chapter the works of the first enemy, the flesh, were exposed. We know that if the flesh was not present, we would not find ourselves in a battle. In our fleshly existence, pride rules from the throne of the self-life, while undisciplined lusts can drive our flesh into obsession, oppression, and possession. God's kingdom is never driven by the arrogance of pride or the foolishness of fleshly lusts. It never has to defend what is right and real because truth will ultimately reign. It never has to give way to any form of contention and strife, for it is an immovable rock in the midst of an ever-changing and untrustworthy world. Clearly, the flesh wars against the Spirit of God. It prefers, demands, and pursues after the tangible things of the world, rather than the unseen, eternal things of God.

This brings us to the terrain that the flesh desires to take captive. The flesh must entice and ensnare our *affections*. Once the flesh takes our affections captive, we will find ourselves looking to the world to feed and satisfy its appetites. From this premise pride is quick to justify and secure what is preferred and pleasing to sustain the life it thinks it is worthy of.

It is easy to see how the flesh ensnares our affections. Through our carnal minds, pride uses what appears to be logical to set us up to fall into the lustful traps of the flesh. It convinces us that we have a right to partake of the things of the world. After all, we have the right to be happy, satisfied, and content. Obviously, we need to believe there is something good in us, worthy of such consideration; therefore, we should be able to feel good about our lives. We are also able to console ourselves by doing good deeds so we can feel fine about our present state, even though such deeds are selfish and self-serving. During this time our affections are being stirred up towards those things that offer to bring pleasure and temporary happiness to us.

However, our real selfish motives are exposed when we do not see the results we desire. We become angry, insolent, and mean-spirited. It is at this time that the Holy Spirit can begin to bring conviction to us. Since our pride wants to maintain personal goodness and rights, our flesh will begin to war against the conviction of the Holy Spirit as we struggle with the evaluation that is being upheld against our so-called "righteousness".

How do we overcome the flesh when there is no good thing in it? How do we stop the war raging between the flesh and the Spirit of God? Today the battle between these two enemies rages in many people's lives, including Christians, but many never overcome. The reason that very few overcome is because their strategy is all wrong. They do not understand the enemy, and if they did, they would have to change their strategy. Such change would require genuine repentance.

The Apostle John gave us some valuable insight into the problem that rests in most people's lives when it comes to God. In Revelation 2:1-7, we read about the church at Ephesus. From all appearances this body of believers would be considered acceptable to many in the religious realm. It matters little how religious people evaluate a matter. What matters is how God regards the condition or works of people. If He has a problem with the condition or works of His people, it is up to us to take note of how He perceives a matter and quickly come into agreement with His evaluation.

Jesus commended the church at Ephesus, but He also had a "but" that meant that it came up short in some way. He told the body that He had one thing against it, and that was that it had left its first love. This means that these believers had strayed away from their first works, which is to love God with everything in them. It is easy to fail to do our first works as we emphasize religious piousness and activities. We can do all things right in the physical realm and have it totally wrong when it comes to the unseen matters of God.

The Church of Christ must always choose the excellent way of the love of God, love for God, and love because of God.[1] If we have the love of God, we will be compelled to do what is right and excellent in regard to God. If we love God, we will do right by God because He is worthy of such excellence. And, when our love finds its origins in God, we will do right by others because we can do no less than that which is reasonable and acceptable in light of the goodness of our Lord.

Love is an active choice and an enduring commitment. We choose what we will love. In religious fervor it is easy to lose sight of our first works, but in doing so we also stray away from that which will balance out our lives. We will become lost to our greatest point of inspiration, while our soul experiences leanness and restlessness because something is missing. Without the love of God, Christianity will become mediocre, causing us to experience a crisis in our faith. As a result, we must come back to our first works to be revived and refreshed in our souls.

The flesh has no such love for God. It is selfish in disposition and will compete for all devotion. It wants to be considered and catered to; therefore, it will war against any conviction or reproof of the Spirit in such matters.

The battle between the flesh and Spirit can best be described by the two thieves on the cross. Hanging between the two thieves on the cross was Jesus, the Son of the Living God. One thief was daring Jesus to prove His identity by saving them in their sin, while the other thief rebuked the other one by stating that they deserved to die for their deeds, but Jesus did not deserve such treatment.[2] The pride of our flesh is always daring Jesus to cease to be and serve the disgusting, deadly whims of the flesh. On the other side of the equation, the Spirit is trying to spare the person of death by bringing him or her to the realization that Jesus' death is not about saving us *in* sin, but sparing us of the rightful judgment that hangs over all sin.

The battle between the flesh and the Spirit comes down to the flesh refusing to accept the conviction of the Holy Spirit in regard to how God evaluates a matter.[3] It does not want to believe that its very actions and attitudes are all that bad or deserve such judgment. It wants to deem

---

[1]   1 Corinthians 12:31-13:13

[2]   Luke 23:39-43

[3]   John 16:7-11

that there is some good in it, and if given enough time, the good will outweigh the bad. In essence, it does not want to have to rely on or become dependent on God to experience salvation. It wants to maintain a self-sufficient status apart from God.

God's evaluation about the flesh is clear. That which is of the flesh will not inherit the kingdom of God. It is corrupt through and through.[4] We must repent of its works in order to change strategy. We must recognize that the flesh cannot overcome itself, and that it is the enemy of our soul and lies at the core of the very problem we must humbly and honestly confront and overcome. Yet, many are trying to overcome the flesh with the flesh. They will not give way to the strategy or work of God. They refuse to admit that it is not a fleshly battle but a spiritual battle that requires the intervention of God for us to overcome it.

Once we turn from the old strategy, we must adopt a new one. We do this by redirecting our affections away from the works and ways of the flesh towards that which is heavenly, powerful, spiritual, and eternal. This requires us to take back our affections by setting our focus on that which we must choose to love.

By setting our focus on the right source, we will be able to reclaim and once again take ownership of our affections and direct them towards the person of our focus. It is for this reason that the Apostle Paul gave this instruction in Colossians 3:1-2, "If ye, then, be risen with Christ, seek those things which are above, where Christ sitteth on the right hand of God. Set your affection on things above, not on things on the earth."

In order to take our affections back, we must disown the rule and claims of pride. If we do not disown the rule and claims of pride, the natural inclination and tendency of our affections will remain towards darkness and not the light of Christ. Jesus stated that man naturally prefers darkness because his deeds are wicked.[5] The deeds that Jesus spoke of are the deeds of the flesh. In his selfish state, man prefers the wicked works and ways of the flesh to the penetrating, convicting light of the Spirit. We can only change such preferences through repentance, redirecting our affections, and choosing to come back to our first works.

In order to make the right choices in regard to God, we must first declare a death sentence on the flesh through the application of the cross.

---

4   Romans 7:18; Galatians 5:17-21; 6:7-8
5   John 3:19-21

We must silence its claims as far as its right to exist. The application of the cross to the flesh will entail a daily exercise on our part. With the Apostle Paul, we must die daily. We do this by mortifying the members of our flesh. The apostle related the intensity of this challenge as a race that must be won, as well as a boxing match that requires the members of his flesh to be knocked to the ground in utter defeat. This boxing match was the only way he was assured that he would avoid being considered a reprobate or castaway in his own faith.[6]

We must never underestimate the flesh. Jesus admitted that even though the spirit is willing, the flesh is weak. It will easily give into temptation. It is a coward at best and a raving lunatic at worse, but it is also shrewd. It can come across as being noble while being nailed to the cross. However, if you do not first deny it of its right to exist because it is a criminal worthy of death, a traitor to your soul, and an enemy of God, it will simply become a noble martyr that will pretend that it is dying in an honorable way. In such pretense it is trying to throw you off long enough to regain the sympathy of your affections. At this time, you can deem that the flesh is not so bad after all. It is willing to die. It is at this point that many believe it will die, or they might even let it off the cross thinking it has learned its lesson; therefore, it can be rehabilitated in some way.

We must recognize at all times that the flesh is a fool, an absolute despot with its pride, lustful ways, carnal mind, and worldly attitudes. Its pride must be denied any audience to present its arrogant case in the courts of the mind, and the ways of the flesh must receive their due death sentence daily. We must purge ourselves from what is a matter of dishonorable character and conduct, and flee all youthful lust in order to pursue what is righteous, faithful, loving, and peaceful.[7]

We can overcome the flesh if we believe God and give way to the convicting power of His Spirit. We must agree with God concerning the works of the flesh and properly confront each one. We must also remember that all spiritual battles must be won in regard to our flesh before they can be won on any other front.

---

[6]   1 Corinthians 9:24-27; 15:31; Colossians 3:5

[7]   2 Timothy 2:19-22

5

SATAN'S TERRITORY

We are in a life and death battle. As previously stated, the target is our faith, and the enemies of our faith must gain inroads into our lives to rob us of pure faith, kill the faith that is present, and destroy any hope of possessing unfeigned faith in the end. In order to be victorious, we have to understand the three main enemies that will attack our resolve to maintain a sincere faith towards God. They are the flesh, the world, and Satan.

We must develop the attitude of a good soldier. Good soldiers understand who, what, and how each of these enemies are able to gain inroads into lives when it comes to the battles that must be fought along the way. Such soldiers do not go off to war half-cocked, but in sobriety as they realize the responsibility and seriousness of fighting a good fight. They do not assume they will win; rather, they realize that even if the odds are against them, they must be willing to risk all, even their very lives, to maintain the territory that has been entrusted to them. A good example of this is the revolutionary war. The war was not about gaining new territory, but about maintaining the present terrain that could quickly come under siege by the tyrannical dictatorship of those who had no vision or real concern for the people they were bent on conquering and controlling.

We have to understand the three main enemies of man's spiritual well-being. To be good Christian soldiers, we must come to terms with who, in what way, and how each of these enemies gain advancement when it comes to the battles we find ourselves embroiled in. We have been discussing that the territory man must maintain on a personal level entails the soul. However, each enemy is posed to take possession of different aspects of our soul.

The first enemy that we considered was the flesh. We know how it operates but let us consider how the flesh operates in comparison to the next enemy, that of the world. The flesh wants to take us captive to prevent us from recognizing our potential in the kingdom of God, but the world wants to own, possess, and control us to determine who we become. The flesh wants us to feed its appetites to keep it content and happy in its doomed state, while the world wants us to serve it in utter abandonment to keep us blinded or indifferent to the impending judgment and consequences that await us in our vulnerable, fallen state. The flesh wants us to give way to its desires, but the world wants us to become subject to its demands. The flesh will pervert all that it comes into contact with, while the world has the capacity of perverting our needs, defiling our understanding, and profaning our points of agreement or fellowship. The flesh gives us temporary times of ecstasy, while the world creates pinnacles of excitement that end with people experiencing the down side of emptiness, dissatisfaction, and depression. Both enemies are shrewd and must not be underestimated or lightly confronted. They both know how to gain the influence and power in our lives to take us captive in order to undermine our faith towards God, by subtly replacing our confidence in Him with reliance on them.

As previously pointed out, the flesh represents the barren territory of man. The terrain that must be taken captive in regard to the flesh is our affections. This brings us to the type of attack the world can launch against us. What is the nature of the world, and what must it capture in order to destroy our capacity and resolve as soldiers of the cross?

Like the flesh, it is vital that we understand what constitutes the makeup of the world. The flesh represents what is natural, but the world represents what is necessary in which to function and live. Since we have need of the world to function, it also represents what would be considered normal to our fleshly needs and acceptable to our self-life.

This brings us to the real crux of the battle we have in regard to the world. When it comes to the flesh, we are aware that we are in a battle with it. After all, we know when the flesh is demanding its own way in a dishonorable fashion and that it will be blatantly opposed to the conviction of the Spirit, along with any tenderness that our conscience may pose to us. The battle between the Spirit and the flesh requires us to logic, debate, and justify wrong actions. However, the battle with the world is not that obvious because in most cases the world represents that which is neither good nor bad. For example, the things of the world such as money, entertainment, food, transportation, health aids, etc. are a matter of life. We need some of these things to survive, while we can also enjoy other things without sinning. We also must partake of other provisions of the world to ensure our ability to function. Such matters seem harmless enough so how do we live in this present age knowing that it can in some subtle way become an enemy of our soul, bent on destroying us?

To understand the battle that rages when it comes to the world, we have to understand that there are three definitions of it. It is only by discerning and understanding these definitions can we begin to recognize where the battle rages. Until people have clarity in this matter, they remain confused about the world. Even though Scripture warns us of the destructive and powerful influence of the world, it is hard for people to see how the world perverts reality and causes man to go amiss as his life falls into disarray. This brings us to the first definition of the world. The first aspect of the world points to people. God so loved the world or the people of the world that He sent His only begotten Son to secure salvation for them.[1]

The second definition of the world has to do with creation. God created all that we see to benefit man. In other words, God created everything man would have need of to live and function in the physical, emotional, and even the spiritual realm. If man cares to consider creation in the proper way, he will see that it speaks of and points to the provision, artistic, majestic, and powerful capacity of its Creator. We are told that God has shown Himself in creation, and that man will have no excuse for not believing in the existence, character, and working of the Godhead.[2]

The third definition has to do with the systems of the world. The word "system" is what will bring to light the real crux of our battle with the world. System has to do with organizing or arranging something in order to distribute, control, or determine how something will function or operate. Once again, such organization would seem harmless enough, but if used incorrectly, it provides a platform in which various abuses can be implemented to gain power or control. This power and control serves as a means to influence and dictate to people. Ultimately, the test will come down to the motivation behind such organization.

We are told who the god is behind these systems and what spirit motivates them. The god is Satan who serves as the designer of and

---

[1]   John 3:16

[2]   Genesis 1-2; Matthew 6:25-34; Acts 17:27-28; Romans 1:19-20; Colossians 1:15-18

magistrate or judge over these systems. He is also the spirit which is described as being the prince or ruler of the power of the air who operates through these systems. His spirit is what works in the children of disobedience.[3] From this perspective the world definitely serves as Satan's territory.

These systems of Satan have taken God's creation, including people, captive. We know that God created the world for man's benefit. Every good gift comes from God and He has provided everything we have need of to live. However, Satan has taken all that God has created and systemized or organized it in such a way as to cause people to look to his system to maintain some semblance of life.

A great example of how man can be organized according to Satan's design, and come under the control of the spirit of the world can be seen in Cain's life. Cain is the first man to build a city. Keep in mind, he was a murderer and rebellious. He had no desire to subject himself to the righteous authority of God. We are told in Genesis 4:16 that Cain went out from the presence of the Lord. The absence of God's authority sets up the environment in which man will form his own government.

The purpose for entangling man into the world's systems is to cause him to become dependent on the world for his life or well-being. Man must now barter in some way with Satan and his systems to live or have any real right to function. Even though we are told that God owns the cattle on a thousand hills, we must barter within the confines of Satan's oppressive systems to be able to enjoy or partake of any part of God's creation. The harsh reality is that unless we are willing to first give way or pay homage to Satan's system, we could very well become oppressed or deprived in some way.[4]

We need to understand how these systems work. For example, food has been wrapped up in an exchange system to force us to look to the world for our provision instead of God. Knowledge has been confined to a system of indoctrination where man has been educated to exalt worldly knowledge in an idolatrous fashion, while negating and scoffing at the truths of God. Such indoctrination sets men up to become ultimate pawns in the hands of the elite as these indoctrinated individuals prove to be fools in their conceit.

---

[3]   2 Corinthians 4:3-4; Ephesians 2:2
[4]   Psalm 50:11; James 1:17

Success is often wrapped up in temporary wealth of the world that is based on an economic system that proves to be nothing more than a house of cards that can be blown down by any wind of change that the god of this world may send our way. Government, which often controls all the functions of the other systems of Satan, can gain control of every area of our lives and prove to be the most oppressive through taxation and rules that are often unfair and hypocritical.

The flesh justifies its wicked ways, but the world puts forth propaganda in order to seduce people into its wicked reality. We can see the spewing of propaganda in the political arena. The political system operates in lies, flatteries, and false promises that have been cleverly refined to cause people to buy the propaganda of the world. Propaganda is nothing more than twisted truth that hides an unsavory attitude and agenda.

Then there is also the religious system that creates a quasi environment at best and a radical, insane environment at worst. We can see how this system has influenced the professing Church. Much of the Church has been dulled down by the indoctrination of the world, weighed down by the demands of the age, and burdened down by the vanity of the world's various systems. The religious system can often prove the most dangerous of all systems. While touting religious causes, it can also best represent the cruelty and hatred of Satan towards those who refuse to buy into his lies and deception.

It is for this reason that James 4:4 tells us if we are a friend of these systems, we are an enemy of God. Clearly, these systems are meant to replace any reliance and trust that we should and must have in God. We may be in this world, but we are not to be part of it, belong to it, or look to it as our provider, solution, and hope.

The Apostle John gives us insight into how these worldly systems operate in his first epistle.[5] We are told not to love the world because if we do, the love of the Father will not be in us. Then John goes on to say that the world is made up of the lust of the flesh, the lust of the eyes, and the pride of life. The world will clearly pass away with all of its lust, but those who do the will of God will live forever.

The systems of the world are designed to attract the lusts of our flesh. Take advertisement for example. It is meant to entice the lust of

---

[5]   1 John 2:15-17

our flesh through sights, smells, and sounds. Consider the knowledge of the world, it is meant to set up our pride and entangle it into a false reality. Think about the ways of success. They cause us to pursue false images and the proverbial "carrot" that represents what will supposedly make us happy, satisfied, and credible. However, such pursuits prove empty, illusive, and mocking in the end.

What about the religious systems? Satan has designed an array of religious roads and messages in which to offer to man as to how he can be saved. However, they all go back to the same source of rhetoric, darkness, and false hope. For example, there is the road of "good works," "the road that purports "the good guy" presentation, and the road of "the New Age" to name a few. The latest road is that of "Collective Salvation," where we all must sacrifice everything and become destitute in order to purge ourselves of the past sins of those who have gone on before us. At the core of each of these presentations is humanism which puts salvation on the backs of men, and negates the one true salvation that was purchased by Jesus on the cross.[6]

When it comes to possessing kingdoms and the powers that are attached to such kingdoms, we can find ourselves willing to sell anything to gain inroads, recognition, and favor in order to be part of the inner group. Clearly, to be a partaker of Satan's systems, we must be willing to barter, trade, and sell what we need to sell in order to be counted worthy to maintain some semblance of life, to secure some preferred lifestyle, or possess a type of false security or happiness in the age we live in.

As we have already stated, due to our pride we can be tempted by the world. Remember, Satan's spirit works within the environment of disobedience or lawlessness. The world is cleverly designed to dare us to figure ways around its various rules to forever beat the odds. It encourages us to lie or find loopholes in order to outsmart the systems. It challenges pride to always come out on top of a matter. However, these are simply shrewd traps of the world to cause men to compromise what integrity or decency they may have in order to possess them. In the end the world will declare, "Gotcha!"

The Bible is forever calling us to excellence in our attitude and conduct. We are to offer the best, and maintain our integrity, as well as be faithful to our God in all we do. In God's kingdom there are no

---

[6]   Matthew 7:13-14; John 14:6; Ephesians 2:8-9

experts, because greatness is measured by the inward disposition and character of a man in relationship to his Creator.

What will the world require of us in the end? Jesus summed it up when He asked what will a man profit if he gains the whole world but loses his soul?[7] The world is clearly after our soul. It wants to take our will captive, influence our intellect in order to determine our worldview, and highjack our emotions so that it can wrap up our affections. By wrapping up our affections we will find ourselves falling in love with the possibilities of what we can experience in the world, instead of loving God.

As you can see, the world's systems are about control. The world wants to control how people interpret, perceive, or receive a matter. In the end, such control points to some part of the world playing God in the lives of people, while determining their point of dependence, identity, authority, reality, and purpose. In summation, the goal of the world is to gain the dependency of a person so that it can own his or her soul.

If the world's systems gain such dependency, it will become an authority to those individuals who must look to them. These systems actually set up the type of reality that its servants must accept in order to determine personal potential and purpose. Clearly, for the world to take such a place is idolatrous for only God rightfully deserves to be in such a position. It also points to paganism. The world uses two main avenues to identify people and determine attitudes: culture and images.

The world uses culture which is often influenced by religion. Culture influences our tastes and worldview as to what is morally acceptable. It uses images to erect standards as to what must be considered normal. Therefore, culture influences the various tastes and preferences of the flesh, while images create prideful biases and prejudices that will cause competition, judgmentalism, superior exaltation, or isolation. Biases and prejudices produce indifference, anger, or hatred towards any reality that might challenge such perspectives.

This brings us to what the world is after. We know that its ultimate goal is to own our souls. But, what must the world take captive in order to take possession of our souls? We know that the flesh must capture our affections, but the world must take our imaginations into captivity.

---

[7]   Matthew 16:24

The world takes our imaginations into captivity by offering so many possibilities. It lures the lusts of the flesh by stirring them up to consider the possibilities of how something will prove satisfying to the appetites. It caters, appeases, or dares pride in some way, at which time it will cause pride to serve as the platform between the world and the lusts of the flesh. Of course, pride will logic why it has the right to justify the flesh in partaking of the world. After all, pride perceives that it is deserving of the best the world has to offer, and that it is quite normal or natural to do so.

This brings us to the crux of the world's temptation. As stated, many of the things of the world are neither good nor bad. It is the emphasis that people put on such things that can cause them to become idolatrous and destructive to the soul. In the end, people will play the harlot with the world. In other words, they will come into agreement with the spirit of the world, which is a type of spiritual fornication. Once again, if we fall in love with the things of the world, the love of the Father will not be in us.

Satan uses the world to take ownership of our souls. Along with Satan the world already stands judged. What you see is temporary, and eventually every system that is attached to it will be destroyed.

Jesus stated that since the world hated Him, it will also hate His followers.[8] The truth of the matter is if you do not belong to the world, it will hate you. As believers, we must never underestimate how much those who belong to this world hate or oppose God and His servants. Subsequently, if the world cannot attract you, it will try to charm, flatter, or seduce you. If it cannot seduce or beguile you, it will intimidate or bully you. If the world cannot bully you, it will persecute you, thereby, making you pay for being unwilling to sell your soul to it.

The Bible is clear—we cannot serve two masters. We will love the one and hate the other.[9] We cannot love God without hating the world, and we cannot love the world without hating God. Again, as believers, we must come back to our first works. We must love God with everything in us to ensure that we will never love or belong to the present age in which we live.

[8] John 7:7; 17:12-16
[9] Matthew 6:26

6

OVERCOMING THE WORLD

It is easy to talk about overcoming, but the concept of "overcoming" implies there is some type of travailing that must occur before we can consider the end result of our actions as overcoming. For example, Jesus stated that there is much tribulation in the world, but to be of good cheer for He overcame the world.[1]

Tribulation implies there is some type of struggle that has ensued that had to be overcome before Jesus could make reference to this subject. We are reminded of this struggle when we are told in Acts 14:22 to continue in the faith and that through much tribulation we, as believers, must enter into the kingdom of God. We also have James' warning that as believers we must know that when we fall into various trials or temptations, the resolve of our faith is being tested. Trials and temptations are also designed to work patience into our character so that we may be perfected in our walk before God.[2]

As you consider the world, it is easy to understand the possible struggle that will emerge in the soul. Because of the influence of the world, it is obvious that much of the Church has been dulled down by the world's indoctrination, weighed down by the demands of the age, and burdened down by the vanity of the world's various systems. Clearly, we must consider what it will take for Christians who struggle with the oppressive ways of the age they live in to finally adhere to the Word, exhorting them to come out and be separate from the world's idolatrous influences, evil workings, and rebellious spirit. Therefore, it is obvious that some tribulation is due to the temptation that abounds in the world.

In order to understand what it means to overcome the world, we must consider what Jesus did in regards to overcoming it. Some people would ask where in Scripture does it reveal how Jesus overcame the world. To answer that question, we must once again consider the makeup

---

[1] John 16:33
[2] James 1:2-4

of the world that was designed by Satan. It is made up of the systems that are designed to attract and entangle the lusts of the flesh, the pride of life, and the lust of the eyes. When Jesus was led out to the wilderness by the Holy Spirit to be tempted by the devil, He was tempted to partake of the things of the flesh when presented with the type of bread the world offers. Satan dared Him to give way to pride when he tempted Him to prove that He was the Son of God to silence or suffice the skepticism of the world. Jesus' eyes were tempted by the glory of the world. If Jesus had settled for the systems or kingdoms of this age by bowing down to Satan, we would still be most miserably lost.[3]

Jesus overcame each temptation with the Word of God. In the first temptation of partaking of the bread of this world, He assured Satan that the bread of this world would not sustain Him. Lasting sustenance could only be maintained by living according to every word that proceeds out of the mouth of God.

When it came to proving He was the Son of God, Jesus was quite aware that Satan knew who He was. The real temptation was not a matter of proof, especially since the world had no real intention of believing or recognizing Him as the Son of God. Clearly, the world has never, nor will it ever, be interested in knowing the truth of a matter, for it maintains its own take on reality. However, Satan's real goal was to get the Son of God to meet him on his terms and come into agreement with the despotic ways of his world. To give way to such temptation simply puts God to a foolish test that would prove to be futile and ridiculous.

When it came to the lusts of the eyes, Jesus knew that the kingdoms of the world were temporary. In reality the earth would become His footstool and all the kingdoms of the world would be destroyed. Their glory would cease and the ashes of their remains would be swept away by the winds of judgment to be remembered no more. He also knew that He had not come to secure His reign as king over temporary kingdoms; rather, He came as a Savior and Redeemer who would be offered up by the kingdoms of the world on an altar.

As you follow the Lord's ministry and trial, you will see how the kingdoms of the world were used against Him. The educational system of His time was used to try to entrap Him, the economic system was used to try to deem Him as being part of an insurrection, the religious

---

[3] Matthew 4:1-11; 1 John 2:15-17

system was used to declare Him guilty, and the system of the government was the tool that ultimately was used to offer Him up as a sacrificial peace offering.

As we follow Jesus' response and reaction to the different traps set by the kingdoms of this world to demean His character, thwart His mission, entangle Him into one of its various traps, strip Him of His authority, and destroy His witness, we can begin to see how He overcame the world by standing on the truth of the eternal words of heaven. However, before we can overcome the world, we must establish the premise in which we approach this incredible battle. The Apostle John gives us this premise in 1 John 5:3-4,

> For this is the love of God, that we keep his commandments:
> and his commandments are not grievous. For whatever is born
> of God overcometh the world; and this is the victory that
> overcometh the world, even our faith.

Notice how the apostle gives us insight into what it will take to overcome the world. We are once again reminded that our first work, or responsibility, as believers is to love God with everything in us. However, the goal of the world is to cause us to love it. It will tempt us to desire it in an idolatrous way, possess it in a lustful fashion, and to partake of its attractive but deadly fruits.

From the premise of worldly attraction, the affections of the flesh are stirred up to lust after it and the pride of the self-life is enticed to use it as a platform to exalt itself. As the world gains inroads into people's affections, the possibilities of the world will catch their imaginations as to how wondrous and glorious it will be to partake of its various deadly fruits. As such possibilities gain inroads into their imaginations, people begin to think regardless of the deadly seed that is present in the fruit of the world that it would behoove them to partake of such fruit regardless of the consequences. In other words, their imagination will deceptively convince them that what is gained by partaking of the world will far outweigh the consequences. These individuals will foolishly conclude that in the end the pleasure, contentment, and satisfaction the world could bring would be worth selling their souls for. It would also be meaningful for them to offer up their souls on the many altars along the way to gain what has become dear to their hearts. Clearly, the love of and for the world is what drives and compels many people to sell their souls.

Even in the Christian realm you will find many Demases. Demas started out on the right footing, but the love for the world was never far from him. It remained on the back burner as he followed Paul in his missionary work.[4] Since he failed to change his attitude towards the world, the world's "strings" were still there to pull him back into its seduction and delusion. Clearly, he valued it too much for it remained dear to his heart. At the right time, its attractions, claims upon his life, and call became too great for him. The Apostle Paul said this about Demas, "For Demas hath forsaken me, having loved this present world, and is departed unto Thessalonica . . ." (2 Timothy 4:10).

It was clear that the Apostle Paul was sorrowful over Demas' departure. Demas once again became entangled with the world, causing him to become a fugitive and traitor in relationship to the kingdom of God. The love for the world proved greater than his love for God. Yet, how many of those who claim to be Christians still hold the world dear to their hearts? How many have departed from the truths of God to partake of the deadly fruit of the world because they have not changed their attitude towards it? How many have caused the Lord Jesus Christ's heart to break because they do not love Him enough to value Him above that which is temporary?

If we love God, we will value Him above all else. He will hold our heart strings as we dread the idea of causing any sorrow to come upon Him. We will guard our relationship with Him as we keep His commandments, for such pure love will inspire and compel us to do right in regard to others. However, as the Apostle John so eloquently pointed out, before we can love God in the proper way we must be born again of His Spirit and Word. Until this new birth experience happens within our spirits, we will have no inclination towards Him, as we remain subject to the spirit of this world. And, unless we choose to believe His Word, we will not possess the necessary authority to overcome.

In order to overcome the world, the premise from which we must always approach the battle is from the place of sincere faith. We approach the Word to believe it, which will give us the necessary authority to stand confidently against the lies of Satan, faithfully withstand the attacks of

---

4   Colossians 4:14; Philemon 24

Satan, and to remain steadfastly standing when all seems defeated and insane.

This brings us to what God's Word tells us about the world in relationship to its temptation and goals. First, what does His Word tell us about the kingdoms of the world? We know that the target is the same for all three enemies: our faith. How does the world undermine unfeigned faith towards God?

We know that it subtly draws us into its traps to cause us to change our confidence and reliance from God to the world's systems. But, it is important to understand how this subtle exchange also changes our attitude towards God in regard to faith.

The world uses its various attractions and kingdoms to present options. As pointed out, if one option fails to bring the desired results, whether it be that of happiness, pleasure, satisfaction, or purpose, we can always try another avenue. Obviously, what the world offers seems like endless possibilities to somehow discover the life that our flesh desires and our pride has deemed that we are worthy of. Such worldly pursuits promise to bring some type of purpose to our existence.

Since the world is temporary, it can only present an illusion at best. Each avenue the world offers ends in emptiness, each pursuit in disillusionment, and each accomplishment can only serve as a pinnacle at best that will cause people to either fall or be flung into valleys of despair. This brings us to the attitude the world will ultimately produce in us, that of skepticism toward life, mockery towards truth, and scoffing in regard to hope. Such an attitude can be traced back to the condition of unbelief. Even though the world has produced such a condition in people, it is natural for them to transpose this ungodly attitude upon God.

It is vital that the record be set straight. Satan, the god of this world along with his kingdom of darkness, is the one who pulls the rug out from any real victory, mocks any attempt of maintaining lasting accomplishments, and deems all worldly successes as mockery. You can see this attitude in the most successful people of the world. They see life as a joke, God as a myth or some indifferent force, and righteousness as a travesty. Such an attitude brings into question God's very existence. Even among those in the religious world, some are saying in their heart that there is no true God.[5] In their minds, at best He is an indifferent force that cannot be pleased or He is just too big to be involved in or concerned about the affairs of men.

Due to the fact that Satan does not mean what he says and proves contrary and contradictory to what he does say, everything of this world becomes untrustworthy. In such a treacherous, untrustworthy environment, man simply becomes a pawn who must accept his miserable existence as being his "lot" in life. Once again, this attitude is transferred towards the life that God intents to give us, throwing doubt and suspicion on His character and intentions. It causes man to question if God's words are true, and if they are, they surely do not apply to him or he would not be in such a state.

This brings us back to the Garden of Eden. Through the world's systems, Satan sets man up as a means to question God's words, character, and intent in order to gain man's confidence in what he sees, what he can experience, and in what he ultimately can know. As a result, man will not only disregard God's Word, question His character, and become suspicious towards His intent, but he will choose to partake of the various fruits of the world to find the solution and answer to his life. It is clear that Satan is clever and seductive when it comes to tempting man with his own tree of knowledge of good and evil that is clearly represented by his various kingdoms.

As you consider the world's subtle tactics, you can begin to see in what way the believer could be undermined in his or her faith towards God. If a believer is unable to believe God's Word, he or she will be robbed of his or her joy of salvation. Remember, Jesus stated that He spoke the truths He did, so as believers our joy could be full.[6] If we do not believe what He says, we will be robbed of the abiding anchor of joy. For this reason, we must always choose to love the truth in order to maintain our joy towards what He has said about our life in Him.

If we do not believe what Jesus said, then we cannot live in expectation that He will bring a matter about. This not only puts doubt on His character, but it takes the teeth out of real hope. Clearly, the world's goal is to kill any expectation we have in regard to God bringing forth His promises. Without expectation, we will find ourselves

---

[5] Psalm 14:1

[6] John 15:11; 1 John 1:4; 2 John 12

drowning in a pool of despair. After all, hope deferred makes the heart sick with despair and depression. Once the teeth are taken out of hope, then our faith has no means to survive the affronts that will rage against our soul. Without unfeigned faith, we will not be able to possess our souls in patience. Keep in mind that in the end days the enemy will try to wear out the patience of the saints. To counteract the devil's attempts, we must possess our soul and endure to the end. This requires us to keep the faith.[7]

When you consider how the systems of the world work, you can begin to see how you overcome them. The first thing the systems of the world have to do is to present the possibilities that stir up imaginations in order to cause an individual to come into agreement with it. In other words, imaginations will cause a person to agree with the world that it possesses the means and possibilities to produce a life that is desirable, pleasing, and worthwhile. Once a person agrees with the world that it is his or her provider, then he or she will begin to look to and partake of the world, coming under the influence of the spirit of the world.

When a person partakes of the world, then spiritual death begins to work within a person's soul, causing him or her to become lukewarm, indifferent, or unresponsive towards the things of God. The more a person partakes of the world, the more he or she loses any real spiritual edge or discernment as the conscience becomes desensitized towards what is holy. If a person has any real spiritual sense in the first place, it becomes dulled down by the environment of the world, bringing the person under the influence of the spirit of the world even more so. It is at this time that the spirit of the world can subtly change a person's attitude and worldview. For this reason we can begin to understand Jesus' candid description that the world chokes out the authority and power that the Word of God has had in a person's life. After all, the more an individual is dulled down by the world, the more he or she falls into the state of unbelief towards God, creating the environment of complacency towards the matters of God.

By recognizing the path the world uses to attract and seduce us, we can begin to understand some of the instructions in regard to it. The Bible is clear that the world stands at enmity with God and works rebellion in those who belong to its age. For this reason we are to walk

---

[7]   Proverbs 13:12; Daniel 7:25; Luke 21:19: John 15:11; 1 John 1:4; John 12

by faith towards God, and not by sight (lusts of the flesh and eyes) or by worldly understanding (pride of life). If we fail to walk by faith, we will never be able to please God.[8]

We have already discussed our need to deny self the right to life on its terms and to crucify the flesh. Once we shut down the avenues of the soul that Satan will tempt by using the attractions of the world, we will become crucified to the world.[9] To be crucified to the world means that the world has no means in which to attract us to it, thereby, causing us to fall into its various traps. However, this crucifixion of the flesh must take place daily to close down the inroads the world can make into our souls.

This brings us to the type of attitude we must have towards the world. If our attitude towards the world is not decisive, we each will find ourselves coming into agreement with it and partaking of its deadly fruits. When it comes to the world we must keep our imaginations intact. Imaginations often become obsessive strongholds when it comes to our pursuits, agendas, and priorities. In order to keep our imaginations realistic in regard to the world, we must take captive our thoughts and bring them into obedience to Christ. This will ensure that we maintain the right mind when it comes to the world.[10]

However, it is not enough to take thoughts captive, we must put on the mind of Christ to properly discern and know what will be the good, acceptable, and perfect will of God. The Apostle Paul and the Apostle Peter give us valuable insight into the proper attitude we must adopt towards the world. In order to prevent us from partaking of the corrupt fruit of the world, we must become strangers to it and pilgrims in it.[11] The way we become strangers to the world is to count everything associated with it as being nothing more than dung. Once we count the things of the world as being worthless and unacceptable, then we can begin to recognize what must become valuable to us. The Apostle Paul counted the things of the world as dung in light of gaining Christ. To gain Christ, Paul would have to partake of the things of God through obedience to His Word and become identified with Jesus in His death,

---

[8]   2 Corinthians 5:7; Hebrews 11:6; James 4:4

[9]   Galatians 6:14

[10]   2 Corinthians 10:3-5

[11]   If you would like to understand more about this subject, see the author's book, *The Victorious Journey*, in the sixth volume of her foundational series.

burial, and resurrection. The Apostle Peter concurred with this when he stated that we needed to be partakers of the divine nature of Christ since we escaped the corruption that is in the world through lust. Paul's emphasis of gaining Christ made him a spiritual pilgrim in the world. He would not be content until he reached his goal of gaining the real prize in his spiritual pilgrimage.[12]

Once we adopt the attitude of a stranger to the world and become spiritual pilgrims in it, we will not be tempted to come into agreement with it and risk our spiritual inheritance; rather, we will separate from it. Keep in mind, we must flee that which would stir up our youthful lusts, but we must separate from that which would bring us into agreement with a wrong spirit, exposing us to an unholy environment. Hence enters Paul's warning concerning coming into agreement with the unholy. We are to come out from being part of such a system or environment, and separate ourselves from such agreement to ensure that our status as children of God remain intact.[13]

The more that I understood the battle with the world in regard to faith, the more I realized why the world clearly hated those who, because of their unwavering confidence in God, were strangers in it. They were walking according to a different drum beat. Their focus was on something unseen by the world and foreign to it. No matter what type of attraction or glitter the world offered, these individuals' attitudes towards it reveal that it was dung, insignificant, and worthless. The world could not attract, seduce, bully, or force them into agreeing with it. It was from this premise that I finally understood what Hebrews 11:38 meant when it said of such saints, "(Of whom the world was not worthy); they wandered in deserts, and in mountains, and in dens and caves of the earth." The world was not worthy to witness such faith, for this reason those who walked according to it meant that the witness they were displaying was hidden from the world as they wandered through it until their spiritual pilgrimage came to an end.

The question we must ask ourselves as believers is, are we overcoming the world or are we a Demas, still entangled by the world so that at any minute it will reel us back into its clutches to reclaim us? We need to be clear and decisive about who or what holds our heart, and what attitude

---

[12] Philippians 2:5; 3:1-14; 1 Peter 2:11; 2 Peter 1:3-4
[13] 2 Corinthians 6:14-18

46

we have towards the world. If we are not clear and decisive, we could easily find ourselves entangled by the age in which we live, making us vulnerable, indecisive, and a potential casualty of its lies and deadly seeds.

7

THE GOD OF THIS AGE

One of the greatest challenges in the quasi religious environment that exists in America is to awaken the Christian realm to the battle that Christians are in. The Bible is clear that we are in a conflict, but to talk to Christians, they either have a fanatic, unrealistic, romantic take on this battle or they live in complete denial that it even exists.

Much of the attitude about the battle that rages for man's soul can be traced back to the type of attitude that Christians have about Satan and his kingdom. The Apostle Paul makes it clear that we are in a struggle. However, we do not struggle against flesh and blood; rather, we wrestle against principalities, unseen powers, rulers of the darkness of this present age, and with spiritual wickedness in high places.[1]

The first thing we must mark in regard to this battle is that it begins as a wrestling match. When I studied the concept of wrestling according to my *Strong's Concordance*, it points out that it is a personal struggle of contention and strife that will prove to be ongoing and trying. If you have witnessed wrestling matches, it must be noted that it takes different maneuvers where there is often a wearing down of one's opponent. Such maneuvers can prove to be clever, subtle, and crafty. As we will see, these three words have been used in relationship to the final enemy we will be considering.

These wrestling maneuvers can also find each challenger gaining the upper hand at different times, only to often watch the other opponent escape the grip and throw down the challenger as a means to gain the necessary hold to claim victory. In wrestling, one must be on guard in order to defend self against any maneuver, as well as be alert to become offensive when the opportunity presents itself. In this match, we as believers must keep in mind that the final enemy has a tendency to play dead, act as if he has been rendered helpless, or give the impression that he no longer poses any real threat. Don't let him fool you. He patiently

---

[1] Ephesians 6:12

waits for us to put down our guard so that he can take us down for the final time.

Scripture confirms the battle is much like a wrestling match. In the end days, the opposing system of the antichrist will try to wear down the patience of the saints in order to take control of the world. Jude reminded us of the target or goal of our opponent when he exhorted us to contend or wrestle for the faith that was first delivered to the saints.[2]

It is important to remember that as Christian soldiers, we are not after new territory, we are simply contending for the territory of our souls, our homes, and churches. We are to maintain our spiritual bearing by standing for truth, withstanding with faith, and continue to stand in light of our blessed hope.

In a wrestling match, two parties are trying to prevent the opponent from gaining personal victory over them. I cannot tell you how much I shudder when I hear songs about going up to the high places to take territory away from Satan. Satan must be mocking such foolishness while he gains more inroads into people's souls, homes, and churches.

Christians, as a whole, remain ignorant and uninformed about the real battle that is before them. The Apostle Paul is clear about what is on the line in these Scriptures. As soldiers, we are not responsible for taking the kingdoms of the world, but we are responsible for maintaining the presence and power of the kingdom of God that resides within the saints of God by faith in the Son of God. Jesus was offered the kingdoms of the world in His temptation in the wilderness, but He was not interested in reigning over them. He left us with an example to follow, but it appears that many have failed to take His example to heart.

This brings us to a very important aspect as to the battle we are in as believers. Satan is forever trying to get us to take the bait that we can somehow gain the necessary access into his kingdoms and take control of them without paying some consequences, or even the price of our soul. Such control or victory appeals to the pride of man, but it will prove his downfall as pride sets him up to fall into Satan's clever traps.

In Jesus' temptation we see that Satan is the great tempter. He is forever trying to gain inroads into the soul of man through the lusts of the flesh, the pride of life, and the lusts of the eyes. He uses the attractions of his kingdoms to gain access into the souls of men in order

---

[2]   Daniel 7:25; Jude 3

to throw them down on the mat of the world as a means to oppress or possess them. It is vital to point out that temptation is not what proves to be deadly: it is when people come into subjection or agreement with Satan as to his temptation that the devil gains the necessary access to take their affections and souls captive. This is when the real seeds of death are planted into the very soul of man in order to take root and grow as he is dulled down by the world's conditioning, desensitized by the leaven of indoctrination, and made complacent towards the things of God.

The Apostle Paul made this statement in regard to Satan, "Lest Satan should get an advantage of us; for we are not ignorant of his devices" (2 Corinthians 2:11). We know that people perish for lack of knowledge.[3] The tragedy is that many people are ignorant towards Satan and his devices. The Word is clear as to how Satan works, but many Christians work in the extreme when it comes to the devil. They either are giving him too much credit or they are acting as if he is simply a "doctrine" or a figment of imagination.

For me, I had to throw out much of my theological understanding before I could come back to center in order to gain a balanced perspective about this worthy foe. It is the tendency of those who believe that he does exist, along with those who believe he is very active in the world to give him too much credit. This brings unrealistic glory or attention to him. The reason people do this is because they do not know how to recognize him.

On the other hand, to deny or ignore his activity is to give him free access to do as he will under the cover of darkness. Either extreme is dangerous. We must be able to recognize how he works with the intent of overcoming his attempts to take possession of our lives. Again, this requires us to know our enemy, whether it be the flesh, the world, or Satan. We must recognize how each of these enemies works and what they are really after.

This brings us to the nature of Satan. We know he is the great tempter, but how does he tempt us? We know that he uses the world to gain entrance into the soul's arena to capture our lusts by taking our affections captive in order to take possession of our souls. Clearly, he wants to own our souls. However, he cannot claim our souls until he can

---

[3]   Hosea 4:6

wrestle us down into an oppressive hold as a means of taking possession of them.

We are first given various insights into this powerful foe. Let us begin with Jesus' temptation in the wilderness. It is here where we gain much insight into this capable enemy.[4] As already noted, from the first two temptations of Jesus, we know that the tempter uses the attractions of the world to gain inroads into our soul. But, what can we learn from the last temptation? We can learn what the devil is after when it comes to man.

We know that the flesh is after our affections, the world wants to take captive our souls, but Satan is after one thing. He is after our worship. This is constantly brought out in Scripture. Revelation 13:4 talks about worshipping the dragon and the beast. The dragon is Satan and the beast is the last great world leader. We know him as the antichrist and are also told this leader will erect an image of himself and demand everyone to worship it.[5]

Satan will use any means to gain our worship. However, he knows he cannot gain worship unless he is a god, a prince who wields power. Man will not bow down where there is no attraction or power. He will not pursue something unless it possesses some type of glory that can influence, has the ability to gain admiration, or be desired.

Hence, enters the attractions of the glory of Satan's kingdoms. He was tempting Jesus to consider the beauty associated to his kingdoms. He told Jesus that he would give him the glories of his kingdoms if He would bow down and worship him.

It is important to point out that Satan is considered the god of this world or age and the prince of the power of the air. The term "god" can point to magistrate, lord, or owner. As god of this world or age, he is the founder and owner of all the worldly systems. If you belong to the world, you belong to him. If you are serving this world in any way, you are serving him. If you are a slave to sin, he is your real master. If you operate according to this world, you do so because he allows it. If he owns you, he has the right to demand you allegiance, devotion, and worship.[6] If Jesus gave in to his temptation to possess the things his

---

[4]   Matthew 4:1-11

[5]   Revelation 19:20

[6]   2 Corinthians 4:2-4; Ephesians 2:2

kingdoms offered, He would have brought himself under the lordship of Satan. And, Satan could claim ownership of Him.

The word "age" is also a very interesting word in light of Satan being the god of this present age. The word "world" can be interchanged with the word "age," but the word "age" points to a period of time. For example, in relationship to "age" God has planned the ages. Each period of time follows a distinct principle as to the method or means God uses to deal with man to bring a specific result. Whether we like it or not, Satan plays a part in what way God deals with man. In each case, we are reminded that Satan has been allotted specific times and boundaries as to his involvement with man and history. We see this in the case of Job and Peter.

God clearly set the boundaries for Satan in relationship to Job, and Satan had the right to sift Peter.[7] Satan's dealings with God's people will always prove to be great times of testing for their faith. Take heart! What Satan intended for evil was turned around for good because in the end the faith of these men won out. Job came out with a living witness of God and Peter was humbled and came out being converted towards the ways of God to serve as a pliable instrument in His hands. Do not be mistaken: the God of the universe is always in control. He is never caught off guard by events or situations, for He is the one who has planned the ages, including the age we live in. This age is known as the dispensation of grace, the age of the Church, and it has also been referred to as the age of the Gentiles.

We know that the environment can change for man in relationship as to the types of temptations and challenges he may face in the age he lives in. Each age has its own flavor as to the temptations and idolatrous influences that may tempt and ultimately take man captive. We must recognize the age we live in, in order to properly confront Satan.

The end of this age is described as one that will be marked by great tribulation. This tribulation will be upon the face of the whole world. It will be unmistakable to God's people. The environment will be much like the one Noah lived in before the great flood. The wickedness of humanity will be so great that it will be unimaginable to the Noah's of the world, but be assured that the cup of iniquity will be overflowing, demanding a response from the just God of the Universe. Jesus stated

---

[7] Job 1:6-12; 2:1-6; Luke 22:31-32

that this time will be marked by great deception, especially where He is concerned. Many wolves and heretics will claim to be "the Christ."

As believers, we must mark Jesus' warning about the end days. He stated that if it were possible, even the very elect would be deceived. Note, if it was possible, the elect would even be deceived. The only reason the elect will not be deceived is because we choose to know the real Jesus, love the truth about Him, and cling to what the Bible clearly establishes about the end days, knowing that the Lord knows how to deliver or save those who are His. You better belong to Him or you will be swept away by the great delusion coming on the face of the world. You already could be in the clutches of this wave. If you are not sure, cry out in humble repentance to your Lord. Admit your inability to save yourself from the incredible delusion sweeping this world, and ask Him to pull you out from the grasp this wave has upon your soul.

Perhaps you are saying how can this be? There is no way I could be deceived. Beware, when you think you are standing on truth, due to your arrogance of what you think you know about Jesus, you are ready to fall into the trap of this great delusion. We cannot stand unless we are established upon the Rock, hiding in the ever-abiding shadow of His hand, knowing that He alone is the only One who is able to save us from our deceptive arrogance and high opinion of what we think we know.

In 2 Timothy 3 the Apostle Paul describes the attitude that will be prevalent in the last days. Mark well what he says for it is evident that we are living in such times. The attitude of many will be expressed in indifference, lawlessness, and contempt for that which will not bow down to their fleshly desires and idolatrous preferences. They will tout much knowledge, but in all of their learning they will become more foolish and deluded as truth eludes them. In their arrogance and foolishness they will resist the truth as their minds become increasingly corrupt and reprobate concerning the real faith. And, those who truly know the pure doctrine of Christ and what it means to possess the true faith of heaven, the ways of compassion, the disposition of charity, and the attitude of patience will be persecuted.

The age we are living in is winding down to a climatic event that will usher in a new age, known as the millennium age or the kingdom age. It will be at this time that Jesus, as King of kings, Lord of lords will usher in His one thousand year reign.

The amazing reality about Jesus' last temptation in the wilderness had to do with Satan's kingdoms. There is so much confusion about the subject of the kingdom. There are those of the religious realm that believe they must usher in or establish this new kingdom on earth before Jesus comes back. However, the Bible is clear about the kingdom of God. It is not of this world for it is unseen. It is contrary to the kingdoms of this world for it resonates with the light of His life and truth, while all other kingdoms will prove to belong to the darkness of this present world. God's kingdom presently resides within man and is empowered by His Spirit. We are also told we will not take up a sword to usher this kingdom in. At the completion of this age, Jesus will return and set up His kingdom, not man.

It is vital to understand the difference between these two diverse kingdoms and how Satan works in and through the periods of time that have been allotted by God. As god of the age, the devil is able to adjust the emphasis and workings of his systems. This brings us to how the devil rules in regard to his systems. According to Ephesians 2:6, he is the prince or ruler of the power of the air. What does this mean to you and me?

As believers, we must remember that we have been translated from the kingdom of darkness into the kingdom of God's dear Son.[8] Even though we have been translated, we are still in a world that is ruled by the unseen kingdom of darkness. Satan is the ruler of a kingdom that exists and operates between the visible world and the heavenly kingdom of God. In summation, he rules over his earthly kingdoms from a spiritual plane. Since he rules from a spiritual plane, this makes him a spiritual, unseen entity that serves as the power, authority, and influence behind all man-centered and worldly systems.

Satan is a spiritual enemy; therefore, he must be discerned. The Apostle John concurs with this. He exhorts us to test or discern the spirits. There are three main spirits in operation. There is the Holy Spirit, the natural spirit of man, and the spirit of the world. We know the Holy Spirit is of God, but the natural spirit represents the unregenerate man. The natural spirit of man makes him a city without walls, causing him to become vulnerable to the spirit of the world. Since he is fleshly and earthly, he has no real inclination towards God and is in the habit of

---

[8]   Colossians 1:13

justifying the ways of his flesh. Satan is often blamed for the rebellious activities of man's natural spirit. To overcome the natural spirit, man must repent of giving way to its preferences for darkness.[9]

The spirit of the world is Satan. This spirit stirs up people to oppose God. The natural spirit works from within man, tempting him to give way to the enticements and attractions of the world. However, the temptations of the spirit of the world come from without. Temptations are like darts that are flung at a person as a means to hit his or her vulnerable spots in order to make inroads into his or her soul.

To falsely accredit Satan for the works of the natural spirit is to avoid overcoming the flesh, while opening the door for this foe to hit the unguarded targets and vulnerable parts of our soul. It is in the soul area that man experiences oppression or possession.

In light of this, can you or I expect to successfully fight Satan in the flesh, overcome him with the methods of the world, or overthrow him with the kingdoms of the world? The answer is "no." This is why the Apostle Paul stated we do not fight against flesh and blood, but against principalities, powers, rulers of the darkness, and spiritual wickedness that is taking place in high places.

I have studied these different positions. Some could rightfully argue with my conclusions and be correct. However, this is my breakdown and understanding of these different rulers in the kingdom of darkness.

Principalities point to chief or principle rulers over something. This reveals that there are ranks in the kingdom of darkness. These ranks begin with Satan the god of the age, followed by principalities. In the book of Daniel, we get insight into one of these principalities in Daniel 10:13. The prince or ruler of the kingdom of Persia was able to withstand one of God's messengers until Michael the chief prince of heaven helped the messenger to push this principality back in order to get the message through to the prophet, Daniel. Such principalities point to the unseen principle ruler over actual nations or kingdoms of the world.

Principalities are followed by powers that have jurisdiction or authority to wield some type of influence or power in certain arenas such as over armies. These powers oversee the work and missions of the different factions of darkness.

---

[9]   Proverbs 25:28; Ephesians 2:2; 1 Corinthians 2:12-14; 1 John 4:1

Rulers of darkness point to that which rules over certain environments. Good examples of those who rule over environments would be spirits and demons. There is confusion as to whether spirits and demons are the same. Clearly, spirit points to air, while demons are known to manifest themselves through some form. The confusion comes because spirits are known to come and go and often rule within certain environments. In a sense, these spirits could represent the essence of the air or presence that hangs in the environment, where demons are associated with seeking out some body in which to possess the soul. However, the difference between spirits and demons may not be a use or twist on words; rather, it could point to rank where there is a certain order or hierarchy within this group. For instance, a couple of prevalent spirits that reign over the environment of churches are the antichrist and religious spirits. In the case of demons these restless spirits seem to rule over people's lives or in designated areas such as a particular room, space, or place. This brings us to rulers of darkness.

The final groups of leaders fall into rulers in high places. Rulers in high places point to the darkness that influences governments, orders, and organizations. Such darkness is behind wicked leaders who serve as conduits for demonically inspired activity. The goal behind these influences is to bring all systems of the world into a one-world system.

The leaders who are doing the bidding of the kingdom of darkness are not always known because they operate under the cover of deception, but in certain cases some of them are very aware of the fact that Satan is the one who has empowered them. In fact, some have sought such power.

Satan simply uses these individuals as pawns to do the bidding of His kingdom. Good examples are George Soros and Obama. These are wicked leaders, and sadly there is never a shortage of those who would sell their souls to enjoy the power that comes with high positions, or to see wicked, anti-God agendas and dreams come to full bloom. However, these individuals do not always recognize that they have been exalted by Satan, who will one day require their souls and sacrifice them as he mocks their descent into hell itself. In fact, in the case of Soros, he thinks he is God; and, due to the declaration his adoring fans make about him being "the Messiah", Obama appears to agree with their conclusion. Therefore, between these two wicked men, the world has its partial godhead. All they need is some false prophet to promote them as such.

The one fruit that sets these leaders apart is their incredible arrogance that is expressed through indifference, cruelty, and mocking attitudes.

Even though some of these leaders are flesh and blood, you must not forget that they are empowered and exalted by Satan. For this reason, the battle will never be won in the flesh. To use the methods or the ways of Satan's kingdoms to secure victories is to look to the enemy to help you defeat his own kingdom.

A good example of this is the visible Church. This church has tried to use the different systems of the world, such as the political system, to push back moral wickedness. How successful has such an attempt been? The church has become more worldly in its approaches, while the world has waxed more wicked, not only in its practices but in its defiance against what it considers to be interference on the part of the church.

I remember being involved in a move to get creationism taught alongside the evolution theory in our schools. As we were exposed to the education system, we could see that besides lacking a fair and balanced presentation regarding the matters of man's origin, we could also actually see where the quality of the school books was designed to dumb down our children. For example, reading books marked for sixth graders were written at a third grade level. As we made our way through the different systems of the world to address what was blatant indoctrination of our children, our greatest opposition often turned out to be educators who also viewed themselves as being Christians. It was appalling to see that those who took the greatest offense for the perverted practices of the different systems were the religious people, while the unbelieving sat on the sidelines watching the fiasco of what appeared to be a divided kingdom. It was obvious that the reason why these religious people took offense is because it was a matter of personal pride attached to position and not one of righteousness.

This experience taught me much about the battle that rages. It will not be fought and won in the arenas of the world, but in the prayer closets. It is not a matter of changing the moral flavor of an environment, it is a matter of changing the hearts and mind of those who are bent on the ways of hell and carrying out the wicked agenda of those in high places.

This also brings us down to the harsh reality that the attitude the professing church has taken on concerning the world reveals that it is part of the world's system. According to Howard Pitman in his book "Placebo," the church was taken over by Satan in 1982. It became one of his systems. The truth is the visible church has no real distinction from the world. Its approach and handling of matters are very worldly. Its attempts to use the worldly systems have made it more subject to the world. It has not only lost its edge, it has lost its way. Although Jesus is tacked on to many messages, and many activities are being done in His name, He is not in any of it. For many churches they are either presenting a watered-down gospel or a different gospel altogether.

Where did the church go wrong? It failed to recognize that it was never meant to fight the battle for men's souls according to the world, but according to the Spirit of the living God. It was never meant to change the strategy established by the Bible by adopting the political ways of the world to address the spiritual matters plaguing man's heart. It was never meant to institute the world's methods in addressing that which causes conflict within man's soul, for such conflict exists because man is at odds with his Creator and not the world.

Due to the church agreeing with the world, it has been conditioned by the world to speak on its behalf, preach its message, and promote its idols. Granted, Jesus has been tacked on to some of the presentations, there have been some truths mixed in with worldly philosophies, and there have been various good deeds done as means to promote the so-called "goodness of man". However, it is nothing but a façade, a false presentation of what is real. It is a lie.

It is important to understand that Jesus is the Rock who in the end will judge and grind into powder all the systems associated with the world. These false systems have been established on the shifting sands of the age and not on Jesus. God is beginning to shake everything to reveal the faulty foundations of such systems as He allows the storms of this age to reveal and topple each wrong foundation. That which is not founded on Jesus already stands condemned and judged. In the end, all that is associated with this world, including the religious systems, will collapse.

As believers, we need to come out and be separate from such systems, knowing that if we do not, we will be judged with them and ground into powder. Our spiritual lives will collapse as our faith becomes shipwrecked when the wave of delusion that is carrying many towards judgment, collides with the reality of the wrath of God that already abides upon those who refuse to believe the message of the Gospel. Make sure you are not part of the wave of delusion that is sweeping the whole world towards that great and final judgment of God.

8

INROADS

When we consider the instructions found in Ephesians 6:10, we are being called to be strong. We can be strong as His soldiers, not because we are capable of taking on our enemies in our own power, but because the battle belongs to the Lord. The war has already been won at the cross of Christ. We must not forget these facts because our enemies are like Goliath who loom in front of us. These enemies will exaggerate their strength and greatness as they mock us in an attempt to intimidate and convince us that we already stand defeated. They want us to believe that they are too great to be brought down. Such claims are nothing but hot air when brought to the light of our God.

One of the facts Christians must recognize about Satan is that he cannot gain territory unless he has been given some access or inroad. Satan needs either our permission to gain access or he must find a weakness in order to gain inroads into the terrain of our souls, as well as the sanctuaries of our homes and churches.

We will be talking about the devices he uses to gain such access in the next chapter, but before we can see how his devices work, we must understand the inroads where he can gain entrance into our lives.

As previously stated, this enemy of the Most High God wants to be god, lord, and master of our lives. It is not because he is necessarily looking for a following, for there seems to be no end to those who will become subservient to him in some way, but his real motive is to compete with, oppose, and defy the Living God. The reason I say all of this is because the biggest and most popular inroad in which he gains access into our lives is what brought him down from being a high ranking cherub in God's kingdom. The fact that he is after our worship gives us a powerful introduction into what originally caused him to fall from his first estate, and what he uses in fallen man to gain inroads into his soul to take him captive. And, just what brought Satan down from such heavenly heights to the abyss of hell?

Isaiah 14:12-15 and Ezekiel 28:11-18 give us insight into Satan's character that brought him down from great heights to great depths.

It was pride. This well-known fact was made obvious by the prideful claims he made in Isaiah 14. From the heights of arrogance he declared sovereignty from the God of heaven. He made five declarations of "I will." I will ascend to heaven to rule, I will exalt my throne above the stars of God (angels) to proclaim preeminence above His host, I will sit in the mount of the congregation (among His people), and I will demand and receive worship from his creation, and in the end I will ascend above the heights of the clouds for I will be as the Most High, sovereign in my rule and independent from any other rule.

It is important to point out that your pride and my pride has the same goal as Satan, and makes the same declarations. Our pride wants to be worshipped. It does not matter how or in what way it receives such worship, it wants to be adored, recognized, exalted, and honored in some way. It declares "I will" accomplish this feat. "I will come out on top," I will gain the upper hand," "I will subdue," "I will conquer," and "I will receive worship." In his arrogance man does not want to be ruled; rather, he actually thinks he is an exception to the rule. Nor, does he think he should have to pay any real consequences for being arrogant, rebellious, and foolish.

Ephesians 2:2-3 makes this statement,

> Wherein in time past ye walked according to the course of
> this world, according to the prince of the power of the air,
> the spirit that now worketh in the children of disobedience;
> Among whom also we all had our conversation in times past
> in the lusts of our flesh, fulfilling the desires of the flesh and
> of the mind; and were by nature the children of wrath, even
> as others.

Satan is the prince of the power of the air, the spirit that works in the children of disobedience. Keep in mind that he is spirit and he operates between the earthly and heavenly dimensions. He works within those who are children of disobedience.

Disobedience points to rebellion and stubbornness. According to 1 Samuel 15:23, rebellion is as the sin of witchcraft and stubbornness as iniquity and idolatry. Rebellion is lawlessness that refuses to come into subjection to any authority. Rebellion is the same as witchcraft, which attempts to get around all authority to gain control of a situation or someone in spite of his or her will. Stubbornness, on the other hand, is being stiff-necked by refusing to humble itself and come under any type of rule. Iniquity is moral deviation that refuses to acknowledge true righteousness. We know pride is the epitome of idolatry. This sin is behind all rebellion and ungodly stubbornness.

Clearly, the disobedience inspired by the ruler of the air can clearly be seen as a form of rebellion which is enhanced by witchcraft and stubbornness. Such practices reveal deviation in character (motives, attitudes, and conduct), as well as encourage personal idolatry. Pride makes it very easy for the enemy to set us up to fall into his snares. How does Satan set our pride up to get us to fall into his traps?

Satan is the expert of pride. It started with him before man ever fell from his state of innocence. Pride has four companions that make it very susceptible or vulnerable to Satan. They are fear, confusion, complacency, and delusion. As we will see, Satan knows how to find inroads via our pride through these four companions.

Hence enters the ranks of the kingdom of darkness the Apostle Paul brings out in Ephesians 6:10-12. These ranks are set up in such a way as to bring about the reality of Satan's declarations. Principalities rule from heights over earthly kingdoms. We gain insight into such a principality in Daniel 10:11-13. The first thing we must recognize is that this principality can hinder the work of God. We see where it took Michael, the archangel to push back this principality that was over all of Persia, so that the messenger could bring understanding to Daniel.

With this information in mind I came to the following conclusion: Principalities are those rulers in Satan's kingdom who create the evil coverings or veils over nations that are mentioned in Isaiah 25:7. We know that as the god of this age, he blinds people to the real light of the Gospel so that they will not be saved. Some will not see any need to be saved. Others might sense they need a little intervention, but they want to somehow be part of their salvation by earning or working their way to some meritorious accomplishment. And, there are those who choose some religious avenue or affiliation for salvation. Each approach simply means the person is blind to the real provision of salvation that comes solely through Jesus Christ.

These coverings set up the environment that will create a certain breeding ground as to the type of idolatry that people will be inclined to pursue or give way to. Coverings cause two reactions from people: fear and confusion. Fear demands our worship as it paralyzes or drives us, while confusion either can cause us to question what is real and true, or it will close us down because nothing makes sense.

There are two types of environments you will see working within societies. Both environments are extreme. This brings us to the reality that Satan must use man's pride to push him into extremes in order to cause him to seek some semblance of control, meaning, or purpose. The extremes in which he works are that of oppression and prosperity. Oppression will cause people to go into superstition and fear, and the abundance of prosperity will often make them self-sufficient, causing them to become greedy in their pursuit of wealth, or complacent and indifferent towards their spiritual state.

It is for this reason that I appreciate the request made in Proverbs 30:7-9,

> Two things have I required of thee; deny them not to me before I die: Remove far from me vanity and lies: give me neither poverty nor riches; feed me with food convenient for me; Lest I be full, and deny thee, and say, Who is the LORD? Or lest I be poor, and steal, and take the name of my God in vain.

It is vital that we keep to the center of that which is true and real: God. We must not forget our humble beginnings and the One who truly provides our every need.

With the environment in place, next come the powers of Satan's kingdom. Powers point to those entities who have been given specific powers to carry out their missions. Satan is not all-powerful or all-knowing; therefore, he must disperse power and assignments to certain entities to seek out means to bring about a desired end.

My co-laborer met one of these powers. She admitted without Christ's authority and protection, it would have been a frightening meeting. The spirit was big and wielded much power. He was scouting out the premise to determine weaknesses, along with sizing up the best strategy to use to bring about destruction. Sadly, the weak link turned out to be my pride and the strategy almost proved fatal to this ministry. However, God was faithful to make the necessary moves to protect us, teaching me some valuable lessons that I will not easily forget.

Rulers of darkness are able to establish Satan's throne in the midst of those who would prove to be shining stars on earth. To me the most predominate rulers of darkness that are busy working within the different environments are seducing spirits. The Apostle Paul warned us that these spirits in 1 Timothy 4:1 would indeed be working in the last days. It is natural for these spirits to work under these wicked coverings. Once a covering is thrown over nations, then seducing spirits will come into the environment to create a different reality among people. These spirits suck people straight into a false reality through conditioning and indoctrination. They make them open to buy a lie or a false light. We know that Satan is the false light that many will embrace and worship.[1]

For the religious environment, these seducing spirits will condition and indoctrinate people to embrace an antichrist spirit. This spirit works within the various religions, as well as the New Age philosophies and teaching. It will spread heretical teachings through false apostles and deceitful workers who will present themselves as ministers of righteousness. Since these individuals are working according to an antichrist spirit, they will be presenting another Jesus and preaching another gospel.[2]

This brings us to the final rank in the kingdom of darkness, rulers in high places who will work within governments, godless orders, and organizations. These entities in high places will gain the devotion and worship of subjects. I believe some of these rulers in high places could also be in reference to devils who plant the seeds of false doctrines through religious organizations that are based on the philosophies and lies of the present age. The Apostle Paul warns us that in the latter days some will depart from the faith because of the ongoing dripping of the conditioning and indoctrination that is taking place within our age, while others will not be able to endure sound doctrine after giving way to their various lusts. Such individuals will heap to themselves teachers who will tickle their ears with fables. He goes on to say that in some cases these people will have their conscience seared with a hot iron, unable to have their conscience pricked by truth.[3]

---

[1] 2 Corinthians 11:14

[2] 2 Corinthians 11:2-3, 13-15

[3] 1 Timothy 4:1-2; 2 Timothy 4:3-4

In Satan's mind the working of darkness in each sphere will allow him to ascend above the heights of his present kingdom. His perception and presentation is that ultimately he will become as the Most High, not subject to the sovereignty of any ruler. Due to his incredible pride, he perceives that in the end there will be no greater than he to whom he will have to answer to. However, we as believers know that Satan can make all the declarations he wants but it will not make it a reality.

This leads us to the harsh reality as to how our pride works within us. As previously pointed out, pride is what sits on the throne of the self-life. It serves as the platform between the flesh and the world. When it reigns, idolatry is at its height within man. It will declare its right to rule, as it boasts of its abilities to be self-sufficient. It will declare that it has the right to be happy; therefore, it can pursue such happiness through whatever avenue is available, whether it be through the flesh or the world. It will not be subdued no matter what pose it must take to maintain its independence. Ultimately, it will reign supreme as it takes its place as god to ensure that all who are in its world come into subjection to its way, its reality, and its idea of truth.

This brings us to how pride serves as one of the main inroads into the soul. Scripture tells us that pride sets people up for a big fall. It warns us not to think so highly of ourselves, and that when we think we stand, we are about to fall into the traps we are setting through our own forms of craft that we have devised along the way.[4] Don't kid yourself, we have devised such crafts to gain the control we desire.

Man cannot take control up front, any more than Satan can. This is where witchcraft comes into play. Subtract the word "witch" from witchcraft, and what do you have. In this text, "craft" points to being subtle, clever, and shrewd. Our craft can entail games we play with people's emotions, perceptions, and reality. It can be smokescreens we create with conning or exuding some type of charisma. However, we look at it or justify it, it is a craft. Like Satan, we use this craft to create a false way or reality so people cannot figure out what we are doing. We ourselves may even be deceived about what we are doing, whether we think we have a right or that we are right, we will justify creating a false way or reality to get our way. This is why we are clearly told by the writer in Psalm 119:28 that he hated every false way.

---

4   Proverbs 6:16-17; 11:2; 13:10; 16:18; Romans 12:3; 1 Corinthians 10:12

We develop these games early in life as a means to keep the peace or placate people to keep them off of our backs. Sadly, when we become adults, we think we can use these games in our relationships with others. However, the world is much more clever than we are about such matters, and is on to such games.

Satan uses our pride against us. He is forever daring us to get around the rules, ignore the consequences, and demand our rights. Our pride often takes up the challenge and obliges him, especially in the area of our spiritual life.

Consider the real test put forth to Jesus in the wilderness in Matthew 4. Satan tried to dare Him to prove He was the Son of God. Satan knew who He was but he wanted Jesus to give way to his test. Consider this for a moment—if Jesus gave way to this test, He would have been bowing before Satan.

It is important to know that pride wants everything to humble itself before its whims to prove it's supremacy Such schemes are a clever way for pride to get its way. It has nothing to do with right or wrong, truth or deception. In the case of Jesus, Satan wanted to humble the Son of God and our pride is no exception in that it wants to humble God before its throne as well. It wants God to save us in our sin as a proof of love, and make an exception for us rather than deprive us of our right to do as we please without paying consequences. When God refuses to become humbled before our pride and do it our way, like spoiled children we become angry, insolent, and accusing towards Him and others.

One of the things we warn Christians about in this ministry is that there is a very thin line between the kingdom of light and the kingdom of darkness. This line is created by our pride. Our susceptibility to give way to whatever excuse or craft we devise in order to have life on our terms will cause us to take the low road of deception, instead of the high road of truth and transparency. We often must throw up a smoke screen of justifications and excuses to convince ourselves and others that our way of thinking, doing, and being is what others should believe, exalt, and honor. Satan is always there to help our endeavors to take the low road. He will use such times to gain inroads into our lives reinforcing our deception, while planting divisive seeds of control through arrogant elitism, the isolation of indifference, and the conflict of wills. Ultimately, he will cause discord in relationships and death in our inner sanctuaries.

One of my concerns when I encourage people to simply ask God in prayer questions about different matters in regard to His will and trust He wants to show them, is that so many times these people can allow personal pride to take captive their motive and present reality without their knowledge. Often people end up with a quasi environment where wrong motives and agendas are exalted, as they begin to run ahead of God's real plans into the wilderness of absurdity. Scripture is clear—we are instructed to ask, seek, and knock. However, if our motive is wrong, the answer we receive will be in conjunction with the motive or agenda. We must know how to test the spirit behind our motive, recognize our Shepherd's voice, be honest about what we are seeking, and make sure we knock on the door to see if God is really going to open it for us or whether it remains closed.

It takes much integrity to test our motive, be honest about our attitude towards something, and hold ourselves accountable for our responses. It takes something called humility to properly test ourselves to ensure we are walking in the light. It is only by walking in the light that the real intent of our deeds is exposed. From this premise we can be assured that all matters of our lives are considered to be righteous. Righteousness results in right standing with God, being right before God in regard to our motives and intents, and doing right by others.

Most Christians know about the armor, but how many realize that armor is what covers our uniform. For the Christian soldiers, their uniform is humility, the complete opposite of pride. Before the Apostle Peter dealt with the subject of Satan in 1 Peter 5, he first instructed believers to clothe themselves daily with humility. If God resists our pride, there is no protection against Satan. As Christians, we cannot stand against Satan in our own prideful strength, we will not withstand him with our arrogant ways, and we will not remain standing in our foolish state of thinking that our crafty way, subtle justifications, clever games, and shrewd calculations will outsmart him. As they say, he will have us for dinner.

Without humility our armor will not properly fit on us. Humility is a state that allows us to humble ourselves to be reasoned with, to be honest about our motives, and take accountability for what is not right. It is in such a state that we can afford to become responsible for our state, our ways, our attitude, and our conduct. You can't fake this state.

You might give the appearance of godliness, but down the line the lack of humility will reveal the real state of your folly.

Humility clearly reveals that there was a pivot point in your life where you really got it. In other words, you finally saw the depths, workings, and insidious ways of your pride. This pivot point, points to real repentance where the reality of your pride was exposed in light of Jesus' humility on the cross and it broke you. You saw how this sinister culprit works in every fiber of your being, way of thinking, and doing. It also revealed how wretched, base, and depraved you can become because of your pride. There is no getting around it or getting away with it. It is what it is.

As we can see, people's pride attempts to humble God. It puts Him to a foolish test, as it competes with Him in regard to other people's lives. It wants to be exalted as an expert, as well as maintain the right to determine truth and reality to receive undue credibility and honor. It wants to avoid justice and responsibility while making everyone else responsible to make it happy with itself and smug with its importance. It is an insatiable appetite that will never be satisfied, and is a haughty look that speaks of how abominable it is before God. However, take the air out of pride and you will discover that it is the part of our character that makes each of us so very small.

Pride's smallness is brought out in Isaiah 14:15-17. We know that like Satan, those who are ruled by pride will be brought down to the pit of hell. But, consider what is said about such prideful personalities once they stand in the light of God's judgment: "They that see thee shall narrowly look upon thee, and consider thee, saying, Is this the man who made the earth to tremble, who did shake kingdoms, Who made the world like a wilderness, and destroyed its cities, who opened not the house of his prisoners?"

In light of this information, will you find yourself exalted in humility or exposed and made quite small by the insipid, hellish ways of pride?

9

THE TRIANGLE OF EVIL

We have been considering Satan and how he works. The Apostle Paul tells us we must not be ignorant of the devices Satan uses.[1] Sadly, it appears as if many, even in the Church, are ignorant about the enemy of God and how he affects men's souls. As soldiers, we must recognize our enemies and how they work if we are going to overcome them.

The one thing we can count on with Satan are the ways in which he tries and often succeeds in counterfeiting the things of God. His attacks are often a three pronged, triangle in shape. Perhaps, this is why his symbol is a hexagram with a goat's head or image in it. Hexagram is basically two triangles placed on top of each other to form six points. The number "six" points to the number of imperfection, as well the number that is going to identify people in the end days to Satan systems. Satan is determined to come out on top of every point as he tries to counterfeit, cover up, or override God in some way. We cannot see how he is weaving his plan into the intricate workings of the world's systems, but we can be assured that he has been working according to this diabolic plan from the beginning of his fall.

In order to gain worship, Satan is striving to be supreme ruler over all. His attempt to bring all man under his auspice as a means to humble God is known as the mystery of iniquity. It is no secret that he is after this supremacy. You can see it in the event of the tower of Babel. What makes it a mystery is that it was being done in darkness.[2] Even though many people mock the idea of a conspiracy taking place in the world to bring about a desired result, the idea of Satan working to bring about supremacy through his systems would clearly classify such an attempt as being a conspiracy. If you know anything about history, you will know he has attempted to do this many times, but there has always been an unseen hand that has somehow pushed him back.

---

[1]   2 Corinthians 2:11

[2]   Genesis 11:1-9; 2 Thessalonians 2:7

Satan's attempts to gain supremacy may cause confusion, but as you consider his methods, there is a "triangle" that can be seen no matter which way you look at how he handles a matter. If you can pinpoint the "triangle," you will be able to cut through a lot of confusion. For example, the world is designed with various attractions to take a person captive through the lusts of the flesh, the pride of life, and the lusts of the eyes. In the end those who come under his auspice will surely be led away to the slaughter to serve as Satan's personal scapegoats and sacrifices.

We know Satan is after our worship. However, we must overcome in those areas that he uses to gain such worship. Once again, a "triangle" appears. For example, the world demands our alliance and allegiance, self desires adoration, and the flesh strives for our compliance and servitude. However, we see the simple command of Jesus requiring us to respond in three ways to Satan's counterfeits: Deny self, pick up your cross, and follow Him.

We see this triangle of evil in many other areas. We know in the end days there will be the dragon (Satan), the beast (antichrist), and the false prophet that will head the one world government that will be put into place. Clearly, this triangle of evil is to counterfeit the Godhead: The Father, the Son, and the Holy Spirit.

Jesus tells us of two other triangles of evil in regard to Satan in John 8:44 and John 10:10. In John 8:44, the Son of God made this statement, "Ye are of your father the devil, and the lusts of your father ye will do. He was a murderer from the beginning, and abode not in the truth, because there is no truth in him. When he speaketh a lie, he speaketh of his own; for he is a liar, and the father of it." In this Scripture, we see where Satan is the father of all that which is contrary to God, life, and spiritual liberty. His goal is simple. It is to entangle the lust of the flesh and murder all that is of God. He does this through lies. Clearly, there is no life in that which comes or originates with him. There is only the triangle of death which is hidden by darkness as a means to produce deception.

In John 10:10, Jesus gave us this insight into the triangle of evil, "The thief cometh not, but for to steal, and to kill and to destroy: I am come that they might have life, and that they might have it more abundantly." Our Lord referred to Satan as the thief whose goal is to cheat us by stealing our faith, killing our testimony, and destroying any life of God we may possess.

We have also seen this triangle of evil in 2 Corinthians 11:13-15. In these Scriptures we are told that Satan transforms himself into an angel of light while false apostles and deceitful workers transform themselves into the apostles of Christ. Satan counterfeits himself as the light of the world, while his false apostles and deceitful workers present themselves as ministers of righteousness. According to 2 Corinthians 11:3-4, their goal clearly forms another triangle and is quite simple. They want to move believers away from the simplicity of Christ so that they will receive another Jesus, spirit, and gospel.

The main inroad Satan uses to gain access into our lives, homes, churches, and societies is pride. Pride is also a triangle in that it produces a self-sufficient disposition and an arrogant attitude that manifests itself in a haughty look. Remember, its four companions of fear, confusion, complacency, and delusion that will set us up to fall into Satan's traps. These "friends" of pride will cause us to fall into some type of idolatry, unbelief, and paganism.

As we consider these avenues that Satan uses, we must recognize that the four companions will tell us something about the attitude we have developed towards God, while the products of these avenues, idolatry, unbelief, and paganism will speak of our inward condition. For example, idolatry reveals a person has a divided heart, unbelief a hard heart, and paganism a worldly heart. But, what do the four companions tell us about our attitude towards the matters of God?

It is important to point out that temptation can begin from the premise of confusion. In many cases we assume that we know something when in reality we have not been grounded in a matter. Consider what the Apostle Paul stated in 2 Timothy 1:12-13:

> For the which cause I also suffer these things: nevertheless I am not ashamed: for I know whom I have believed, and am persuaded that he is able to keep that which I have committed unto him against that day. Hold fast the form of sound words, which thou hast heard of me, in faith and love which is in Christ Jesus.

The Apostle Paul had suffered much for his faith in Christ, but he was not ashamed to have such identification. After all, he was persuaded by what he knew about His Lord, and as a result he was able to commit all matters to Him. He told others that they could hold fast to the words they had heard him speak.

We must not assume that we know a matter; rather, we must be able to give an account of the hope that is in us with meekness and fear as instructed by the Apostle Peter. Assumption leads to presumption which has to do with self-will trying to bring a matter about. However, if you take assumption and presumption, they both reveal that one is ignorant in regard to God's ways and will. Here lies another triangle. Acts 17:30 states that God will not wink at such ignorance; instead, He is calling men everywhere to repent. We can know our God, and we need to know our God, and as Daniel 11:32 tells us, those who know God will be strong and do exploits.

Fear tells us that we do not trust God. There is also a triangle when it comes to how fear affects our spiritual life. The Apostle Paul declares in 2 Timothy 1:7 that God has not given us a spirit of fear but of power, love, and a sound mind. Although there is a natural fear that man must recognize, there is also a powerful spirit of fear. It will paralyze us, preventing us from overcoming. The reason fear can take such power over us is because we do not trust God in different circumstances or with important matters.

The reason we do not trust God is because we choose not to love Him. If we do not love Him, how can we trust His character when everything around us seems to be closing in on us? In the end days we are warned that men's hearts will wax cold as fear grips them in unbearable ways when they see and experience unleashed iniquity taking center stage. Hebrews 12:3 tells us that to avoid becoming weary and fainting in our minds we must consider what our Lord endured on our behalf. The Apostle John reminds us that perfect love casts out fear.[3]

Fear also causes people to be confused or double-minded. They will not know which way to turn. Their faith is being tested, their foundation shaken, and their understanding is becoming dark. Nothing makes sense and everything appears hopeless. This is where people must choose to trust what they know about God. Once again, if you do not know

---

[3]   Matthew 24:12; 1 John 4:18-19

God, how can you choose to trust Him and His Word or promises? No wonder the Apostle John stated that the young men had overcome the wicked one because the Word of God abided in them.[4]

The third companion to pride is complacency. Complacency points to being dulled down by the environment, causing one to become indifferent to God. Such an environment will prove to be self-serving in its attractions and pursuits. The complacent attitude wants to "feel" good or comfortable in everything it does. However, it is simply a form of spiritual slothfulness and emotional laziness that often produces procrastination. In such a state things do not get done. People entrusted with a few responsibilities in His kingdom will drop the ball and never be entrusted with more responsibilities. The Apostle Paul exhorted Christians to wake up and then stir themselves up to do what is right. He also talked about running the race to obtain the prize, but to run it you have to bring aspects of your mind and body into subjection to avoid being a castaway.[5]

Delusion is the fourth friend of pride. It brings us another triangle of evil. It has to do with the subtle or clever ways in which Satan works within the confines of his evil triangle to deceive people. In Ephesians 6:11 the Apostle Paul tells us that we have been given armor to stand against the wiles of the devil. The word "wiles" points to trickery. Keep in mind, witchcraft has to do with using some type of craft to deceive as a means of controlling. Satan has devised his form of craft or trickery to take us captive with lies.

The tendencies of people are to live in denial as to Satan's capabilities or be flippant when making any real reference to him. Yet, the Apostle Paul is clear that he is an enemy that must be recognized, respected, and properly confronted. We cannot afford to be ignorant or foolish about his devices. To combat his "wiles" requires us to wear our complete armor. In spite of the foolish claims that Satan has no teeth in which he can do any harm to God's people, the Apostle Peter assures us that he is able to devour those are not sober or vigilant where he is concerned. In fact, we must clothe ourselves in humility to ensure that we are sober

---

[4] 1 John 2:14

[5] Psalm 35:23; Luke 16:10-12; 1 Corinthians 9:23-27; 15:34; Ephesians 5:14

and vigilant in regard to properly stand against this enemy, withstand his attacks, and to keep standing as a means to resist steadfastly in the faith.[6]

The trickery of Satan is also brought out by different Scriptures such as Genesis 3:1 where it points to the serpent being more subtle or crafty than the rest of the beasts. In 2 Corinthians 4:2 we read that we must renounce the hidden things of dishonesty, not walking in craftiness, nor mishandling the Word of God in deceitfulness. Ephesians 4:14 talks about how people can be carried away with every wind of doctrine, by the sleight of men and cunning craftiness, whereby such individuals lie in wait to deceive. Once again, we see Satan's triangle in how he works his craft. There is the element of dishonesty at work, the trickery in which to get man to buy such deception, and the device that is used which is the mishandling of God's Word or truth in some way.

This brings us to the second part of the meaning of "wiles." It points to our enemy lying in wait. Notice the last part of Ephesians 4:14 about those who are using the tricks of Satan's trade to deceive people. They are lying in wait. In other words, he, along with his workers are waiting for the right opportunity to take us captive with deception.

We can clearly see this in the case of our country. The progressive movement that has taken center stage in this nation was rejected by the people at different times in our history. Each time it went under cover to lie in wait for the right opportunity or right environment to once again raise its ugly head. Each time if has cleverly worked in darkness to condition our younger generations to buy its perverted, gross, murdering lies.

In the last chapter it was pointed out how Satan must first condition us to believe his false reality. Whether it is within the confines of his world's systems that include religion, politics, education, and so forth, he knows we must be conditioned to buy his particular deceptive reality. In the last chapter, we considered how he uses the ranks of his kingdom to bring about such a receptive environment so that people will fall like flies into his destructive traps.

This triangle of evil and trickery as to how Satan conditions his targets can clearly be seen at work in the Garden of Eden. We see Satan cleverly setting Eve up to fall into his trap of deception. When we study the fall in the garden, it is often noted that the "silly" woman was

---

[6]   Ephesians 6:13-14; 1 Peter 5:5-9

deceived. Instead of pointing the finger as to who got who and who is to blame for what, we need to learn how the enemy works and the lessons that both Eve and Adam have left us for our edification.

We must first note that according to 1 Timothy 2:14, Eve was deceived and as a result was in transgression, but Adam was not. This stipulates who was the most vulnerable of the couple. Why was she vulnerable? Where do you think Satan positioned himself as he waited for the right opportunity to deceive Eve? No doubt he was waiting at the location of the forbidden tree for a time when Eve would walk by it. It is for this reason that we are told to flee that which would stir up our youthful lusts and to separate from that which would entangle us into the affairs of the world which would bring us into agreement with it.

The Apostle Paul explains how great the deception was that Eve came under in 2 Corinthians 11:2-3 by stating she was beguiled by the serpent. "Beguile" in this text implies that she was actually cheated through exceedingly clever seduction. What happened to Eve was not a minor attack or affront. Satan cleverly and thoroughly robbed her of her life in God.

It is important to understand that Satan does not invent new tricks, he simply repackages the old ones. There is nothing new under the sun, including his tricks of the trade, but he knows how to make them attractive to each age. He cleverly changes the intent or meaning of words in order to create a different reality as a way to attract people to that which would be considered new or better in the light of his deception. Let us see how he uses the triangle of evil in regard to Eve in Genesis 3:1-6 to cause her to become beguiled, cheating her of her life in God.

The first thing we must note about Eve is that she was a bit confused about the instruction in regard to the tree. She stated that they were not to eat or touch the fruit of the tree, but God's instruction was not to eat of the fruit of it. To add or subtract from any of God's instructions is to pervert it. Clearly, this is why Satan tempted her and not Adam.

It is in a state of confusion that Satan starts with his first affront by throwing doubt on God's Word. Did He really say such and such? The way Satan throws such doubt is to cause us to begin to wonder if God meant what He said. If the environment does not fit our desired reality, this is the first thing we will do. We will speculate about whether God means what He says in His Word. We see Eve's first big mistake when she tried to reason with Satan rather than rebuking him with what she knew to be true. It is for this reason that Jesus stated in His temptation in the wilderness that we live by every Word that proceeds out of the mouth of God. We also know that genuine faith approaches the Word to believe it, not speculate or debate about it. Faith comes by hearing, and hearing by the Word of God.[7]

The second affront Satan made was an attack against God's character. He does this by implying that God has ulterior motives. If you do not mean what you say, then you are untrustworthy. Clearly, he was tempting Eve to put God to a foolish test to see if He really did mean what He said: the lie being that she would not die; rather, she would become enlightened by experiencing evil. The lie was that it was not enough to know something was evil, she had to personally experience it to know why it was evil. This is why Jesus stated that we are not to put God to such a foolish test, because it will result in consequences.

God is not like earthly parents who often idly threaten their rebellious children. The Lord warns or admonishes us that we will pay the consequences for our actions. He does not need to lecture, nor does He need to clarify or defend what He has said. It is the way it is. In the case of Eve, it was clear: if you eat of this tree, be assured you will die. This is where we see Eve make the second big mistake: she began to think about the tree. It was now becoming a point of attraction to her, where before she may have not given it much consideration. Temptation can only gain inroads when we begin to consider or toy with the possibilities of something that had no significance in the past.

This brings us to another triangle that involves knowledge. Knowledge is not only a grave test, but often serves as a powerful avenue for Satan to gain inroads into our lives. It is vital for us to understand how Satan uses knowledge to enslave us in our thinking. The Bible makes reference to destructive knowledge in relationship to God in three Scriptural texts. There is knowledge inspired by pride, knowledge that is moved by fleshly zeal, and knowledge that has not been tempered by virtue.

According to 1 Corinthians 8:1-2, knowledge that is puffed up by pride lacks love. Even though a person may think he or she has a corner on a particular subject, he or she must remember that a person can only

---

[7] Genesis 3:3; Matthew 4:4; Romans 10:17

know in part. In our fleshly tabernacles we house carnal minds that must be transformed by the Spirit. Note, our minds must not be transformed by more knowledge or a particular type of knowledge such as doctrine, but by the Holy Spirit. Therefore, we must not assume our conclusions constitute truth.

The problem with undisciplined knowledge is that the arrogance and conceits of the carnal mind would have us believe that there is no way we can be wrong about a matter. After all, we researched it on the internet, exposed ourselves to what we believe to be reliable sources, and turned over every stone that was made obvious to us to gain insight into the situation. However, the exalted opinion of such knowledge finds its source in pride.

Deep will call to deep. This means I will go with the natural preference of what first catches the imagination of my mind. Such knowledge will appeal to my arrogance for it will seem logical to my way of thinking and feed my conceits for it will satisfy my sense of knowledge as to what I would consider a sufficient explanation. Therefore, my conclusion will be based on that which made me feel smart in light of those I respect, sure in what I think I know, and superior in my knowledge towards those who are not, thus far, "enlightened".

Clearly, such a state is not interested in the truth. The mind at this point is actually indifferent to reality, unteachable, judgmental, touchy, and mean spirited towards anyone who dares to challenge its fragile, empty foundation. The Apostle Paul puts knowledge in this perspective in 1 Corinthians 13:2, "And though I have the gift of prophecy, and understand all mysteries, and all knowledge; and though I have all faith, so that I could remove mountains, and have not charity, I am nothing."

According to the Apostle Paul in Romans 10:2-4, those who have a zeal towards God based on limited knowledge will prove to be ignorant of what constitutes God's righteousness. Subsequently, knowledge that lacks understanding of righteousness, according to God, will operate from the only known premise: the philosophies of the world. Paul warned believers in Colossians 2:8 of being spoiled through the philosophy and vain deceit of traditions established by man that find their source in the rudiments or foundations of the world.

As Christians, our pursuit of knowledge must not be an intellectual or fleshly pursuit. We must keep in mind that our initial encounters with God are often exciting, new, and fresh, but to mature in such understanding we must learn who God is. It is not a matter of what I think I know about God; rather, it is a matter of growing in the knowledge of who He is. As I understand the character of God, I will begin to distinguish what would be considered righteous to Him.

It is for this reason that the Apostle Peter exhorts us in 2 Peter 1:8 that we must not to be barren or unfruitful in the knowledge of our Lord Jesus Christ. We are told in 2 Peter 1:5-6 that knowledge must follow virtue. In other words, integrity must be present to properly handle all knowledge. Such integrity includes having the wisdom to discern the credibility of such knowledge and walk out godly insight in order to make it a reality.

Knowledge that can be properly discerned and handled will always be tempered by the Word of God. The problem with most people is that they have no standard in which to test their knowledge. In most cases, God's only sure standard, the Bible, has been undermined in some way. Therefore, people test their knowledge according to how a matter makes them feel and not the Word of God. We clearly see how the environment of delusion has escalated because in most people's minds there is no sure foundation in which to test anything other than by their own personal understanding.

The final affront against God in the Garden of Eden was directed at His glory. This is very important to understand. "Glory" has to do with that which distinguishes you. God's glory stipulates that He is who He says He is, and He is worthy of unfeigned commitment, service, and worship. He is God and His glory verifies this. In Jesus' last temptation, Satan showed Him the glory of his kingdoms. We read the Apostle Paul's words in Romans 1:23, "And changed the glory of the incorruptible God into an image made like corruptible man, and birds, and four-footed beasts, and creeping things."

How do you change God's glory in the minds of people? Well, now that you have created doubts about the integrity of His Word and questions about His character, it is easy to cause people to question the goodness or sincerity of His intentions about a matter. If you get people to question the sincerity of God's intentions, you will change His glory as to what distinguishes Him. In other words, you will either make Him an indifferent force, very human as far as motives, or even common like the rest of creation as to how He handles matters. He will cease to stand out in people's minds, as their affections are being drawn elsewhere. Like much of humanity, if His intentions are considered hypocritical because He has some underlying motive or concern in regard to competition, He is not someone to fear because He really does not have the necessary integrity or power to bring about a matter. He is not someone worthy of consideration or obedience because He is untrustworthy. And, one will conclude that He is not someone to worship because He does not stand distinct from the rest of creation.

Now that God has been made untrustworthy, Eve made the final mistake. She looked upon the tree according to a false light created by Satan, causing the tree to be regarded in a whole new way. Clearly, her affections and imaginations had been taken captive. It was from this so-called "enlightened premise" that the tree looked good, pleasurable, and would cause her to perceive that she would come out wiser for taking of its fruit, especially in lieu of becoming as a god, knowing good and evil. Who or what is being exalted at this point? It is from this premise that God appeared less desirable. Don't forget Satan's last declaration, "I will be like the most High" (Isaiah 14:14). But, he must in some way lower God by changing His glory in the eyes of people in order to accomplish it.

The Bible is clear as to God's intentions towards us. Consider Jeremiah 29:11, "For I know the thoughts that I think toward you, saith the LORD, thoughts of peace, and not of evil, to give you an expected end."

Perhaps, you can see why Eve was totally beguiled by Satan. These three affronts against God represent what we would call a slam-dunk when it comes to deception.

We know that Adam was not deceived, but it is very interesting to see how Adam gave way to Satan. First of all he let him enter the garden, apparently Adam did not see how he could be a threat. Perhaps he assumed in ignorance that Satan was harmless or presumed in some type of arrogance that his presence was no big deal. Remember, Satan lies in wait, watching for the perfect opportunity to set his trap.

Perhaps Satan did not pose a threat to Adam, but he was not after Adam. He was clearly after Eve. This is the problem with most people when they allow a bit of "leaven" or evil into their home. Perhaps they can handle it, but what about those who are vulnerable such as children? When evil that is present in our midst is left unchallenged, it will allow it the opportunity to gain a foothold where it will one day rule in some way. Do not fool yourself, a complacent attitude towards Satan and evil is a matter of pride.

Next, he let the serpent tempt Eve, while knowing the truth and did not rebuke this enemy or set the record straight. In complacency we omit righteousness. We do not think any affront against truth or righteousness is any big deal. However, lack of response is the same as agreeing with it or partaking of the lie or sin.

Finally, when confronted by his disobedient actions, he went into self-delusion by justifying his actions at the expense of Eve and God. Like Peter during Jesus' last night before His crucifixion, Adam was being sifted and was found wanting in regard to his character. Clearly, Adam was hiding underlying motives that no doubt would be traced back to some form of pride. The fact that he willingly partook of the sin pretty well gives us insight into this man's commitment to his Creator. Job brings out the inner character of Adam in Job 31:33, "If I covered my transgressions as Adam by hiding mine iniquity in my bosom."

As you can see, Satan works in a triangle. If you can discern what device or trickery he is using, you can overcome him. A good place to begin is with repentance, where you come into a state of humility in order to humble yourself before God in submission to His conviction. Once you submit to His conviction, you can begin to be converted to what is right. Righteousness will become part of the transforming work of the Spirit upon your mind. Once your mind is converted by the transforming work of the Spirit, your heart will naturally follow to embrace a matter as truth.

What about you? As Christians, each of us should be like Jesus, standing on the Word, refusing to put God to a foolish test, and rebuking Satan for trying to gain inroads into our souls so that he can receive underserved worship. Or, are you like Adam, complacent towards the presence of evil in your midst or like Eve, vulnerable and ready to be taken captive by evil. By repenting you can come to a humble state where you can claim the promise that whosoever has been set free by the Son of God has been set free indeed.[8]

---

[8]   John 8:36

10

The Armor Of God

Satan is a big topic, yet in many ways he is treated as a minor subject in some Christian circles. He is limited by God, yet in other circles he is greatly empowered and often becomes a scapegoat for the immoral deviations and practices of man. He is the god of this age that works utter spiritual devastation in men's lives, yet the God of heaven is angrily accredited with the destruction Satan works in the lives of those who hate their Creator. In their hatred these individuals justify their unbelief towards God and the wickedness of their own lives. In the minds of some people, Satan is a toothless lion who bluffs his way through the den of the present world, instead of a roaring lion who is capable of devouring those who do not soberly understand who he is, and vigilantly discern when he is present and ready to take someone captive.

For the last couple of chapters we have been stripping away the layers, or I should say the coverings in which Satan works. Shrouded in confusion, as well as in the darkness of ignorance and unbelief, this enemy of God often works unhindered and unopposed as he gains inroads into people's souls, homes, churches, and societies.

Satan's target is our faith. For this reason Jesus asked if He would find genuine faith when He came back the second time. This enemy's goal is simple: to become supreme ruler in order to receive our worship. He desires to humble God instead of being subject to His rule. It is for this reason that he is forever trying to change the glory of God in the minds and hearts of people. He does this through clever deception.[1]

Deception is a way of setting up the environment in which man will in some way worship and serve Satan as the god of this age. The greatest environment he sets up is that of idolatry, and the greatest avenue in which man can be taken captive is through his pride. We can see this scenario where the Apostle Paul talked about our pride in relationship to temptation in 1 Corinthians 10:12-14. His exhortation is clear, flee idolatry.

---

[1]   Luke 18:8; Romans 1:23-28

Satan wants to set up the necessary environment that will condition us to fall into idolatry, which entails paganism and unbelief. Once again, we have the triangle of evil. These three elements point to the inward disposition of man. According to Ezekiel 8:11-13 and 14:3-7, idolatry occurs on two fronts: in the high places of the mind and the secret chambers of the heart. It is for this reason that the flesh entices our affections and the world is poised to entangle our imaginations in order to own our soul. It is the mind that exalts idols by giving them some form of identity and authority, while it is in the heart that such idols become preferred causing people to pursue after, bow down to, and worship them. Once the mind exalts an idol and the heart begins to worship the idol, you will see the body give way to pagan practices that will be sensual and fleshly, in spite of such images being dead, lifeless, and reprobate. Such practices reveal that people are walking in unbelief towards the true God of heaven. Jesus made reference to this idolatry when he stated that people of His day drew near to God with their lips but their hearts were far away from Him.[2]

Idolatry is found at the core of fleshly ways and worldly attitudes. It is often expressed through paganism. However, there is also a subtlety that exists in paganism when it comes to idolatry. For years it was observed that in some nations such as Africa, the worship of idols was blatant and obvious as the people's pagan ways of witchcraft took center stage. These individuals openly worshipped their idols in sensual ways. Often driven by fear and superstition, these people would enter another state of mind to pay homage to a frightening world of darkness that entailed the unseen demonic forces through means such as magic, music, dance, and drugs. Since Satan is after the worship of man, we must reason and keep in mind that demonic activity is behind all idolatry.

I recall the story of a missionary from America who was confronted with this reality when in Africa. A new convert to Christianity told her that they appreciated the American missionaries bringing the Gospel to them, but they could not understand why they continued to ignore or deny the influence of the demonic world on people's lives. Clearly, it had been their reality in Africa, and one that they could not ignore if they were to overcome as believers.

---

[2] Matthew 15:8

Through the years I have watched the different attitudes of Christians in America swing from one extreme to another about the presence of demonic activity. The consensus I was most acquainted with is that in America, demonic activity is restricted to a few isolated cases. Even in spite of the trans-like beat of music that inspires rebellion or an altered state of consciousness, along with the New Age beliefs and practices that would yoke people to demons, as well as the rise of drug use that open people up to the demonic kingdom, many in the Christian realm have acted as if America is immune to such demonic activity gaining any inroads into our society.

This is when I realized how clever Satan has been in gaining inroads into our culture. Paganism is the breeding ground for all demonic activity. The only difference between paganism in Africa and America is that America has civilized its paganism. It is at this point that I came to realize there is nothing more seductive or deceptive than civilized paganism.

In civilized paganism, idols have been window dressed or hidden under various cultural activities; nevertheless, they are still present. For America, its idols have come in the form of money, education, entertainment, sports, religious and political leaders, along with the concept of worldly power and success. Even though we cannot see people physically bowing down to such idols or dancing around their altars, they are nevertheless bowing down in their hearts as their minds honor such idols, while they speculate how to pursue, possess, or model themselves after that which they highly value. In the end, such individuals become rebellious, indifferent, and lawless, as they become more ignorant and unbelieving towards God. Some will be turned over to a reprobate mind that no longer retains any real knowledge of God. At this point their conscience has been thoroughly seared, for the world now clearly determines their worldview or premise, while their pride of self stubbornly determines their reality. The flesh has become their final authority as to what they will pursue and what altar, such as TV, sports, worldly philosophies, positions, or events, they will dance around or stand before in sensual or fleshly abandonment.

The Apostle Paul in Ephesians 6:11 instructed the soldiers of the cross to put on the whole armor of God to stand against the clever advancements of the enemy. Once again, we must note that we are not to "take territory," but to maintain it by standing against the wiles of the devil.

In Ephesians 6:12, we are once again reminded that we do not wrestle against flesh and blood, but against that which is unseen, powerful, and has a mission of wickedness. For this reason we are again exhorted to put on the whole armor of God, not just a couple of pieces when we feel like it or when we perceive it will serve our purpose. We must put on the whole armor of God if we are going to withstand in the evil day.

The one aspect of popular Christianity that is presented that causes revulsion in me is people's attitude towards Satan and the armor. In the past I have watched Christians go through the so-called "process" of putting their armor on to combat the evils of the day, without having any real concept as to what it means. In its place was a flippancy that if they went through the outward motions of putting some imaginary armor on that they were protected from the wiles of the enemy. The truth is, although Satan may be an unseen enemy, he is not an imaginary enemy. He is real and He plays for keeps.

The battle for Christians is not just a matter of standing; but, we must also withstand the attacks that will be leveled at us. And, when we have withstood, we must continue to stand because Satan will continue to make his advancements until he realizes that there is no vulnerable spot in which he can take a soldier captive or destroy him or her. He will have to withdraw to fight another day or flee because he no longer possesses the authority to continue his assault. However, such retreat will only be for a season for he will devise a new game plan, and once he does, he will lie in wait for his intended target to be tempted to fall into his trap.

As believers, we have the necessary armor to stand and not retreat or surrender, regardless of what is thrown at us. Although much of our battle is fought in the spiritual arena, our armor is not imaginary. It is real, but we need to understand how we put such armor on in the spiritual realm. We must understand how it protects us and the implication behind it. However, before we can put on our armor, we must remember to put on the proper undergarment.

The armor of God is the outer protection that is put on over our daily garment. If the right undergarment is not properly in place, the armor of God will not protect us. Before we can understand what it really means to overcome Satan, we first must come to terms with getting our undergarment right in order to put on the armor of God to ensure our personal protection and well-being.

A couple of chapters ago we talked about how Satan gains inroads into our lives. The greatest avenue is that of pride. Pride serves as the platform between our flesh and the attractions of the world. It judges God for not bowing down to its judgments. It falsely accuses Him, while touting how just it is and how unfair God is in light of its so-called "justice". It questions God's intention as a means to demean Him, while daring Him to prove Himself by saving us in sin or making us an exception to the rule by sparing us of the affects and consequences that our stubborn, perverted ways can have upon our lives.

Obviously, we must first address the matter of pride in our lives before we can confront the flesh and the world. We must shut down this avenue altogether. It is for this reason Jesus stated that we must first deny the right of the self-life to govern, judge, and exalt itself in any way, shape, or form.

This brings us to the undergarment that we must put on daily to ensure that our armor fits properly. We are once again reminded of this garment in 1 Peter 5:5. Peter instructs us to be clothed with humility for God resists the proud and gives grace to the humble.

We know that we are saved by grace.[3] In other words, everything we are provided with in our spiritual life is a matter of grace. God does not have to provide the armor. He does not have to regard us in our plight, but because He is full of grace He has shown us favor by regarding our predicament and providing the necessary means to overcome the enemy of our souls. However, He can only show this grace towards us when we are ready to receive it and appropriate it in our lives in a proper way.

In 1 Peter 5:8, we are told to be sober and vigilant. This means being sober in doing right and vigilant in guarding what is of God. Satan is like a lion who will devour our life in God. We have a tendency to be flippant towards our enemy and foolish towards his deceptive ways. In fact, I have been told that Satan is a toothless lion. This is an example of how even Christians regard the devil in a foolish light. Humility is the best way to address such an attitude.

Obviously, the only state in which we can receive God's grace is from a state of humility. James 4:6-10 reveals the necessity for humility to be

---

[3]   Ephesians 2:8

in place when it comes to Satan. It is only from this state that we can properly submit to God. It is in such submission that God becomes our point of authority to stand against the wiles of the devil, our place of refuge to withstand his onslaught, and our source of strength to remain standing when all seems lost. By submitting to God, Satan will see there is no inroad for him to gain any access into our lives. We are under God's protection, leadership, and direction, and that in Christ we are able to resist the devil's temptation, lies, and maneuvers to gain some type of hold on our lives.

James also reveals what such submission entails. After all, there are those in the Christian realm who think highly of their form of humility. They perceive that they have submitted to God when in reality they have simply given way to the deception of the fake nobility of their pride.

Submission involves drawing near to God as a cringing beggar who recognizes that without His intervention there is no hope. Jesus put it best when He stated, "Blessed are the poor in spirit for theirs is the kingdom of God." Once we draw near to God in need, we will be broken at the point of our pride and sin, and will become contrite, pliable, and receptive to His mercy and grace. Hence, enters Jesus' declaration of, "Blessed are those who mourn for they shall be comforted."[4]

Such a state points to coming to a place of repentance and meekness before God that allows cleansing. Out of cleansing comes spiritual healing and restoration. Our hands can be washed clean of touching that which was profane and begin to pursue what is righteous. Jesus promised that those who are meek shall inherit the earth, and those who hunger and thirst after righteousness shall be satisfied in their souls. At this point, we can be assured that our hearts can be cleansed from divided loyalties, allowing us to see God in the beauty of His holiness, as our minds are transformed so that we can be clear about what is important to Him. What is important to God is that of reconciliation with each of us which will bring peace to our souls and minds.[5]

It is only from the state of humility that our minds can be changed about a matter. Our understanding about something will determine our attitude towards it. Consider what our attitude must be towards the world. We must cease to worry about the matters of the world, cast all of

---

4   Matthew 5:3-4

5   Matthew 5:5-8; Romans 12:2-3; 2 Corinthians 5:18-19

our cares upon the Lord, knowing it is His business. We must then gird up the loins of our minds.[6]

The word "gird" points to binding something up. There should be no loose ends that can cause inconsistency, confusion, or uncertainty in the mind. The concept of "loin" points to the procreative power to resolve a matter in order to be confident as to what needs to be done.[7] We know that the cares of the world can cause a person to become agitated, and that fear can grip a mind that has not been girded up or disciplined. In summation, we know that the cares of the world can bury us and fear can paralyze us.[8]

The results of "girding up the mind" will produce a right attitude in facing what is before us. The attitude is that of sobriety that is void of foolishness, as well as vigilance which points to a mind that is alert and on guard. It is with such a mind that we can resist Satan as we hold fast to our faith towards God. In the end, we can be assured of exchanging a spirit of heaviness with a garment of praise. After all, God inhabits the praises of His people. Such praises often become those precious sacrifices to Him when it comes to withstanding the enemy of our soul.[9]

With the proper undergarment in place, we then must gird up the undergarment with truth.[10] Humility allows the armor to be placed on us in an orderly fashion, but truth ensures that the armor fits tightly against our body as a means to distinguish the importance of our life and mission. It points to that inner resolution that everything about our walk must be disciplined by the Lord's immutable truths.

When I was in the military, the belt is what brought out the sharpness of the uniform. Without such sharpness, the uniform became disheveled, losing its attraction and distinction. This is what truth does for our armor. It ensures that it will distinguish us as to what we stand for.

To gird up the undergarment with truth means that we must bind all that we know to be true to every aspect of our Christian life. This means lining up to the cornerstone of our faith, Jesus Christ. Jesus is the essence of all absolute truth. We must believe the truth about Him, believe that

---

[6]   1 Peter 1:13; 5:7

[7]   Strong's Exhaustive Concordance: #328, 2224, 3751

[8]   Hebrews 12:3; 1 Peter 5:7

[9]   Psalm 22:3; Isaiah 61:3; Hebrews 13:15-16; 1 Peter 1:8-9

[10]   Ephesians 6:14

He is truth, and believe in His work of redemption. We must resolve in our inner being to love the truth as a means to stand against any false reality or way that would spiritually dull us down, delude us as to what is going on, and cause us to walk in unbelief towards the matters of God.[11]

The final purpose for the belt is that it is where the sword hung, until it was ready to be used. The Word is truth. It is upheld by the reality that when the sword of the Word is being used, it will be ready and available to be effectively used against the enemy. But, until the sword of the Word needs to be used, it will rest on God's eternal truths that there is no need for another weapon for it is capable of defeating any of the enemy's advancements.

After we gird up the undergarment with truth, we are able to put on the breastplate of righteousness. The breastplate guards our heart against all that would rob us of a credible testimony in regard to our lives in Jesus Christ. Many walk in shame because they failed to do right. Granted, these individuals may have justified the deviation in their attitude, character, or actions, but their conscience reveals their guilt. If there is any tenderness in their hearts, the Holy Spirit will also convict of such deviation. Such individuals are not able to stand before the Lord in confidence. As a result, they will not be in right standing with Him.

People know what is right and wrong. However, they fail to guard the affections of their hearts by resolving in their inner man that they must not toy with or give way to the preferences and feelings of the flesh and the justification of pride. When it comes to their attitude and conduct, they must discipline their affections by directing them upward as a means to set them on the only one who is capable of ensuring their integrity, Jesus Christ. Once their focus is directed towards the right source, they will flee that which could take their affections captive, and effectively pursue after what is considered right and acceptable to the Lord. Such a soldier will fight the good fight of faith as he or she lays hold of eternal life.[12]

It is active faith that allows God to reckon our status as being in right standing before Him and our obedient actions as being righteous. Righteousness certainly lies at the heart of a matter. With all of our heart we are to first seek the kingdom of God and His righteousness,

---

[11] John 14:6; 2 Thessalonians 2:10-12; 1 Peter 5:6-9

[12] Colossians 3:2; 1 Timothy 6:11-12

as well as pursue His ways with tenacity and resolution. Without faith that can be accounted as righteous, we cannot effectively stand before God, withstand the accusations of the enemy, and continue to stand in confidence that God is for us. And, like Job we would not be able to maintain or defend our ways before Him.[13]

Next our feet must be shod in the right way to carry out the orders of our commander. When I was in the military, we were issued shoes that were not very attractive to the eye, but they were made to endure the ways of a soldier. Without good footwear, soldiers would not be able to march, stand, and fight the good fight.

It is important to understand that the Lord has prepared and will empower us to march or walk through the rough terrain of this world to carry out our commission as His soldiers. Our commission is to preach the Gospel. The Gospel is the power of God unto salvation.[14] Our walk is what will set us apart and give our message credibility in light of all of the other claims that are being presented in this world. Without the walk to back up our message, it will sound unpleasant, lifeless, and hypocritical.

It must be noted that the message we have been entrusted with is a message of peace. The goal of the Gospel is to bring peace to the sin-laden, lost soul. It results in reconciliation with God and restoration of what was lost to man in the Garden of Eden. It restores us to an incredible status as being children of God, cleansed by His Word, purified by His Spirit, and kept by the power of His grace. Jesus stated that happy are those who are pure in heart for they shall see God, and blessed are those who are peacemakers because they shall be called the children of God. We must be at peace with God before we can offer such peace to others.[15]

The prophet, Isaiah gives us this insight in Isaiah 52:7, "How beautiful upon the mountains are the feet of him that bringeth good tidings, that publisheth peace; that bringeth good tidings of good, that publisheth salvation; that saith unto Zion, Thy God reigneth!" The feet that are prepared to bring the good news of peace established by our

---

[13]   Job 13:15; Matthew 6:33

[14]   Mark 16:15-18; Romans 1:16

[15]   Matthew 5:9-10; Colossians 1:20-21

sovereign ruling God are beautiful in His sight. After all, the message can bring salvation and hope to despairing, desperate souls.

The next article in the armor is the shield of faith. It is important to realize that shields vary in size and use. Some were smaller and were used in hand to hand combat. Some were large enough for the soldier to hide behind. In such times, soldiers would be able to move forward against any barrage of spears and arrows that was being sent their way. However, when attacked by a barrage of spears, arrows, or darts, they either had to crouch behind such shields or raise them as a means of protection before they could move forward.

In different Scriptures we are told that God is our shield or buckler. Buckler was also a type of shield. The picture that God serves as our various sizes of shields reminds us that our faith must be towards God who will not only be our means of protection from Satan, but in Him we are able to advance forward in our spiritual lives without being defeated. Granted, we may be hindered as we out of necessity stop to raise up our shield against the onslaught of fiery darts or crouch behind it in humility to avoid the barrage of spears being flung at us, or obediently lift it up in protection, but once the enemy flings his darts and spears, we can move forward to victory in confidence as we can take the offense.

The helmet is represented by our salvation. Although it does not present as a great of a target as the area protected by the breastplate of righteousness, we must remember that our salvation is nevertheless a target that Satan will take aim at. This is especially true in hand to hand combat. Keep in mind, if we receive a blow or wound to the head it can be fatal.

As we consider the helmet, we must remember there is only one head to protect. For the Christian that Head is Christ. God only had one Son who can save us. Clearly, this helmet is not just about protecting our relationship with our Lord, but maintaining a right understanding of who He is. The problem is there are many different Jesus' being presented. The present attitude in the environment is very apathetic when it comes to Jesus. It is as if any "old" Jesus will do. However, is that the attitude one would take towards those he or she loves? Will any "old" person serve as one's spouse? Come, and let us scripturally reason together. Such an attitude is not only ridiculous, but dangerous.

People's attitudes towards Jesus carry over in their understanding about salvation. Only the Jesus of the Bible can save us. It is His life in us that identifies us as children of God. Therefore, we cannot afford to adopt a casual attitude towards salvation and assume we are saved; rather, we must understand our place in Christ to be assured of our salvation. We cannot stop short in the matter of our souls, and presume we are saved because of titles and associations. We must know we are saved because His life is evident in us. We must not hope we are saved, but we must be abiding in the confidence that we stand saved because of His redemptive work on the cross. Satan often throws doubt upon God's Word as to what constitutes salvation, causing people to speculate as to the Lord's character and integrity towards them when it comes to salvation. Speculation and doubt will bring accusation against our personal standing in regard to salvation when we encounter our human ways and vulnerability.

Clearly, we must understand the real work of salvation in our lives. We have been saved by faith through justification wrought by redemption. We are being saved by the work of sanctification being brought forth in us by the Holy Spirit, and we will be saved in the glory that awaits us. We may not understand the full work of salvation, but we must realize that it is being done in us and will be realize fully in the world that is yet to come. We must also by faith believe that we have been delivered from the law of sin and death by Jesus' death, we are being delivered from the tentacles of this present age by the Holy Spirit, and we will be delivered from all workings and claims of spiritual death when we are delivered unto our Lord as His children and legacy.

We know that salvation is followed by the sword of the Word. We have already considered this sword and its power to put Satan on the defense. We also know that the sword of the Word reminds us that the words of God are a matter of Spirit and life. It points to the Living Word, Jesus Christ. In Jesus we stand on His authority as the Son of God, withstand according to His power, and can remain standing because of His life that resonates in us and His resurrection that is present to raise us up when the time comes.

As I consider the reality of the armor provided by God, I realize that we simply are putting on Jesus Christ. We must let His meek mind or attitude be our mind and attitude. We must take on His disposition of lowliness or humility. However, before we can put on the life of Jesus, we must put off the old life. We cannot put on something new until the old has been taken off.[16] We begin by repenting and agreeing with God about its wicked and filthy ways as a means to convert to that which is righteous. The truth is, we cannot put the old life off until we humble ourselves, and we cannot take on the new life or new man until we come to a place of humility.

As already stated, the new man or new life is the very life of Jesus. He is the essence of truth, our place of righteousness, and the light of life and the bridge of peace in the Gospel. He is the author and finisher of our faith. In other words, He is the beginning and end of our faith. We must walk by faith in Him in order to please God. He is also the author of our salvation. We can wear the helmet of salvation because our hope of glory is Christ in us. He is our all in all for He can be found in all that is necessary to ensure our spiritual well-being and He will be found in all that will secure us in our life in Him.[17] There is nothing we have need of as long as we take refuge in Him.

We are once again reminded of what the Apostle Paul stated in Romans 13:14, "But put ye on the Lord Jesus Christ, and make not provision for the flesh, to fulfil the lusts thereof." As the life of Jesus fills us, the ways of the flesh will have no inroads in our lives. Keep in mind that if it was not for the flesh, temptation would be rendered ineffective. Our affections could not be taken captive and our imaginations would not be able to serve as strongholds to strip God of His true glory in our minds in order to honor creation in some way.[18]

As believers, we must consider and discern if we are putting on the Lord Jesus. His life in us serves as our armor. Our life in Him ensures that He is our protector, shield of faith, and refuge of peace and rest. He is the one who ensures we stand, withstand, and remain standing in each test, battle, and challenge.

---

[16]   Matthew 11:28-29; Ephesians 4:22-27; Philippians 2:5; Colossians 3:8-17
[17]   John 14:6 Romans 13:14: 1 Corinthians 1:30; 2 Corinthians 4:3-6; 5:7; Colossians 1:27; 3:11; 1 Thessalonians 5:8; Hebrews 5:8-9; 11:6; 12:2
[18]   Romans 1:23; 2 Corinthians 10:3-5

11

THE INDICTMENT

We have been stripping away the layers to expose the real works and ways of Satan. We know the devil's goal is to become supreme ruler in order to receive worship. As a means to accomplish such a feat, he must become as God, not subject to any other rule. To oppose God and compete with Him, he must also gain man's worship. We see that through his means of deception he is forever trying to change the glory of God to entrap man into his destructive web to be exalted, honored, and worshipped.

To change the glory of God means establishing some other glory that will from all appearances outshine God's person, character, and ways. After all, we humans are attracted to what stands out as being distinct in what we consider to be the beauty or glory of something. Satan can only diminish God's glory in man's mind by demeaning, downplaying, and offering a substitute that will be more attractive to the flesh. Hence, enter the glory of his kingdoms.

The glory of Satan's kingdoms is designed to attract the fleshly appetites and appeal to the pride of man. In Jesus' temptation in Matthew 4:8-10, Satan showed Him the glory of his kingdoms and offered all they possessed if Jesus would simply bow down and worship him. In other words, Jesus would have to bow before him and sell His soul as man to partake of the glory of his many worldly kingdoms.

We know that Jesus understood what was on the line. He was not attracted to the false, fading, temporary glory of Satan's kingdoms. In His prayer on the night He was betrayed He made this request, "And now, O Father, glorify thou me with thine own self with the glory which I had with thee before the world was" (John 17:5).

Jesus understood that He possessed and had available the glory of deity, the very life of God, and the heavenly light of heaven. On the Mount of Transfiguration in Matthew 17, His flesh temporarily parted, revealing His glory as deity to Peter, John, and James. The Apostle John talked about the glory he witnessed on the Mount of Transfiguration in John 1:14. He referred to it as, "the glory as of the only begotten of the

Father." Hebrews 1:3 describes Jesus as being the brightness of His glory, the actual express image of His person. His actual person has and will always depict His real glory as God that was manifested in humanity 20 centuries ago.

You might be wondering why I am taking the time to discuss the matter of Satan's kingdoms. The reason is because there are misconceptions about his kingdoms. As believers, we know that the essence of Satan's kingdom represents darkness, rebellion, and unbelief, but what we often fail to realize is that his kingdom of darkness is also made up of the kingdoms of the world that manifest a false life and light. They are presented to us as possessing some type of glory that is worth possessing. Since they are designed to attract the flesh and appeal to the pride, we must realize that we will not see them as darkness, but as kingdoms that radiate some type of light or life that is worth possessing. This is the cleverness of Satan in regard to his kingdoms.

Today we are witnessing people who call themselves followers of Christ presenting various heretical teachings regarding the kingdom. Some camps are calling for a separation from the systems of the world, but they are advocating setting up a physical kingdom that will declare its sovereignty as immunity against the one-world government, economic, and religious system that will take center stage. What these people fail to realize is that the kingdom of God is unseen and will not take on any physical identity until Jesus comes back as King to rule from the throne of David over His own kingdom.[1]

There are various camps that believe that we, as Christians, must take possession of the kingdoms of the world to ensure that Jesus comes back. Some of these people are quite militant in their attitude and believe that their mission is to subdue earthly kingdoms. However, as Christians our commission in Scripture is quite clear. It is not to subdue earthly, worldly kingdoms for our Leader, but to preach the Gospel in order to ensure that the unseen kingdom of God resides within the heirs of salvation.[2]

Clearly, there are two unseen kingdoms at war in this world. These unseen kingdoms are known as the kingdom of light and the kingdom of darkness. Standing in the middle of this great conflict between these two kingdoms are men's souls.

---

[1] John 18:36; Revelation 19-20:6
[2] Mark 16:15; Luke 17:20-21

This great conflict was brought out in the book of Job. Job did not know that God had pointed him out to the accuser of the brethren, Satan. The Creator made this statement about Job to Satan in Job 1:8, "And the LORD said unto Satan, Hast thou considered my servant Job, that there is none like him in the earth, a perfect and an upright man, one that feareth God, and escheweth evil?"

By God pointing Job out as a man who worshipped Him in service, devotion, and consecration, a target was put on this righteous man. Did God understand what He was doing? No doubt He did, but He also knew something else, Job could be entrusted. In the end, Job's faith towards God would sustain him. Job would stand on what he knew about God, withstand according to what God promised him, and would remain standing in light of what God would accomplish because of the great trial he was enduring. Granted, it would bring Job to the abyss of utter despair, but he would choose the way of faith and be brought forth from the fiery ovens as a man of great faith, one's whose very testimony could not be snuffed out by the best affronts that Satan could level against his faith towards God.[3]

How is it that Christians think our target in the battle that rages between these two kingdoms has to do with taking the kingdoms of the world by some type of force when they are what Satan cleverly uses to entangle us as soldiers of the cross? The move to take into captive the kingdoms of this age in order to control or offer them to Jesus when He returns is unscriptural. It covers up the fact that these people have already been entangled by Satan in some way to his kingdom. These individuals see Satan's kingdoms as having value and worth that will usher in Jesus' coming and bring great pleasure to Him. However, when you consider Jesus' attitude towards these worldly kingdoms in His temptation, it becomes quite clear as to how the Lord values them. Jesus' example shows us that in spite of the initial glitter of these kingdoms that easily catch one's eye, they were not worthy of His consideration; therefore not worthy of our regard either. In truth, this glitter simply hides the empty, temporary glory of the world that will one day be unmasked when judgment renders it no more. Since these people are subject to Satan's worldly kingdoms, they will find themselves being deemed enemies of God, not soldiers doing His bidding.

---

[3]   Job 13:15; 19:25-27; 23:10; 1 Peter 1:6-9

The Leadership Series

The truth is the kingdoms of this world and the kingdom of God will never be brought together. Jesus made it clear that His kingdom was not of this world. In other words, it was not part of the world, did not function like the world, and had no agreement with it. The kingdoms of the world are temporary, while the kingdom of God is eternal. The kingdoms stand judged with the god of the world and will pass away in judgment, while the kingdom of God will be brought forth in the power and glory of His Spirit. The kingdoms of the world may be attractive to the natural man, but to the spiritual man he already knows that he has been translated from the kingdom of darkness into the kingdom of light. He is a citizen of the kingdom of God, and will ultimately have no identification or association with the kingdoms of the world. The world has become strange to him, and in his heart he has become a pilgrim who, like Abraham, is looking for the city made by the hands of God. He knows that he has been commanded to come out and be separate from that which is of this present age to ensure his status with God.[4] Therefore, why would the spiritual man want to revert back to, or try to gain that which is already doomed, as well as oppose the type of work the Spirit is doing to bring forth the life of God in him?

We clearly must understand our place, status, and position in Christ. The more we take on the attitude of Christ about the matters of the age we live in, the more the systems of the world will become foreign and strange to us. If we fail to have our mind transformed when it comes to our attitude towards this world, we will never overcome. We will find ourselves being subdued by the world, taken captive by its illusive glory, and possibly selling our souls to it to secure some type of life, purpose, and meaning that can only lead to death and ruin.

This brings us to one of the books of the Bible that gives us much insight as to how to overcome Satan and his wiles in relationship to our flesh and the world. It is the book of Revelation. This is the book that holds the promise of a blessing to all who read it. However, many people find this book depressing rather than serving as a blessing.

The problem is that most people fail to understand the real intent of it. It was not inspired to necessarily show us the harsh reality of the end times, but to unveil Christ to us in a greater way. When I approach

---

4   John 16:11; Romans 14:17; 1 Corinthians 2:14; 2 Corinthians 6:14-18; Ephesians 2:19; Philippians 3:20; Colossians 1:12-14

the book of Revelation, it is to see Jesus, not try to wrap up the end days into some understandable theology that I can be at peace with.

As I recently discussed with a friend the unveiling of Jesus that is brought out in the book of Revelation, it dawned on me what the main revelation is that is being brought forth in Scripture. This revelation is found in the very first chapter. Granted, the first chapter of this book drives home that Jesus is God who came in the flesh, the Great Alpha and Omega, the Almighty. The Apostle John clearly understood this about Jesus, but the revelation that brought John to a place of utter fear and caused him to fall at His feet was Jesus being unveiled as the ultimate Judge of all.

Jesus said in John 5:22 that all judgment was given to Him by the Father. As believers, we know according to 1 Peter 4:17 that the judgment of God begins in the house of God. Why would we be surprised that in the book of Revelation the great judge would begin judging the condition of the different churches that existed?

There were many different bodies of believers during the time these exhortations were given by Jesus, but instead of defining them as seven different church ages, I believe the seven churches that Jesus confronted represented the different types of conditions the local bodies can and have possessed throughout the ages. Much of their spiritual condition depended on the environment that they were living in. However, if we consider the whole world, we can also see similar environments existing, whether it be that of prosperity, indifference, or persecution. These different conditions must be properly discerned, confronted, endured, and overcome by individual church bodies in light of the promises of eternity.

It is also important to recognize how each church body is regarded and what distinguishes them. There are seven angels or messengers that were to carry the different messages to the churches. The churches were considered as the seven candlesticks.[5]

Candlesticks or lampstands were to stand out in the midst of darkness. Surely, this reminds us of a couple references in the Bible. The first one can be found in Matthew 5:14-16. As believers, we are told that we are to be the light in this world, and that we must avoid hiding our

---

[5]   Revelation 1:19-2:5

96

light under any bushel of compromise or sin. Rather, our light must so shine that people will see our works and glorify the Father.

The other reference to light has to do with the parable of the five wise virgins and the five foolish virgins in Matthew 25:1-13. They all had lamps, but not all had oil. Lamps without oil have no means to set forth a light. Granted, the lamps had to be lit in some way, but they had to have the oil.

The oil is the Holy Spirit, but through the years I have discovered that what lights the oil in my lamp is godly love. Godly love is the flint that creates the spark. Without godly love I am not compelled to shine or even stir myself up to see if I have any oil to even endure a dark night of testing and waiting. Romans 5:5 tells us that one of the responsibilities of the Holy Ghost is to shed the love of God abroad in our hearts. The presence of oil and a love for God will set the candlestick ablaze with passion and urgency.

Jesus' exhortation is that if each local body fails to repent, endure, and ultimately overcome, He will remove their candlestick out of the place each of them held. As we will see, some of the churches do not possess the necessary oil, while others must maintain the passion to keep them shining through challenging times. If the Lord removes their candlestick, it is because they have no real distinction or purpose. They will simply represent a dark place that no longer has any real message or testimony that is able to serve as a light in this dark world.

This brings us to what would cause a church to lose its oil or passion. As we will see, it comes down to the enemies of the soul. Christians lose their edge when they forget what their purpose is. This often occurs because they lose sight of what is truly important to the Lord in the midst of religious activities. Some churches are indulging self with the things of the world, while others have come into unholy agreements or have let too much of the world's influence in. In fact, they are so worldly there is no distinction.

To lose one's spiritual edge implies the Holy Spirit is withdrawing because there is a lack of passion for what is true and righteous. When Christians indulge themselves with the things of the world, they will grieve the Spirit, forcing a battle to take place that will end in some type of separation or division. When churches come into an unholy agreement, they will quench Him, causing Him to lift from off all activities. When churches allow the world into their midst, they will greatly vex the Spirit, causing Him to depart.

The Church at Ephesus clearly teaches us that to overcome we must maintain our first works of loving God to keep our spiritual lives in balance. If we keep our love towards God fresh and our love towards others honorable or upright, we will be assured of eating of the tree of life.

The Church of Smyrna assures us that there will be tribulation on this earth. It reveals that even though God's people taste the poverty of this present world, they can be rich in faith that assures them of the blessings of the next. Although they may suffer because the Church resides among those who would persecute it, if the believers of the body are faithful, they will receive a crown of life. Clearly, we are reminded once again that if we are not willing to lose our present life in regard to the world, we will lose the future life we have been promised in regard to eternity.[6]

It was also in light of the suffering of those at Smyrna in not loving their lives unto death that the churches were told that if they overcame, they would not be hurt by the second death. The second death is the lake of fire. Smyrna was being persecuted by the religious people who represented the religious system of the world. We know persecution will come to those who live godly. Instead of hating those who persecute us we are told to love them and rejoice that we could be counted worthy to become identified with Christ in His sufferings.[7]

The message to the church in Pergamum is clear. Although this body had notable works even in light of Satan's throne or government being set up in its midst and experiencing martyrdom to one of its faithful members, Jesus had a few things against it. As you read the indictment being brought against this body, you begin to realize it is a very serious indictment. This church was committing spiritual fornication by holding to the same doctrine of demons that had proved to be a stumbling block to the children of Israel when they were in the wilderness. This idolatrous doctrine not only resulted in the people succumbing to pagan and sensual activity, but to immoral conduct that brought swift retribution

---

6   Matthew 16:25-26; Acts 14:22; James 2:5; Revelation 2:8-11
7   Matthew 5:10-12, 44-48; 2 Timothy 3:12; Revelation 20:6-15

on them.[8] We can once again see that Satan's tricks of the trade are not new, but simply repackaged in some way and served up on a variety of platters. These tricks of the trade possess the same seeds and fruits of death that can be ingested by those in the religious realm.

Unlike the church of Ephesus who hated the deeds of the Nicolaitans, the church of Pergamum was actually holding to their heretical doctrine. According to F. W. Grant's small booklet on this subject, the Greek meaning of the word "Nicolaitane" means "conquering the people." Our commonly used term "laity" is derived from this word.[9] From what I could learn about this teaching, it was acceptable for certain people, referred to as clergy, to be exalted over the masses. The leadership was considered as being superior. This concept of leadership is not only contrary to what has been clearly set forth in Scripture, but it allows such individuals to unduly lord it over the people.

In Scripture, the greatest type of leadership comes through example and service. Even though there are those who have been called to lead God's people, it was for the purpose of edification or building up the believers into one functioning Body. Each member of the body is equally important for the function of the whole body. One member was not to be honored or exalted over another member, unless it was for the purpose of taking the member who was considered inferior and exalting the individual to the place of like importance in regard to the whole body. For this reason believers were and are to come into submission to one another to ensure that which is honorable and worthy is upheld. The ultimate leader of the Church is to be Jesus Christ.[10] Clearly, the doctrine of the Nicolaitanes would allow for abuses in relationship to authority and power to occur. As the Apostle Peter admonished the pastors in his first epistle,

> Feed the flock of God which is among you, taking the oversight thereof, not by constraint but willingly; not for filthy lucre, but of a ready mind; Neither as being lords over God's heritage, but being ensamples to the flock. And when

---

[8]   Number 22-25

[9]   Nicolaitanism (The Rise and Growth of the Clergy), F. W. Grant

[10]   Matthew 20:25-27; 1 Corinthians 12:12-26; Ephesians 4:11-16; 5:21

the chief Shepherd shall appear, ye shall receive a crown of glory that fadeth not away (1 Peter 5:2-4).

According to Revelation 2:6, Jesus hated the type of works that were produced by Nicolaitanism. And, here you have the church of Pergamum holding onto what Jesus hated. Perhaps there were only a few members who might have held onto it, but a little leaven will defile the whole lump. The Apostle Paul was quite clear about how to confront heretics in Titus. After twice admonishing those who advocate heresy as a way of establishing a record or testimony against them, they were to be rejected.[11]

In most cases where such sin is allowed to remain, people become indifferent to what is true. Indifference is opposite of love. Jesus stated that if those at the church of Pergamum did not repent of their indifference towards the spiritual fornication among them, He would quickly come and fight against them with the sword of His mouth. This should serve as a sober reminder that Jesus will not tolerate any form of spiritual fornication or heresy among His people.

Once again, Jesus exhorted the churches that if they overcame, He would give them the hidden manna to eat and a white stone with a new name written on it that will be known only by Him and the recipient.

The next message was to the church at Thyatira. Jesus commended this body of believers for their works, love, service, faith, and patience. The love, service, and Christian virtues were present, yet Jesus had a few things against this body. The members allowed a false prophetess in their midst who had been given leeway to seduce others through teaching that would cause them to commit spiritual fornication through unholy agreement and deeds.

Today there is an influx of false prophets and teachers that are being allowed to seduce others with an unholy mixture. This unholy mixture contains false teachings and profane practices, which involve partaking of the depths of Satan. Jesus is clear about what He will do with such people along with their followers. Out of longsuffering He will give them a space of time to repent as a standard of truth is lifted up to challenge them, but if they do not repent, He will cast them into great tribulation and kill the offspring of such an unholy union. This should serve as a

---

[11] 1 Corinthians 5:6-8; Titus 3:10-11

testimony to others that He searches the reins (minds) and hearts, and will ultimately recompense people for the quality of their works.

For those of the church of Thyatira who refused to uphold this unholy union and the doctrine it produced, He would put no other burden on them except for the one that they already held fast to.[12] We know our main burden is to love God and others. However, there was something else that was clearly established for the new Church in Acts. It is very interesting to take note of what the early fathers set forth as a record in regard to Gentile believers.

There was much conflict over what obligation the Gentiles had towards the Law of Moses. Much of the conflict was over practices or statutes such as circumcision. The elders at the time had to make a decision as to what the responsibilities of the Gentiles were concerning what they were obliged to observe at all times. They agreed that the burden of the Law proved even too great for their fathers. It was decided by the elders as to the practices the Gentiles needed to observe. This is the essence of the ruling that came down from the council that was convened to decide this matter, "Wherefore my sentence is, that we trouble not them, which from among the Gentiles are turned to God: But that we write unto them, that they abstain from pollutions of idols, and from fornication, and from things strangled, and from blood" (Acts 15:19-20).

Keep in mind, the Gentiles were exposed to various pagan practices. The call in the different letters penned by Paul, Peter, and John was to flee all idolatry, abstain from all fleshly, corrupt practices and ways, and avoid being a stumbling block to others who might be tender in their Christian faith.[13] James who was one of the elders wrote this in his epistle, "Pure religion and undefiled before God and the Father is this; to visit the fatherless and widows in their affliction, and to keep oneself unspotted from the world" (James 1:27). These instructions were in accordance set forth by the judgment passed down by the elders in Jerusalem.

The indictment that Jesus brought against the next church is that it was dead. There was no semblance of spiritual life to be found in it except those who had not yet defiled their garments. The church, Sardis,

---

12   Revelation 2:18-29
13   1 Corinthians 10:14; 1 Peter 2:11; 2 Peter 1:3-4; 1 John 5:21

once had life in it, but somehow it had been spiritually dulled down by that which was defiled, became complacent towards what was true and right, and was now totally unresponsive.

We are given a few clues as to why this church was in its present condition. It had ceased to watch and guard what it did have in Christ, and it failed to strengthen what was truly Spirit and life. Even though it had works, they were deemed imperfect or defiled before God.

Jesus exhorted this church to remember what it had in Him. Clearly, it had received the Gospel message and had been taught the truth. After remembering, it needed to repent and once again become watchmen and guardians over what had brought life to it in the first place. In a sense, the Lord warned this body that if it did not wake from its dead state, that He would come upon it as a thief in the night.

Clearly, the church of Sardis was like the five foolish virgins in Matthew 25. The members did not possess enough oil nor had none to speak of. As the Apostle Paul instructed in 1 Thessalonians 5:6 in regard to Jesus coming as a thief, "Therefore let us not sleep, as do others; but let us watch and be sober." The members needed to stir themselves out of their lethargy, and buy truth, for they had become unworthy in their present state to incur any real consideration by the Lord. The Lord will not accept a church that is tainted by some type of defilement. He is coming back for a Church without spot and wrinkle.[14]

The Lord goes on to declare that those who overcome such a state, will be clothed in white raiment and He will not blot their names out of the book of life. Rather, He will confess their names before His Father and the angels.

The sixth church was the Philadelphia Church. Jesus declared that it was holy and true. Since He possessed the keys of David, He was capable of opening and shutting doors. At this point we must be reminded that we must also ask the Lord to show us the way, seek it out and when we come up to the right door, to knock on it in faith and prayer so that He will open it to us.[15]

From what I have gathered in my studies is that those who falsely claimed they were Jews were buffeting this body in some way. Jesus stated that in the end, these foolish liars would come to Him and worship Him

---

[14] Proverbs 23:23; Ephesians 5:25-27; Revelation 3:1-6
[15] Isaiah 22:21-23; Matthew 7:7-11; Revelation 3:7-13

before the feet of these precious saints. Philippians 2:10-11 tells us that every knee will bow before the Lord and every tongue will confess that He is indeed Lord. If we compare this text with Philippians 2, we must wonder if every blood-bought saint will witness those who insist on their arrogance, tyranny, disobedience, deception, lawlessness, hatred, unbelief, and so forth kneel before the Lord and confess what they had blatantly rejected in their hearts. They will do it for the glory of the Father, but the saints will also witness it because of the love the Lord has for them. It is clear the Lord had great love towards the members of the Philadelphia Church because of their heart, devotion, and testimony.

It is important to note that Jesus set before this body an open door. He knew the members' works and recognized that they had little strength, but in spite of their weariness, they had kept His Word and had not denied His name. We are told that in the end days, the patience of the saints will be worn down. However, we are also exhorted by Jesus to possess our souls in patience. The Apostle Paul encouraged those who were weary to maintain the integrity of their works, and that in due season they would reap. Clearly, due to inner strength and character the Christian life can maintain and present itself as enduring even during grave trials. As believers, we have been given the necessary tools to endure.[16] We must keep our eyes on Him and be true to our testimony and obedient to His Word.

Jesus reminded this church that when He comes, He will come quickly. His point of encouragement is that that He will keep the members of this body from the hour of great temptation that will try all men's souls. However, He warned those who live in this day to not be foolish; rather, they must pray that they are found worthy to escape such a time.[17]

Whether we as Christians are delivered from this great tribulation or through it, we must hold fast to what we know is true and right in order to maintain the crown we already possess. Our crown is His life that is being formed in us, and when He comes, we will freely offer what this life has produced in and through us back to Him as a testimony of His abiding faithfulness on our behalf.

---

[16] Daniel 7:25; Matthew 10:32-33; Luke 21:19; Galatians 6:9; 2 Peter 1:3-4
[17] Luke 21:34-36

The promise given to those who endure and overcome is that they will be made pillars in the temple of God. They will forever abide in His presence. He will also write His new name on them, as well as the name of His city that they will be abiding in. This mark will truly identify them as belonging to Him.

The final message went to the church at Laodicea.[18] The indictment against this church was harsh as well. The members were lukewarm in their works towards the Lord. To show His displeasure towards their works, He stated that He would spew them out of His mouth. The concept of works being considered a byproduct of what once was, and now being nothing but vomit in the mouth of Christ, is a pretty hard reality to grasp.

The works were the product of the Laodicea Church's spiritual condition. Even though the people perceived that all was well with them, they were by every account, belonging to their present age. In other words, they were worldly, not spiritual. They judged themselves according to worldly standards. For example, they thought themselves to be rich, when in fact Jesus judged them as being wretched. These people may have been rich according to the world, but they were not rich in faith. They had a mixture that spoke of pride, fleshly ways, and the influence of the unseen idols of money, greed, and indifference that are often present in times of prosperity.

They may have considered themselves possessing the goods of the world, but they did not possess the goods of heaven. As a result, Jesus counted them as miserable before Him. Granted, they may not have sensed such misery, but according to His action towards their works, it implied that He was fed up with them.

This church body saw itself as being self-sufficient, but Jesus saw them as being spiritually poor, inept, and unacceptable. The problem with self-sufficiency is that it will always blind people to their real needs as they stand naked and vulnerable to the consequences and judgment that will come upon them in due time.

Jesus counseled this church to buy the real gold that has been tried in the fiery ovens that brings forth true faith towards God. Job spoke of coming forth as gold after his fiery ordeal that not only refined his very faith, but his character.

---

[18] Revelation 3:14-19

The Lord went on to counsel the members of the Laodicea Church that once they possessed what is valuable, they could then clothe themselves with white raiment. "Raiment" points to righteousness and purity. It we are not clothed in the righteousness of Christ, we will stand ashamed. He also counseled them to put salve on their eyes so that they could clearly see their spiritual condition.

Even though this church's works had become repulsive to Jesus, and its members stood wretched before Him, He reminded them that He chastens those whom He loves. He then rebuked them as He called them to be zealous about repenting of their wretchedness, miserable state, and shameful ways.

Jesus reminded this church that He stands at the door of hearts, knocking and calling out to those who will hear Him to open the door of true communion. If people hear the voice of their Shepherd, and open the door, He will come in and commune with them. He goes on to state that those who overcome, He will grant them to sit with Him in His throne.

It is clear that as we study the different churches, the three enemies of man's soul were clearly at work. Occasionally disguised behind appearances of righteousness, religious cloaks, and activities, as well as unholy mixtures, the churches' light (testimony), life (covenant), and quality of lifestyles were being robbed and compromised as a means to bring them to a place of total spiritual ineffectiveness and ruin. As Judge, Jesus not only brings forth points of judgments, instructions, and warnings to the churches, but He clearly establishes the promises that await those of each body who truly overcome.

It is obvious that overcoming is a personal responsibility. We see that in the midst of the churches that were indicted that there were those who had not succumbed to the enemies that were working within the different bodies. God will always have a remnant of saints who will not compromise their testimony, life, or conduct by bowing to, coming into agreement with, or ignoring Satan in order to partake of his kingdoms to live at peace with them.

Are you part of such a remnant?

12

THE WINNING COMBINATION

The book of Revelation gives us incredible insight into what it means to overcome. Sadly, most people see it as a book that becomes overwhelming and frightening. Granted, from the perspective of the happenings surrounding the last days of the dispensation of grace, it can be quite depressing. However, the truth is, in the midst of such depressing reality is the fact that through Jesus Christ, God will judge all matters and bring an end to the reign of Satan as the god of this age and the prince of the power of the air. He will usher in a new millennium of righteousness and peace.

The harsh reality in Revelation is that for the kingdom of God to come forth in regard to the millennium, there will be a great time of travailing. Such is the way of any birth. Travailing is not only a time of tribulation, but a type of death where what has been will be judged and cease to be, so that which represents new life will come forth. It will demonstrate to be a great time of sorrow that will prove to be intense. Such a time will put men on their knees or cause them to faint in utter fear and terror.

Before the new can come forth, the fruits of that which exists in darkness must be brought to full fruition. The cup of iniquity must be allowed to not only become full, but it must be allowed to spill over and run out. There will be no doubt that God's judgment upon what has been nurtured in the midst of darkness rightfully deserves to be consumed by the fires of His wrath.

The need for judgment will be made obvious due to the extent of man's rebellion against God. This judgment will also be in light of Satan's rage directed against God's creation, especially mankind, resulting in God's wrath on all unrighteousness. These three factors will culminate in the events described in the book of Revelation. However, the beauty about this devastating time is that it marks the end of the reign of wickedness and terror on the earth. In the end, Jesus will remain standing as the victorious King and the righteous Judge who will overcome all wickedness and make all things right. Everything will have been brought to the light, shaken, and exposed for its lawless, wicked abominable ways.

In the midst of this great conflict are men's souls. People will be brought to the crossroads of who they will choose to serve. Many will sell their souls for the bread of this world to maintain some semblance of life, while others will offer up their souls to be part of the power play, and some will fling their souls on the altar of Satan to do his bidding. However, there will be a remnant of God's people that will choose the way of the cross. They will deny self the right to partake of the world. They will consecrate their lives unto God for His work and glory. As a result, the Morning Star, the Christ, will not only arise in greater ways in their hearts, but His light will intensify in their lives as they take on His likeness. They will truly become those lights on the hill that will clearly shine through the darkness to attract those poor souls who desire to see hope in the midst of the carnage of ruined souls, and despair, and hopelessness.

As Christians, we are commanded to be prepared for times of tribulation. According to Acts 14:22, it is only through much tribulation that we are able to enter into the kingdom of God. Once again, we must recognize and acknowledge that there will be a time of travailing. The Apostle Paul also stated that Christ is coming back for a Church that is without spot or wrinkle.

There is no way that the Church can be presented to Christ in such a way unless the proper cleansing of water, heat, and fire is applied to it. Hence enters the exhortation for us to watch when such times are near at hand so that we will not only warn others, but we will be ready spiritually to do what we must do to keep our light burning through the long, dark night of waiting. We must not be foolish like the five foolish virgins who were unprepared, or like those who are part of the world's scene, thinking they will be able to get their act together in time for the coming of the Master. We must be sober and vigilant in our spiritual lives. We must be soldiers, always ready to adhere to our Commander's call if we are going to overcome the darkness that is engulfing the world and encroaching into our lives.

Revelation is a book about God's people overcoming even in the greatest of tribulations. It is a book that reveals what we must discern, watch for, and be ready to overcome in all manner of darkness. The Apostle John's revelation of Jesus is that of the great Judge. He will not only judge all matters in righteousness, but it will be done in a swift manner. In the twinkling of an eye, He will once again enter on the scene of history and mankind as the great Judge. We are given insight into how the wicked will react to His appearance in Revelation 6:15-17:

> And the kings of the earth, and the great men, and the rich men, and the chief captains, and the mighty men, and every bondman, and every free man, hid themselves in the dens and in the rocks of the mountains; And said to the mountains and rocks, Fall on us, and hide us from the face of him that sitteth on the throne, and from the wrath of the Lamb: For the great day of his wrath is come; and who shall be able to stand?

Is it not amazing that those who denied the reality and work of Jesus recognize who He is? Is it not incredible that they who lived without fear or dread of meeting Him, now dread seeing Him? Is it not amazing that they who defied His authority now ask the rocks and mountains to fall on them to hide them from His wrath because there is no recourse? Their day of reckoning has finally come upon them and they know their dreadful end.

Like those who recognize and worship Jesus at His throne in heaven in Revelation chapters four and five, these unbelieving, lawless people could have been spared from facing His wrath if they would have believed in their hearts what was written about Jesus in His Word. They could have known authority and power in His Spirit. They could have been people who impacted the world with the peace that only comes from above. They could have and should have been on the right side of truth and righteousness, but they were fools in their hearts for they refused to believe that the God of Abraham existed. Rather, they sold their souls to the devil in order to partake of the glory of his temporary kingdoms in the hope of gaining the devil's false promises.

As Christians, we must be assured that we are not ashamed when we stand before the Judge of our souls. All religious facades, worldly attitudes, and self-serving ways of the heart will be stripped from us, to expose our real motive and character before the One who is holy. We cannot afford for Jesus to walk among us as the light of the world and reveal that we have become candlesticks that no longer possess any real oil. We must take seriously our lives in Christ and must avoid neglecting the salvation that was given to us.[1]

This brings us to the winning combination. In Revelation 12:7-9 we are told that the great accuser of the brethren will be cast out of heaven along with his angels. In other words, the accuser of the brethren will no longer have any access to heaven. Once Satan is cast out of heaven, his wrath will escalate and become more intense for his time on earth is short. It is within this text that we are told what it will take to overcome him, "And they overcame him by the blood of the Lamb, and by the word of their testimony; and they loved not their lives unto the death" (Revelation 12:11).

Jesus tells us that to be His disciples we must deny self, pick up our personal cross, and follow Him. His instructions are simple. They are not rhetorical ramblings that are laced with idle words. We can clearly see how simple and forthright God's instructions are to His people. In Revelation 12:11, we are given the simple winning combination of overcoming Satan's wrath that will be leveled against God and His people.

If we are going to overcome the frontal attacks of the devil regardless of the age we live in, we need to understand how this winning combination works. First, we have the blood of the Lamb. Jesus' blood is significant in that it reminds us that we have been redeemed. His blood was used to purchase or ransom us; therefore, we belong to God.[2] As previously pointed out, Satan cannot touch us in any way, shape, or form unless God first removes the boundaries for him to sift or test us. We also know that the Lord gives him permission to try our souls with the intent of refining our character and faith.

Whether we like it or not, Satan is part of our process of preparing us for a glory that will never fade or cease to be. It is an eternal glory that will ensure us that we will live in the presence of our Lord and Savior for eternity. Oh, what a glorious time that will be for each of us as His saints! We will never be homesick for His presence again, nor will we know sorrow in our spirits because of the wickedness that abounds in the world, or leanness of soul due to stagnation in our spiritual lives and the influence of the flesh. How we will rejoice in His presence as we worship

---

[1]   Hebrews 2:3

[2]   Ephesians 1:7; Colossians 1:14

Him around His very throne and enjoy the beauty of His countenance as we see Him face-to-face.

The blood of Jesus affords us the privilege of walking in His light and fellowshipping with Him and others. We must walk in the light in order to know where we are spiritually and to be aware of what is going on around us.

Today there are many people groping in the dark when it comes to their spiritual lives. They have no real assurance that they are connected to heaven in sweet fellowship with God. Such individuals have no real consensus as to their spiritual status. Whether they have been walking contrary to God's ways or in total unbelief, these poor souls will be devoid of any real assurance that in the end, they will not be standing spiritually naked before the great Judge and with no recourse; for, it is appointed for man to die once than face judgment.[3]

As believers, we know that through the blood we can find forgiveness or pardon from the Judge of our souls. This pardon is possible because the blood of Jesus cleanses us from all unrighteousness. However, we must confess our sins to Him, and then receive His pardon by faith. Active faith produces the response of obedience to His holy ways, which will manifest itself by a cessation from living a life that is not only contrary and offensive to our Lord, but trespasses His very Law.[4] The blood of Jesus clearly allows us to be positionally in right standing with God as our faith ensures we stand right before Him, and our obedience reveals our sincere intentions to do what is right and pleasing before Him.

The blood of Jesus also identifies us as being part of an everlasting covenant that Satan cannot touch or do away with.[5] Covenants point to an agreement that in most cases is not one-sided. Both parties come into agreement about the requirements that must be met to ensure the integrity and keeping of the covenant.

People in today's world, where the philosophy is, "The end justifies the means", regardless of how deceptive such means may be, do not understand the significance of a covenant. The main reason for a flippant or indifferent attitude towards the covenant that God established with

---

[3]   Hebrews 9:27; 1 John 1:3-6

[4]   Hebrews 11 John 1:7-10

[5]   Hebrews 9:11-22; 10:16-23

the Church of Jesus is that according to the pagan philosophies of the world, a person's word does not have to have any real substance or clout behind it.

Most people do not mean what they say or say what they mean. Most words are a front to throw people off guard as to the real intent of the speaker. Such intents will often prove to be questionable and untrustworthy. Even though such practices deem those who use them as liars and fools that will ultimately be judged for all idle, fraudulent words and cast into the lake of fire, there is clearly no real fear on these people's part when it comes to paying consequences for such wicked deeds. Sadly, there are always ears that seek after and want to be tickled by the flatteries and foolishness of such liars.[6]

Without substance or clout there is no authority in which to stand. As believers, we stand in accordance with, and because of, the authority of our Lord, Savior, Redeemer, and God. We withstand in our Lord's authority because of the covenant or agreement we have with Him. However, this covenant means nothing unless we are keeping our end of it. The New Testament serves as the terms of our agreement with the Lord. Obviously, we have godly responsibilities to ensure the integrity of the authority of this excellent covenant.

When it comes to our testimonies, we will be able to stand against Satan, withstand his devices, and continue to stand because we know what we believe and speak of is true. Truth is unchangeable and immovable. Our Christian life is based on the truth; therefore, when our foundation is shaken, it will remain standing *because of truth*. When our cornerstone is challenged, we will be able to give a defense of the hope that is in us because we know *what is true*. And, when the integrity of our testimony is being questioned, we will remain standing because we know in the end that we will not be ashamed for putting our confidence in what we *know to be true*.[7]

What does our testimony consist of? Most people think testimony has to do with them, but in reality it has to do with Jesus. Many times people's testimonies are about how bad they were, instead of how far reaching the love of God had to extend itself when it comes to saving

---

[6]   Matthew 5:37; 12:36; 1 Thessalonians 4:6-7; Revelation 21:8

[7]   John 14:6; 1 Corinthians 3:11; Colossians 1:27; Hebrews 12:27-29; 1 Peter 2:5-8; 3:15-16;

each of us from the abyss of utter ruin. As I have stated many times, the bottom is the bottom. Some people may have to taste greater devastating circumstances than others before they hit the bottom, but the impact is the same: Broken lives.

When a life has been utterly broken, there is only One who can put it back together. The One I speak of is Jesus, the great physician of man's spirit and soul.[8] He has certainly put my life back together more than once. Broken by bad choices, unbearable sins, and miserable captivity, I had to cry out to Him many times to show mercy to me in my wretched state. Out of mercy He showed me pity, offered me forgiveness, bestowed on me His healing grace, and restored my soul.

However, testimonies are not simply about how the Lord has saved us from our miserable selves, but they also possess a record of who He is and who He has become to us. Our testimony as to who Christ is serves as the source of light we are to emit from our very lives. Remember that the light of the Gospel that is hidden from those who are lost is the very person of Jesus Christ.

Those who are lost do not have a testimony. There is no light in them. As a result, God is lost to them and they are lost to God. They are groping around in spiritual darkness that prevents them from seeing the abyss of damnation that is awaiting them.

When I have studied the seven churches in Revelation, I have noted that in each rebuke or point of encouragement, Jesus gives a testimony of Himself, which is in correspondence with the revelation that John had of Him in Revelation 1 as the great Judge. I cannot help but think that each testimony He gives of Himself is the very testimony the church is missing or needs to embrace in order to endure their time of testing. Let us consider each of these testimonies in light of John's revelation. Perhaps it will stir us up, fan some coal in our soul to once again become aflame with the very Spirit of God, a flame that will inspire us to possess a greater witness or testimony of Christ regardless of what it may cost us.

The church of Ephesus lacked their first works which were to love God. Consider how Jesus presented Himself. He comes to them as One who holds the seven stars in his right hand and walks among the seven golden candlesticks. When John turned to receive instructions to the seven churches, he did so because a voice spoke to Him. He first sees

---

[8]   Luke 4:18-19

Jesus as standing in the midst of the seven candlesticks as the Son of man.[9]

We cannot love what we cannot personally associate with or relate to. Jesus came as man so we could relate and interact with Him. Even though He was and is the Alpha and Omega, the first and the last to all matters, He came as the Son of man. He made God real to mankind and opened up the way that God could once again fellowship with man.

The right hand points to a position of authority, preeminence, and preference. Jesus sits on the right hand of the Father.[10] Clearly, without love there is no real preference for the lover of our souls. He will hold no real preeminence in our lives. Jesus is also holding these stars. Love ensures that those who are dear to us, we will indeed hold close to our hearts. He is walking among the candlesticks. This points to our need to walk and fellowship with Jesus, but without love there will be no desire to do so.

To the church of Smyrna, He presents Himself as the first and the last who was dead and is now alive. Even though the persecution I have experienced for my Christian faith seems relatively minor compared to that which takes place in other areas of the world, it has made me aware of how much of a victim it can make you feel. It seems as if there will be no end to it, and that even though death is eminent, it can make the present suffering seem useless or a mockery.

Jesus clearly is establishing that all matters will begin with Him and end with Him. He holds the keys of death and hell. There is nothing that will escape Him, and in the end He will have the last say. It is in relationship to the revelation that He is the first and the last that He also reminds those at Smyrna that at one time He tasted death, but the grave could not hold Him. Clearly, he is no longer dead, and will live for evermore. He is indeed the firstfruits of a new creation that has been brought forth through death. It is with this backdrop that He is encouraging those at Smyrna to be faithful even unto death.[11]

To the church at Pergamum, He states that these are His judgments for He holds the sharp sword of the truth of the Word that has two edges to it. In Revelation 1:16 we know that this sharp two-edged sword came

---

[9]   Revelation 2:1-3

[10]   Hebrews 8:1

[11]   1 Corinthians 15:20, 23; Revelation 2:8-11

out of His mouth. We also know that the sword is in reference to the Word of God. Jesus is the Living, active Word of God, who will proclaim and bring forth the righteous judgments of God.[12] His judgments are not only true and just but they will stand. It is important to point out that the sword of the Word not only penetrates and cuts one way, but it will also come back and cut through the whole matter exposing all that may be hidden. Hebrews 4:12 best describes how effective and powerful it will be, "For the word of God is quick, and powerful, and sharper than any two-edged sword, piercing even to the dividing asunder of soul and spirit, and of the joints and marrow, and is a discerner of the thoughts and intents of the heart."

There is no way that those at Pergamum would ever escape the righteous judgments of His truth. They had to cease to be indifferent to the wicked doctrine that was in their midst and repent of their casual attitude towards what was right. They had to expose such doctrine with the sharp truth of His Word if they were to overcome or know the personal sharp, but liberating penetration of truth upon their hearts and souls.

To the church of Thyatira, Jesus came as the Son of God whose very eyes were like a flame of fire and His feet like fine copper or brass. This is the very same revelation that John witnessed in Revelation 1:14-15. Remember, those of this church were allowing spiritual seduction and prostitution to take place in their midst. They were given a space to repent before being cast into great tribulation. They would see that the offspring from this agreement would be killed, and that the other churches would know that hearts and minds would be tested by Jesus and works proven in the fires of judgment.

What can we learn from this aspect of the revelation of Jesus? Jesus is God and will not tolerate iniquity, transgression, or offense against His holy character or name. Fiery eyes pointed to anger, while brass or bronze in the Old Testament was symbolic of judgment on sin. Jesus' anger towards this unholy agreement and the fruits it produced would result in judgment.

Those at Thyatira may have possessed charity in regards to their deeds, but they did not really love who the Lord was. If they had loved His person, they would have been cognizant of the great anger or

---

[12]   John 1:1-3

114

displeasure their spiritual prostitution would cause Him. They needed to see His holiness and be broken by their sin to revive godly love in relationship to His holy person and ways.

To those at the church at Sardis, Jesus revealed Himself as the One who possesses the seven spirits of God and the seven stars.[13] The seven spirits have to do with the works of the Spirit who convicts us of sin, quickens life in the inner man, leads to all truth, refreshes the soul, empowers us to take forth the message, enables us to pray and worship, and does the work of sanctification. The seven stars remind us of the messages that need to be or will be delivered to His Church depending on the people's spiritual condition.

As Christians, we know that we can do nothing except by, through, and with the prompting of the Spirit of God. The Apostle John was in the Spirit when he heard the great voice in Revelation 1:10. The Spirit is the air that pulsates through our spiritual lives, the wind in which we soar above the present age, and the power in which we walk out the life in us. He is the One who speaks to our spirits. It is for this reason that Jesus states if we have spiritual ears, we need to hear what the Spirit is truly saying to each of us in regard to our spiritual condition. We need to discern His presence and be sensitive to His leading, as well as believing and being obedient to His voice.

Clearly, the condition of the church at Sardis revealed that the Spirit was missing from the people's midst and works. They were unable to respond to God, and their works were barren, reprobate, and useless before the Lord. They needed to return to square "A" by remembering the message that was first delivered to them.

The message is the Gospel of Jesus Christ. However, this message has the power to produce life and fruit that is displayed through godliness. The Apostle Peter speaks of becoming barren in the knowledge of Jesus because of failing to put the life of Christ in us in action.[14] He put the reason for people being barren in the knowledge of the Lord Jesus in 2 Peter 1:9-10,

> But he that lacked these things is blind, and cannot see afar off, and hath forgotten that he was purged from his old sins.

---

[13] Revelation 3:1-3
[14] 2 Peter 1:3-10

Wherefore the rather, brethren, give diligence to make your calling and election sure: for if ye do these things, ye shall never fall.

To the church of Philadelphia Jesus reminded them that He is the one who is true and possesses the key of David that is able to open and shut the door. We know that He has the keys to hell and death. He alone controls the keys and doors in which people will be allowed to pass through.[15]

Recently, I heard of the passing of a supposedly "Christian" pastor that I had some encounters with in the past. I was aware that this pastor had preached blatant heresy. In his mind, he was on his way to heaven, but some of his close friends related a story that brought absolute dread to my soul.

Just before his death in his drug-like state, he began to cry out this unusual, eerie request, "Open the door, open the door!" What door was this known heretic talking about? My prayer has always been that he would see the error of his teachings and ways and repent before he entered into eternity. I cannot judge his heart, but his request must cause us all to stop and ponder what door will be opened to us. Scripture is clear that only Jesus holds the keys to the doors. While hanging between the state of physical life and eternity, this man apparently was trying to enter into a door that remained close to him.

Jesus was encouraging the Philadelphia Church in its weary state. He knew that it needed to know that even though the members of this church felt like they were banging their heads against every door in their attempts to serve Him, that He truly held the keys to the doors, and that He would in due time open the door that would keep them from the hour of great temptation.

To the church of Laodicea, the testimony He brings of Himself is that He is the faithful and true witness, the beginning of the creation of God. This church had ceased to maintain a faithful or true witness of Jesus. They had forgotten that He is the Alpha, the first begotten of the dead. Everything must begin with Him if it is going to end right. The Christians of Laodicea had gotten off the mark of Christ as the Alpha, and had veered away from what was true, causing them to lose sight of

---

[15] Revelation 1:18; 3:1-8

the Omega in His glory. They had no sure gauge in which they could properly discern their real spiritual condition. They needed to zealously repent for their unfaithfulness to Him.[16]

As I studied the revelation of Jesus in regard to the history of the seven churches in Revelation, I was reminded that from all appearances the influence of the Muslims has snuffed out the light where these churches were once located. Muslims love to build their churches on the former sites of other known religious buildings and tout their success of becoming the world religion in the future. We can actually see them making the same inroads into America. Eventually, this heretical cup will come to fruition and these deluded souls will know the taste of God's wrath upon their ungodly, evil belief systems. Meanwhile, we must examine our own testimonies. Can they withstand the frontal attacks of Satan, or will such testimonies become dispensable when the trials and tribulations become too uncomfortable to the flesh or our relationship with the world?

When it comes to the true Church of Jesus, the very gates of hell will not prevail against it.[17] Meanwhile, if the light of a local church ceases to be, it will not be because of any moves made by Muslims or God-hating philosophies, but because the church failed to adhere to Jesus' exhortations, and did not fan the flame of their light in the darkness. Clearly, its members failed to keep their testimonies burning bright. As a result, Jesus, who walks among the candlesticks, will remove those lampstands that have no connection to heaven and are lacking the oil of His Spirit

As believers, we must remember that genuine testimonies are bought with a price. They have been established on the immovable Rock, they line us up to the unchangeable cornerstone of our faith, and will assure us that as the Rock, the righteous Judge will ultimately judge the seen and unseen. He will reward those who are His and will pronounce judgment on those who oppose His kingdom, Law, and sovereignty. It is upon this Rock of ages that we stand as those born-again into a new creation, and it is because of this erected cornerstone that we will withstand as believers. As a reward for such faithfulness, we will be assured of the future hope of His righteousness reigning in and through us.

---

[16] Revelation 1:5, 8; 3:14, 19

[17] Matthew 16:18

The final part of overcoming is that we do not love our lives unto the death. According to Philippians 3:10-11, the Apostle Paul was always being made conformable unto Jesus' death so that he could attain unto the resurrection of the dead. Once again, as soldiers we are reminded that we are always walking towards our demise, ready to be offered up on any battle field for the glory of God, made to look like a fool in any arena of the world, and a foreign combatant when facing the enemy on any frontier.

There is liberty in being dead to this present world. We can choose what we live for and what we will die for. If we are willing to fling aside what is already doomed and considered to be non-essential, we will be able to avail ourselves to live unto that which is much more worthy and honorable of all consideration. If what we live for is not greater or considered more worthy than our present life, it will not be worth dying for. And, if what we live for is not worth consecrating for that which is truly praiseworthy, then it is not worth offering all up as an acceptable sacrifice to strive to gain the real prize.

We must recognize that the self-life is not worthy or honorable and the world stands doomed. There is only one aspect of life that stands worthy, one means that is honorable, and one source that deserves our sacrifice, and that is Christ Jesus in us, the real hope of glory. In light of His redemption, the future glory that awaits us, as well as the promise of gaining the prize of heaven, there is nothing worth consecrating our life, honor, and duty unto.

We surely must count the cost of our self-life and our relationship with the world to gain that which is eternal, praiseworthy, and honorable for our consideration and sacrifice. Such a cost is the real secret behind the Christian who truly overcomes the enemies of his or her soul. It costs to know, experience, and possess the reality of Christ. For example, if we buy truth we must sell our right to insist on our own reality. If we strive to follow after righteousness, we must recognize our best is nothing but filthy rags that must be cast to the wayside in order to follow in the ways of godliness. If we choose the way of peace, we must desire reconciliation with God more than harmony in regard to our present relationships with others and the world. Jesus declared in Matthew 10:34-39 that He did not come to bring peace but a sword of truth that will divide. If we put feet to our faith, it will lead us into a life that will cause us to be considered a fool in the eyes of the world. If we put on our helmet of salvation, we will be able to guard that which is valuable and worthwhile, while we take up the sword against all that would oppose our lives in Christ.

There are thirteen references to overcoming in the book of Revelation. Many of the references are made in light of receiving the promises or rewards that await those who embrace the excellence of the Christian life. Our Lord also made reference to Himself overcoming the challenges presented by His humanity and the world. He is our example, and we must walk in the type of life that will ensure us victory. The victorious life will lead us to inherit all that has been promised to the heirs of salvation. Revelation 21:7 best summarizes it, "He that overcometh shall inherit all things; and I will be his God, and he shall be my son."

As we come to the end of this book, we must examine to see if we are overcoming the enemies of our soul. Are we standing on the right side, withstanding in the strength of the Spirit, and remain standing on what is true and right. We cannot and will not inherit all things unless we remain standing. We need to keep in mind that we have been given what we have need of in order to be more than conquerors in our Christian life. When all is said and done, and we stand before the great Judge, there will be no excuse or reason for not securing the victory that has been made available through our soon and coming King and Lord, Jesus Christ.

13

THE ESSENCE OF OVERCOMING

We have been considering what it means to overcome. Sadly, what the world declares as being victorious or overcoming in a matter is not overcoming, but getting around something, coming out on top of something, stepping on something, subduing something by grinding it into powder, or using it as stepping stones to erect some type of pinnacle. But, such activities do not constitute overcoming.

In the kingdom of God overcoming means just that. You have faced the challenge, responded in a way that allowed you to overcome a matter in an honorable manner. It is almost as if you found the bridge that simply allows you to step over a challenge, thereby, avoiding the base tendency to step on whatever you need to in order to come out on top. And, when it comes to doing what it is honorable, there is no sidestepping a challenge or stepping around what is not convenient or comfortable by using flattery or excuses. Such base practices are a coward's lazy way out of having to stand for what is right. It is not a matter of finding a convenient route or a kink in the situation, for that is the thief's way of robbing a matter of what is right. It is not devising a clever way of coming out on top of something, for that can easily be the despicable way of attempting to kill or murder the essence of what is honorable. Overcoming is not a situation where one is exalted at the expense of another for that is the way to destroy the testimony or contrast of what is right and acceptable to heaven's way of thinking.

An excellent way points to character that possess integrity. Integrity is not related to whether you are stronger, cleverer, or a great game player; rather, it points to the manner in which you perceive and approach a challenge. An overcomer never approaches a matter to come out on top. Rather, a godly person responds with the intent to allow his or her character to be overcome by that which is higher in practice, worthy of consideration, and bigger than the most notable action of the age in which he or she lives. These individuals see challenges as opportunities to overcome self, personal defeats as valuable teachers, and the base ways of their enemies as occasions to be honorable.

The Apostle Paul summarized what it meant to truly overcome in Romans 12:21, "Be not overcome by evil, but overcome evil with good." In other words, the only way to overcome evil is not by resorting to something that is evil, but by demanding of yourself the response of that which is excellent. The instructions and examples of what it means to overcome evil with good can be seen throughout Scripture. As we study the character and dealings of God towards man, we never see Him resorting to evil. His reactions speak of goodness, or that which will benefit those who will humble themselves to be recipients of His excellent ways. It is His way of approaching matters that serves as our example.

For instance, we are told to love our enemies and pray for those who persecute us. The Bible is clear that in our unregenerate state of being sinners, God so loved us that He sent His Son to die on our behalf. In an unregenerate state, we were enemies of God, yet He still commended His love towards us.

After man put Jesus on the cross, His first statement was in the form of a prayer where he sought forgiveness for those who were attempting to snuff out His light. Jesus acknowledged that in such an unregenerate state man has no awareness of what He was doing. He had no concept that he was robbing himself of life, trying to kill what was true, and doing all he could do to destroy what was right. This is clearly the excellent way the Bible speaks of that will overcome a matter. Regardless, of how hatred may destroy something or someone, love will overcome it by its excellent response of meekness and forgiveness. It will bring a contrast that will not easily be forgotten. It will serve as those works that will ultimately speak of the outstanding ways of godliness, subsequently, bringing glory to God.

It is important to understand that what we are truly overcoming is the personal tendency in our own lives to give way to that which is base. It is natural for us to return hate with hate, unforgiveness where ignorance and bitterness reign, unmerciful judgment towards that which offends our pride, and bias towards that which serves our purposes.

As the Bible declares, "the dog will return to its vomit". We are the creature we give way to. Our preferences will always be in line with the person we insist on being. We cannot change the creature we are used to being unless we are willing to experience a radical change that comes from outside of our control and begin to ensure an inward environment to nurture the change. Obviously, we must not insist the change succumb to our base ways and preferences; rather, we must insist on allowing the change to radically forge a new disposition and attitude in us. If we fail to do so, we will find ourselves giving way to the same driving fears of failure and rejection, hiding behind the same walls of obstinacy to hide our insecurities and rebellion, insisting on our perverted realities and ways to cover up our pride, and giving an appearance of agreement through flattery and manipulation in order to hold onto our independence from being held accountable and responsible for the person we are becoming.

This is the creature many of us give way to because this is how the game has been played in the age in which we live. Granted, the world promotes a certain amount of character, but such promotion encourages people to become characters who appear clever, act rationally, pose as gullible or ignorant, and hide their rebellious, hateful, foolish ways behind a veneer of rights gone amiss along with wicked philosophies. However, such character does not possess true character. We may be decent about such a wretched state, but decency often consoles and justifies itself as it slides by that which is righteous and gives way to that which is wicked. We may have an appearance of righteousness, but it is a form of self-delusion that keeps us from facing the fact that in such a state we prove to be nothing more than religious, unmerciful bigots. We may lift up a noble standard, but in light of God it is apt to be nothing more than filthy rags. It is clear, we are what we have chosen to become.

We will never overcome unless we understand that it is often the essence of who we are in our miserable state that we first must overcome before we overcome the rest of the enemies of the soul. Clearly, the wolf will always be a predator to the vulnerable, and the pig will end up wallowing in its pigpen, trampling everything into the mire, regardless of what it is offered. The goat will end up wandering around in the wilderness of nowhere, always searching for some type of pinnacle of self-exaltation to stand on. It is for this reason that we must first and foremost demand excellence from ourselves before we will walk in the excellent ways of godliness.

The ways of excellence will not allow for such base responses. It will call us higher in our way of thinking, and will require us to be realistic about our way of being, as well as transparent about our way of doing. It will demand we deny self from acting according to the seductive, deceitful, hateful, and unforgiving ways of the self-life. It will require us to demand that such ways be nailed to the cross and left to die a coward's death. It is from this premise that we are to insist on the ways of excellence from our character as a means to forge in us the qualities of heaven. It is the mark of heaven that will bring a decisive contrast to a matter.

The contrast will reveal how the excellent ways of heaven will never succumb to the low, base, wicked ways of self, the world, or Satan. Where hatred reigns, the way of love is chosen, thereby, overcoming hatred. Where any form of deception darkens the soul, the transparent light of truth will overcome it by tearing away any veneer, liberating the soul to discover the way of excellence. Where wickedness touts it victories over righteousness, it will be overcome and eventually silenced by judgment with the example of genuine faith towards God and obedience to His Word. Where Satan held one captive, submission to the ways of God will make him flee. Where the world entangled a person, subjection to God will cause a separation from it as he or she is consecrated to Him.

Overcoming always involves giving way to that which is excellent to ensure exaltation above that which is base. Once exalted, it allows the person to walk in contrast to wickedness by choosing righteousness, which will allow one to soar above the claims and entanglements it has upon the soul. And, by coming into subjection to that which is holy or set apart, one will be able to walk in godliness away from the evil traps of spiritual death and ruin.

This is the essence of overcoming. The Apostle Paul puts a face on such glorious victory in Romans 12:9-20. Love must be without hypocrisy to overcome hatred. As Christians, it must be our natural tendency to abhor evil, while overcoming it with goodness. We must possess the necessary disposition to be kind towards those who do not serve our purpose. We must know what it means to possess the type of affections that will allow us to express genuine benevolence towards others, even our enemies.

As Christians, we must not be slothful about doing right before our Lord or we will excuse ourselves from being responsible to walk in the ways of righteousness in regard to others. It is when we walk according to the excellent ways of heaven that we will possess the hope of heaven, and have the character of a true saint who will endure to the end. Such a walk will empower us to be diligent in righteous prayer to see a matter come to fruition for the glory of God. We will know how to genuinely serve others, sincerely bless those who persecute us, and maintain the right perspective that will enable us to refrain from cursing those who do not serve our purposes. Instead of coveting and competing with those who are being blessed, we will be able to truly rejoice with them. We will have the sensitivity to weep with those who weep, be able to reach the same mind with those who have the same spirit, and humble ourselves before others instead of having to hide arrogant conceit and judgment behind a cloak of fake nobility.

Ultimately, we will be able to avoid responding in anger, bitterness, and hatred. We will be honest in all we do, and do all we can do to live peaceably with others without compromising what is true and right. We will leave the matter of judgment and vengeance to our Lord, and if we have the means to minister to our enemy, we will do so in the hope of seeing him or her repent. If such enemies fail to repent, we will know that in the end, such righteous deeds will become a means by which these individuals will have to face their deserved judgment by the righteous Judge of all.

This is the face and action of those who overcome the enemies of the soul with that which is excellent. There will be no reproach or shame in such actions. There will be no need to speculate or debate such responses. There will be no hint of treachery, unfaithfulness, or foolishness in such behavior. It will be obvious that the excellent conduct of godliness finds it source in God. It will always lift the person above the base ways of the world as all guilt and shame lay silently along the former path of sin and death. As the cross has its way, Satan will find fewer and fewer inroads into the territory of the person's life. As the believer follows Jesus, he or she will come to the place of rest for the soul, satisfaction in the spirit, and assurance of glory.

As previously stated, overcoming is not an option; rather, it is the result of the Christian life being lived according to the plan of heaven. It is not an unobtainable goal; instead, it is the ultimate end for the saint when it comes to the matters of life. It is not a future event; but, it is a daily occurrence that will lift believers above the nominal, acceptable, and minimal life that is void of any real contrast or eternal purpose. Instead of living in this world, the Christian will live above it. Instead of tasting the drudgery of this present age, overcoming allows a believer to taste the sweetness of the next. In the place of being subdued by the entanglements of the world, saints will escape the corruption of such entanglements to soar on the wings of expectation in light of the world yet to come. This is the reality for the Christian of overcoming this world. This is the beauty of the overcoming life for the believer. This is the glorious essence of the overcoming victory wrought by every saint who has his or her face and heart set towards the light of heavenly glory.

A Matter
Of
Authority
And
Power

✠

Book Two

INTRODUCTION

One of the struggles and points of confusion Christians have in regard to their spiritual lives has to do with authority and power. There have not only been misunderstandings concerning these subjects, but there has also been abuse in both areas. Due to the mishandling of authority by cultist and heretical leaders, there are also those who purport the extreme view that there is no real authority or miraculous power to be found in today's modern, quasi-type of religion that is being promoted. However, those who often purport such unscriptural nonsense are often abusing or misusing the very authority and power they so proudly claim that they have rejected.

Sadly, misunderstanding, misuses, and abuses of these two forces have caused an unbalanced perspective that have, far too often, rendered some of the Church ineffective and powerless. This has caused many to reject the checks and balances that have been put into place to protect each of us who belong to the kingdom of God from abusive authority and demonic power that is often wielded at us by those who are using it for their own agenda.

It is time that the members of the real Church of Jesus Christ sit down and reason together about these two subjects. It is important to set the record straight for those who are wrestling with these matters. Pull up a chair and let us now reason about what it means to be a people who possess authority allotted by the throne of God, and have been endued from above by the Spirit of God with miraculous working power.

1

Authority Versus Power?

If you were to choose between authority and power, which one would you prefer to understand or possess? I thought about this in light of my own Christian life. There are those who prefer power over authority. They perceive power as giving them strength and the ability to carry out a matter. However, is this a proper understanding of power?

To answer any genuine question about a particular subject, we must understand the nature of it. In the Scriptures authority and power are used interchangeably on different occasions. However, there are places where both are distinguished in Scripture. Are these two aspects of God's kingdom the same or do they have distinction, yet walk hand in hand if properly understood? Do they bring some type of checks and balances to each other to ensure integrity when they are present? These are the questions we must answer in order to bring perspective.

From my own observation, I have seen where "empty" authority lacks power and "abusive" power lacks authority. For example, there are people in authority, but they lack credibility to carry out their responsibility. Such people often hide behind their so-called place of "authority" as they bully others or try to bluff their way through a matter.

On the other hand, I have seen people exert their power, which sometimes comes down to exerting their strength to try to gain the upper hand or get control of the situation. In the case of authority, I had to note that it was about getting one's way, while in the case of power it was about coming out on top or controlling something.

Does authority have to do with the way something is carried out, while power has to do with creating some environment in which someone will come out on top? Once again, we must come back to the nature of these two subjects.

Strong's Exhaustive Concordance of the Bible presents different usages when it comes to the words of "authority" and "power." It is not unusual to see where both words are used in conjunction with one another. However, there is a clear difference between them. Authority has to do with position that allots a person certain rights and privileges when it comes to carrying out responsibilities. Such responsibilities have either been ordained or designated by the position of authority which a person holds. For example, God has given authority or the full rights to parents in regard to child rearing. Such authority establishes an environment of order or jurisdiction. Clearly, people are not to step outside of the proper order or jurisdiction that has been established by their particular position of authority. This brings us to the type of environment that will exist without such authority. In such an environment, chaos and lawlessness will reign.

We see such chaos and lawlessness in our society. The reason for such an environment has to do with the fact that those who are rebellious and lawless do not recognize the authority established over them. They do not see any need to regard or respect such authority because in many cases real authority has never been properly established in their lives in the first place. Without authority there are no boundaries in which to regard or respect the rights of others or their property to ensure genuine honor and justice.

Authority also establishes a place of influence. In other words, parents hold their particular position in order to properly influence their children in a right way. For this reason, Scripture tells parents to train their children in the way they should go and when they are older they will not depart from it.[1] Here we see righteousness is also attached to genuine authority. When proper authority exists, it is to carry out a matter in a right way to ensure both righteousness and justice in the situation. Clearly, where true authority is in operation, it is never for the purpose of doing what is wrong. Proverbs 29:2 bears this out, "When the righteous are in authority, the people rejoice: but when the wicked beareth rule, the people mourn." Notice how the righteous are in a place of authority according to this Scripture, and not in one of power. It does not take authority to do what is wrong. But, it takes authority to have the means and liberty to establish what is right.

Godly people, who are in authority, hold their positions to greatly impact and influence others in regard to right attitudes and behavior when it comes to the matters of order. They lead through example rather than control through power. This is true when it come to the influence parents should have in their children's lives. They are not to provoke

---

[1]   Proverbs 22:6

their children to frustration by being indifferent, cruel, or abusive in their position. They are to encourage, instruct, and lead their children to an understanding of what is right and wrong. Such influence will serve as the children's stake in which they can come back to gain some semblance of purpose or legacy if they lose their way.

In a world of chaos and lawlessness it is not hard for people to lose their way. It often takes the former influences of their life or strong authoritarian figures to bring them back to some type of center to reestablish their sense of identity and purpose. Otherwise, most people flounder in the midst of the unpredictable oceans of the world as they are tossed back and forth by what usually proves to be empty and useless.

Power is different in that it is the ability to carry out a matter. For believers, when we think of power, we think of God. He was able to create the worlds by the power of His words. He parted the Red Sea for the children of Israel. He defeated great armies with supernatural force. In such a text the word "power" points to supernatural power that operates beyond the natural elements of the world we live in. However, the meaning of power entails more than a supernatural work.

Authority points to the necessary position of influence to ensure the integrity of something, but power is the means in which to bring forth a matter to fruition. It is often related to such words as "strength" and "might". Power finds its boundaries in light of what has been authorized. Clearly, it is established by authority. In essence, man has no right to seek power outside of the position he holds. To do so would be a show of contempt and lawlessness towards the position he holds and would be an abuse of power. The fruit of abusive power can be easily detected. It is oppression.

If a person is void of moral responsibility as established by what is right and honorable, power can be easily abused. The ability to carry out something also implies a person has some type of means to carry it out. For example, a person may have the financial means or even the physical force, such as an army at his or her disposal to carry out something. However, the means to carry a matter out and the right to do so can prove to be worlds apart. People who abuse their power simply oppress those who are unfortunate enough to come under their domain of control.

Once again, we are reminded that authority seeks to influence and abusive power seeks to control. The tyrants and despots of the world will use their authority to nudge people into their way of thinking, their power to push people into their way of doing, and their so-called "dominance" to dictate to people how they are to think and live.

Sadly, we see this happening in our own country. The best way to understand how it works is to present it in light of the times in which we live. Despots who have no real moral sense or accountability have been placed in official capacities in the highest offices of our nation. These individuals have no qualms about the methods or means they are using to gain control of people's lives. They have no moral conscience or sense that allows them to recognize that their so-called "values" are morally depraved. Their understanding is upside down as they exalt causes and ideology over the basic rights of people. They tout social justice while denying people of righteous or fair justice. They advocate a "collective salvation" while sacrificing the basic rights of others to bring forth a cruel injustice on the collective masses.

The beauty about the salvation obtained by Jesus Christ is that He became a sacrifice on behalf of the people of the world. He did not simply die for the masses, He died on behalf of every individual who lived before Him, who lived during His time, and who would live in future generations yet to come. In His foreknowledge of all things, each person had a name and purpose, and did not simply recede into the throngs of humanity as an insignificant face. In the redemption of Christ, salvation became a personal issue that was not to be left to the masses to somehow secure through some type of "collective" means.

It is important for people to realize that "collective salvation" will sacrifice the rights and decency of the masses for the sake of certain individuals. Even though it supposedly calls for people to come together as a collective mass to bring about a desired result in the name of "social justice", it promotes a morality that is agnostic in attitude, amoral in practice, and socialistic in ideology. To those who are clueless to the real goal behind this blasphemous gospel and heretical salvation, it may appear noble, but it is quite sadistic. It will hide behind the concept of righting the wrongs of the past by enforcing a Marxist ideology on the masses. Those who enforce such ideology are considered part of the collective group who have the responsibility of reversing the roles of those who have been wronged with those who have supposedly benefitted from such injustice.

Sadly, the first time I ever heard such insanity was in a church. It came in the form of a new movement where everyone had to ask forgiveness for the past sins committed in this country against the Indians and African Americans. As the pastor worked up a few tears of remorse for the actions of past generations, I looked at him in disbelief. The Bible is clear in Ezekiel 18:17-28 that we will not be punished for the sins of others. Our God is a just God and will only hold people accountable for their own sins and actions.

As people blindly followed the nonsense declared by the pastor, I refused to have any part of it. To me it was a fake gesture of nobility that was an affront against true righteousness. Granted, bias and prejudice prove to be forms of sin that are motivated by fear, ignorance, and hatred. Clearly, it does not matter who holds to such darkness of the heart, it is wicked and unacceptable. However, people will be held accountable for their own biases and prejudices, not for others.

Sadly, this movement has become a wicked platform where those who possess prejudice are trying to use the past to justify their own wicked, hateful heart conditions. People who condemn the practices of the past are trying to justify like practices in the name of "collective salvation". They are justifying the very actions they condemn by oppressing those who dare to have acquired something through hard work, by robbing them of such blessings to distribute to the less fortunate, especially throughout the world. Even though many of these same people are also touting social justice, these individuals are not interested in equalizing the field; instead, they want to become the harsh taskmasters and make everyone equal in becoming subjected to their tyrannical dictatorship and insanity. In the end, such wicked philosophies serve as platforms to cruelly oppress the masses.

As you can see, collective salvation and social justice have nothing to do with righting past wrongs and ensuring justice, but with securing the tyrannical dictatorship of a few who have no qualms about sacrificing anyone who might end up standing in the way to bring about their wicked agenda. These people are not after justice that comes with proper authority, but after abusive power. They have no sense of real authority because they are lawless. They see themselves as being part of the "elite", those who are an exception to any rules. These "elite" people see rules as their platforms to bring others under their sadistic leadership, but in their minds they are personally too smart, clever, or intelligent to be brought under what they consider to be obsolete, stupid, and insignificant laws.

Collective salvation puts man down on the bottom of the list as to what needs to be saved. He is nothing but a dumb sheep that will be led to the slaughter. However, those who are considered part of the "elite" make up the collective group. The very ones who must carry out the wicked ideology and agendas are the ones who must be saved to usher in an unrealistic utopia, while the masses are considered as an insignificant inconvenience that must first be used in a collective way to bring about these wicked people's desired results of power. Meanwhile, the masses must be whittled down by whatever means in order to properly use and control them.

The masses must be made slaves to serve the common purpose of the elite. They must be conditioned to be used up for the sake of the privileged and indoctrinated to be sacrificed for the cause of the agenda. As people become part of the masses, they are stripped of their identity. Without any real identity, people can be classified as to their importance in light of the collective. They will be classified, demoted as being dispensable, and randomly sacrificed according to their status, belief, race, or preference. Nothing will be held sacred, and all things have a potential of being offered up whenever it is deemed as necessary to obtain and maintain the collective salvation of the cause and goal of the "elite."

Collective salvation is not a new concept. It has always been around to be used by those who see themselves as being part of the "elite". You see it in Jesus' day. It is important to recognize that social justice and collective salvation often walk hand in hand. In such people's minds there is so-called "authority" to be gained through social justice and "power" to be had in collective salvation.

For example, in Jesus' time the idea of social justice was manifested in the attitude of a man named Judas Iscariot, while collective salvation was presented by a man named Caiaphas. It is important to consider the logic behind these two men because you will also be able to see the sinister motivation behind them. This is the same motivation that exists behind those who advocate such immoral justice and erroneous salvation. It is vital that people tear away the veneer of the insanity and false presentations that are being presented by these wicked people, and see how immoral, insane, and tyrannical their belief system is.

Judas Iscariot was one of Jesus' disciples. Jesus had entrusted the money to his care. However, Judas had his own agendas. Granted, he followed Jesus, but his motive for following him implied that it was very self-centered and self-serving. In a sense, what Jesus was advocating served as a personal platform for Judas to benefit from.

Just before Jesus was betrayed, a woman came with an alabaster box of very precious ointment and poured it on His head. We know that this woman was Mary, the sister of Lazarus. She was the same Mary who sat at Jesus' feet while her sister, Martha, served His physical needs. She was also the same person who fell at His feet after the death of her brother, seeking some type of consolation. Now we see her at His feet anointing Him for His burial. Jesus stated that her actions would actually serve as a memorial.[2]

It is important to consider Jesus' disciples' reaction to Mary's action. It was one of indignation. Their thought was that such ointment could have been sold for much and given to the poor. The attempt to equalize everyone at the expense of the righteous actions of decent souls is the typical cry of those who tout such insanity in the name of "benevolence". Do we not hear the same logic in the name of "social justice"? Only in the case of the American people, it is a matter of stealing from those who have something and giving it to the less fortunate on the basis that their ancestors have been wronged by our forefathers; therefore, these poor wretched people have not had the opportunities to benefit. After all, the logic is that such "justices" and "works" will ensure the collective salvation of all.

What was Jesus' reaction to such logic? First, we must understand that in John 12:1-8, the real instigator behind the disciples' indignation was Judas Iscariot. Did this man care about the poor? No, and I dare say that those who are advocating this type of insanity today on behalf of the less fortunate do not care about their status either. The misfortunes of others serve as platforms for these despots to spew out their hatred against anything that brings clarity or distinction to truth, integrity, and initiative. We are told that Judas was a thief and was only concerned about how much he was personally losing in the deal. As we consider the actions of those who advocate such hypocritical logic, we can also see that they are nothing more than common thieves and thugs.

---

[2]   Matthew 26:7-12; Luke 10:38-42; John 11:2, 28-33

There is a famous saying that proves to be true: "The accuser is the abuser." In other words, I have learned that people who possess genuine concern for others are actually serving among such people and have no need to make any claims about their intentions or work. They actually put feet to their beliefs by living it. Those who couldn't care less are flapping their lips about such causes, do so because of self-serving reasons.

Jesus made a statement that is true today, "For the poor always ye have with you, but me ye have not always" (John 12:8). The idea that we will rid society of poor people is not realistic. Granted, there is one place we all stand equal at—the cross of Jesus. We all need to be redeemed or saved from the tyrannical dictates of sin. Such salvation is freely offered to each person regardless of status. However, when it comes to society, people have different status. Some are rich, while others are laborers, and still there are those who must glean from the fields after the harvest is over. However, there is no place where God advocates simply giving to the less fortunate without them showing their good intention of doing their part. God is aware of how man, who is usually uninspired to do what is right, will often take the road of least resistance. If he sees no need to work, he will not see why he should work. He often lacks the initiative or integrity to realize that it is his responsibility to work as a means to provide for his family and lifestyle. It is for this reason that man can easily sell his soul for free bread and be quickly taken into some type of captivity. The Apostle Paul reiterated man's need to be responsible for his own personal welfare when he told the Thessalonians in 2 Thessalonians 3:10 that if they did not work, they would not eat.

The Bible is clear. The rich are entrusted with much, but such riches serve as a test as to whether they can be entrusted with more. The Bible is also clear that God blesses people so they in turn will bless others. Blessings are a grave test that can become points of great judgment on those who fail to do what is right.[3]

Those who have the means to labor must be faithful to do so. We all must carry the burdens of our own way of living. We must pay all debts but the debt of love. Obviously, we must not incur debt because of heaping upon our lusts or trying to live a certain lifestyle that is far

---

3   Genesis 22:16-18; Deuteronomy 15:7-15; 24:10-22; Luke 16:10-12; James 4:17

beyond our means. We must be responsible in how we live, and live responsibly in regard to what we possess. The Bible is clear that a man who fails to work and support his family is no better than an infidel. The first man, Adam, was told to dress and keep the garden even though his environment was perfect.[4] Work it not only a responsibility, it is a privilege.

It is also made clear that people are to sustain the work of God's kingdom. They are to support those who invest in their spiritual well-being.[5] The idea of a "Nanny State" or giving to those who refuse to work is scripturally and morally wrong. As already stated, even the poor were to glean in the fields after harvest. Nothing was to be handed to people unless they could not help themselves. In fact, it is partaking of people's sin. And, one of the great sins mentioned in Proverbs is "slothfulness." The "Nanny State" advocates slothfulness and irresponsibility on people's part. It is sin to expect others to support you when you have the means to work, and it is immoral to enable people to continue in irresponsible and immoral lifestyles because they are lazy and irresponsible.

The problem with Americans is that they have sat back on their laurels, thinking that we, as a nation, are too great to fail, while failing to stand for what made America great in the first place. We saw ourselves as a giving nation, but we never evaluated whether such giving ensured the integrity or moral responsibility towards those to whom it was directed. Did it guarantee their dignity and create an environment in which they would personally thrive or benefit?

Due to the fact that we failed to stand for what was right, we also failed to ensure what is right. Righteousness points to right standing before God, not sitting back while evil men sow tares into our way of thinking. This is especially true when it comes to the tender ground of those who are vulnerable.

A good example of such tender ground is our children. Seeds of Communism have been sown into the hearts of our children through the various systems of the world. Such systems include our educational

---

4   Genesis 2:15; Romans 13:8-10; Galatians 6:2-5; 1 Thessalonians 4:11-12; 2 Thessalonians 3:6-10; 1 Timothy 5:8

5   Luke 10:7; 1 Corinthians 9:12-14; Galatians 6:4; 1 Thessalonians 5:12-13; 1 Timothy 5:18

system, and the media that has played the perverted psychologist through movies, music, and other art forms. Our young people have been sold lies by those who advocate that success and happiness require no real personal cost. All of these things have caused many to become distanced from being actively involved with actual people who have needs, feelings, and basic God-given rights. It has caused them to become lovers of pleasure rather than lovers of God. In fact, we can go down the list that was presented by the Apostle Paul found in 2 Timothy 3:1-7 concerning the environment of the last days and see how the attitudes and environment of our own society fit his description.

We are told that after Jesus rebuked the disciples for their show of "fake nobility" while He actually exalted Mary for her actions, Judas Iscariot immediately went out and betrayed Him for thirty pieces of silver, the same amount that would have been paid for a slave.

All of these wicked presentations of social justice and collective salvation are to enslave people into a form of tyranny. Ultimately, those leading the crusade will require people to sell their souls to right the wrongs of the past. As you study the people's lives that maintain such ideology, you will see where treachery lies at the door of their hearts and ways. The reason why such treachery exists is because all real boundaries of righteous judgments have been adjusted to fit the wicked ideology and agendas of a few. As a result, such individuals will sell out those who do not fit their idea or agenda in the name of "justice".

Caiaphas was the high priest for the Jewish nation. The religious people of Jesus' day saw Him as a threat to their religious kingdom. Granted, there was a fragile balance between the religious system touted by the Jews and the political system of the Roman Empire. Leaders from both sides walked a narrow tightrope of compromise to maintain a flimsy peace between them.

We are told that the Jewish leadership convinced themselves that Jesus posed a threat to their precarious balance of power. However, Jesus' only real threat was truth that stripped away their religious cloaks and exposed the white washed tombs of their religious practices. He threatened the power they had over the Jewish people, but He did not threaten the delicate balance that was maintained between them and the political machine of Rome.[6]

The Jewish leadership managed to convince themselves that by offering up the man, Jesus, they would save the masses from possible destruction. In a sense, a wrong would be made right by supposedly "preserving" the welfare of others. This sounds much like collective salvation. It would take a collective effort on their part to maintain the unstable balance. Keep in mind, collective salvation will always require some type of sacrifice to cover up that which is wicked, make atonement in some fashion to keep the collective happy, or to "supposedly" right a wrong. We can hear this wicked insanity constantly being advocated by those who hold to its liberal theology. If society offers up unborn babies, it will keep the liberal women happy. If we allow the godless to sacrifice Israel, we will keep the Muslims happy. If we quietly allow the wicked to blame all the ills of society on Christians, it will allow them to direct the gullible away from the obvious reality that they are the real instigators and troublemakers.

The truth is these wicked individuals do not care about the masses that are considered lest fortunate. No movement, group, or person can right past wrongs regardless of the sacrifices made to silence the voices of hatred that are forever crying "foul."

The real objective of these wicked individuals is to rid society of anyone who may oppose them in their causes. They are always looking for the pride and prejudice that is established within every group within society, to use as a platform to create some form of hatred and suspicion among the masses that will be used as a means to divide and conquer.[7] The purpose for such strategy is that it is an effective way for these individuals to hold on to their positions of importance and prominence. They will use the innocence or ignorance of the masses to oppose and destroy that which stands in their way.

Ultimately, someone will be offered up. For example, Jesus, the Prince of Peace, would be offered up as a peace offering.[8] The prophet, Isaiah, even prophesied this in Isaiah 53:5c, "the chastisement of our

---

[6] Matthew 23:14-16, 25-33; 26:57-68; Mark 14:55-58; Luke 22:66-71; John 18:12-14
[7] Matthew 12:25
[8] Isaiah 9:6; Luke 23:13-16; John 14:27

peace was upon him." He would be beaten by the Roman government in order to keep the Jewish leaders happy. However, the religious leadership did not want a peace offering; they wanted a sacrifice to be offered up on the altar of the cross. This was brought out by Isaiah, "But he was wounded for our transgressions, he was bruised for our iniquities" (Isaiah 53:5a).

Today innocent people who have nothing to do with past sins committed against certain groups in this nation, are being swindled and forced to pay. Likewise, the religious leaders in Jesus' day falsely accused Him, claiming it would justify His death as a means to save the Jewish nation. In a sense, the high priest was right. Jesus came to be a sin offering that would bring reconciliation between a holy God and lost, wretched man. The prophet Isaiah brings this out, ". . . and with his stripes we are healed . . . and the LORD hath laid on him the iniquity of us all" (Isaiah 53:5d, 6c). However, for those who offered Jesus up, it was not about reconciliation between God and man, but instead it was a means to maintain their tenuous balance of power and control over their religious world.

In order to understand the abuses often found in authority and power, we must understand what constitutes real authority and power. We must not let the world define these two elements, for it lacks the correct order and jurisdiction to ensure the proper boundaries in which all power must operate in order to avoid creating oppression for the masses.

As Christians, we must truly reason together to make sure that we are not divided in what we know to be right. We must understand what we need to stand for in order to ensure that righteousness is lifted up as a contrast in a world that appears to have gone mad from the wickedness that is taking hold of every fiber of this nation and the world.

2

THE SOURCE

To properly understand genuine authority and power, both must be considered in light of their source. If authority is genuine, it will be based on the integrity and character of the one who possesses it. If power is real, it will be disciplined according to the authority that is present. Clearly true authority keeps power in check and genuine power keeps authority balanced and credible.

The reason authority is used in a wrong way is because it serves as a platform rather than a point of keeping something in check. The basis for which power is abused is because people do not see it as a point of balance or giving credibility, but as a way to exalt their schemes so as to bring about their particular agenda.

In order to understand the real source behind righteous authority and what I refer to as "godly power," we must come to terms with the source that allots true authority and wields such power. Jesus gives us real insight as to where all authority and power comes from when He stood before Pilate. Pilate told Jesus that he possessed the power to crucify or release Him. Consider Jesus response to Pilate, "Jesus answered, Thou couldest have no power at all against me, except it were given thee from above: therefore, he that delivered me unto thee hath the greater sin" (John 19:11).

The Bible is clear that in the hands of God, man is a mere instrument or vessel. God alone exalts people to certain positions or places of authority. It is from places of authority that people are allotted the right to exert certain power. However, a person's character, or lack thereof, will determine how he or she handles the power of his or her position.

We are told that God is the potter and we are the lump of clay that will be made into vessels. All vessels are meant to bring honor to the potter. However, there are vessels who attempt to bring honor to themselves. These vessels become fitted for dishonor and are destined to be destroyed by God's wrath, whereas those who reflect His glory as the great Potter will receive mercy that ultimately will allow them to partake of His glory.[1]

The Apostle Paul tells us in his second letter to Timothy that in a great house there are vessels of gold, silver, wood, and earth. Once again it is pointed out that some vessels are made for honor, while others will be used in dishonorable ways. From this premise as vessels we are instructed that we must purge ourselves in order to ensure that we are used as vessels of honor for the Lord's glory. As such vessels, we will be made fit to be used and prepared unto every good work.[2]

It is apparent that God is the one who determines who is given a place of authority. This brings us to a very important aspect concerning this revelation. What will ultimately determine the type of vessel God will set in places of influence and power?

God is never surprised by events. He sets vessels in positions in order to bring about certain events. For example, He set Pharaoh in his position over the children of Israel, Judas in his place to betray Jesus, and Pilate in his position to offer Jesus up as a peace offering. This brings us to another reality. God sets people in places based on their heart condition. Pharaoh displayed a hard heart towards the truth. God used Pharaoh's responses as a means to show Himself mighty and deliver the people of Israel.

Judas Iscariot took offense against Jesus because He was failing to serve his idea of how He was to benefit him. As for Pilate he was too afraid to stand up to the Jewish leadership. Even though he had the power to save Jesus, he did not use his authority to do so. Even though Jesus stated that he would not be as responsible for the shedding of His innocent blood as those who demanded He be offered up, the leader would still be held accountable to some degree. After all, he had the authority to determine the outcome and the power to carry out his judgments.

These were men that were used in dishonorable ways. They could have not been party to such ways if they possessed honorable character. God knew their caliber, and simply placed them in their position in order to bring about a greater purpose. He used Pharaoh to oppress the people in such a way that they would cry out to their Creator in desperation to be delivered so He could bring them into the Promised Land. He

---

[1]   Romans 9:20-24

[2]   2 Timothy 2:20-21

used Judas Iscariot to betray the Lamb of God so that redemption could be secured. He used the jealousy of the religious leaders to deem Jesus worthy to die, but since they did not have the authority to sentence a person to death, they had to turn to Pilate. Pilate in turn carried out their evil plans to provide a way of salvation.

Even though these vessels were used to bring about God's plan, they were destined to failure and future wrath. For Pharaoh, he lost his firstborn son to a plague and lost his army in the depths of the Red Sea. Jesus said of Judas Iscariot that even though he would be used to carry out God's plan of redemption, woe to him for being used in such a manner. We know later that a remorseful Judas Iscariot committed suicide. When it came to the religious leaders, John the Baptist stated that an axe would be taken to the root system of the Jewish belief. For Pilate, his wife even warned him to avoid becoming involved with Jesus because she had a frightening dream regarding Him.[3] Even though Pilate's historical record seemed to start and end with Jesus, according to the *Eerdman's Handbook to the Bible,* legend has it that he possibly committed suicide. Whether his particular demise was a matter of truth or not, it was clear that down the line he would be held accountable for his part in putting an innocent man to death. Although he washed his hands of the innocent blood that was shed, he could not negate the role he played in Jesus' death.

As we follow the trail of mankind, we can see how certain people were used by God to fulfill His plan, but it was in such a way it revealed their own destructive end. God is never limited in His ability to use man, but how He uses man will depend on the inward character and heart condition of that person.

On the night of His betrayal, Jesus knew what was about to happen to Him. He came to die on the cross. Nothing was surprising to Him, nor was He caught off guard by the reactions of those around Him. He knew that each individual had been placed in their position because of their caliber of character. He knew, but He did nothing to try to reason, coax, or stop them. We see Him telling Judas to do quickly what he had so determined to do. He never tried to defend Himself against the false accusations of the Jewish leadership. In fact, He provided them with the

---

3   Exodus 12:29-30; 14:22-31; Matthew 3:7:10; 27:1-5, 15-26; Mark 14:21; Luke 22:21-22

truth they needed to justify their devilish ways for insisting He die on the cross. We do not see Him giving any type of defense when it came to the Roman government. He told Pilate that he would not be held as accountable for his death in the same way the Jewish leadership would be. He silently took His beatings, asked forgiveness for them who were party to His crucifixion, declared that His mission of redemption was finished, and commended His spirit into the hands of the Father.[4]

As we follow the steps of Jesus, there are matters we must acknowledge about wicked men who hold positions of authority and power. Clearly, we must recognize the natural path that evil will take, knowing that it mirrors where we might be in the scheme of things in regard to the condition of our nation. For example, wicked leaders have been placed in their positions by God. Even though they are not aware of it, God used them to carry out His plan to bring about desired results. For example, we can clearly see that the wicked leaders of the present will usher in the second coming of Jesus. They are setting up an environment that will require God to pour out His wrath on all wickedness. These leaders already stand judged with the god of this world, Satan, and will meet their ultimate judgment and demise in this present generation.

There are many reasons why followers of God need to recognize the ways of wickedness. The first reason is because of the great darkness it brings upon the souls of men. Works of darkness can only grow in darkness. They are shrouded in lies, false promises, and seductive flattery. They cannot afford to be brought to the light before they first produce the system or environment that will allow them to come to full fruition. Jesus said of the darkness of the night that would reign at its height during His ordeal to Calvary that it would be so great that no man would be able to do any work. He also stated that the world would hate Him because He would take away the cloak that hides its sin.[5]

In the darkest of times, wickedness will appear to triumph over what is good, decent, and right. It will make a mockery out of justice and it will cause the world to appear mad with greed, insane with power, and in utter chaos as all is turned upside down. Such great darkness causes great oppression upon the souls of men. It produces sorrow, despair, and hopelessness.

---

[4]   Matthew 26:63-68; 27:11-14; Luke 22:66-71; 23:34, 46; John 13:26-27; 18:4; 19:30

[5]   John 9:4; 15:19-24

This is what Jesus' initial ordeal to Calvary reveals about darkness. However, the reason darkness must have its way is so that its ways and works will be exposed by truth. It is from the premise of truth that righteousness is able to triumph over the darkness of wickedness. Great darkness may at first appear to extinguish the light, but eventually the light of truth will break through the darkness to bring a contrast to people, causing them to make a decision as to what they will ultimately give way to.

As the Bible declares, the wicked will never inherit or rule over the earth, and their seed shall be cut off.[6] Psalm 7:11 tells us that God is angry at the wicked every day. At times the wicked may make what appear to be great strides in gaining rule or control over the earth, but such advancement is because God is using them in their foolishness to test the character of His followers and bring a contrast as to the ways of righteousness. This contrast is necessary in the midst of an environment of indifference where people have become dull of hearing, their eyes glossed over with complacency, and their understanding dumbed down by compromise. Such individuals may have a certain leanness to their souls and a restlessness in their spirits, but they cannot properly discern the times they live in.

When Peter was about to face the reality of his flawed character, Jesus warned him that Satan would be sifting him, but once he was converted, he needed to encourage his brethren.[7] What did Jesus mean about conversion? Was not Peter converted? Peter had a revelation of Jesus, but he still held on to his own standards as to what he thought was right. His standards gave him a false sense of who he thought he was. Peter needed to be converted to God's righteousness. He needed to understand the difference between his hypocritical and unrealistic standards that could prove to be impulsive in decision and deed and the righteousness in regard to God's kingdom.

As we are facing the darkness of night engulfing our nation through wicked leadership, we must remember that even God gives such leadership a season to flourish. In every respect it will appear as if wickedness will truly win over righteousness. It is also clear that a line is being drawn in the sand. Those who believe in the decency of man

---

6   Psalm 37:17-40
7   Luke 22:31-32

will find themselves standing on one side of the line while those who advocate the ways of darkness become increasingly prominent, abusive, and outspoken as they rage against those who dare to oppose their arrogance and insanity.

Psalm 10 speaks about the ways of the wicked. They will persecute the poor as they seek after that which they covet. Such individuals have no desire to seek God, nor are their thoughts towards Him. Their ways are grievous, their judgments are unrealistic, and they will try to intimidate those who oppose them. In their wickedness they will boast of that which is in their hearts. Due to their hatred, they will love violence. Their mouth will be full of cursing and deceit. They will have no qualms about defrauding others. Such individuals have no misgivings about murdering those who stand in their way or setting themselves against those who are poor and vulnerable. Such people despise God, and will rage against His righteousness as they show contempt towards His truth. We know that such individuals will indeed be turned into hell.[8]

Even though we know these individuals will lose in the end, we will taste their destructive ways as they begin to destroy all that is pure, defile all that is right, try to silence all that is truthful, and rage against all that would oppose them. It is vital that as a people we understand what these wicked leaders are saying about us as a nation, and what they are saying about the professing Church. After all, the Church should serve as the mirror that brings viable contrast to the wicked ways of such leaders, as well as solutions in which people can escape the destructive, far-reaching tentacles of the despots and tyrants that emerge in their particular age.

---

[8]   Psalm 9:17

3

THE PLATFORM OF THE WICKED

As previously discussed, the wicked uses authority as a platform to gain power. The way individuals approach their authority will identify the type of leader that will emerge. The ways of wicked leaders become obvious to anybody who will consider the fruits that are ultimately produced by their actions. The wicked have no regard for authority because they are lawless. They use chaos as a means to cause problems in order to gain control. Their motives are clearly wicked, and their ways are evil. In many instances, they perceive that their darkness is light, causing them to call good evil and evil good.[1] Their world is upside down in how they perceive and handle matters. However, to them their conclusions to the issues of life are true and correct.

As for the righteous, they see authority as a way to check their motives, approaches, and ways of handling a matter. They use the discipline and order of authority to keep power in balance or in line with what has been established as true and right. Authority disciplines them while power enables them to carry out their ordained responsibility. Without the accountability of righteous authority, people would automatically abuse the responsibilities that come with power.

We are told that God sets up the leaders. It is hard to believe that God exalts the wicked as leaders to rule over His people. How could a just, fair God allow those who are wicked in their plans and ways to end up ruling over a nation that once maintained a righteous foundation? There is one main reason why God allows the wicked to rule where righteousness once stood. It is the only way in which He can humble a nation that has become arrogant, self-sufficient, and populated with people who have become indifferent to righteousness.

As you study the nation of Israel, you repeatedly see this humbling taking place. The children of Israel were told to remember their God, their spiritual legacy, and their purpose for existing. God did not separate them as a nation so they could become like the rest of the pagan nations,

---

[1]   Isaiah 5:20; Matthew 6:23

He separated them so they could properly represent Him. He called them to be a peculiar or special people, not to blend in with the pagan, idolatrous ways of those around them.[2]

As a holy God, He was always calling His people to an excellent way. His righteous way required them to reach for that which was exceptional, called for honorable behavior and conduct in all matters, and would cause them stand out as a distinct light in the midst of darkness. However, we see where His people wanted to be like the rest of the nations. They did not appreciate the idea of having to be exceptional in regard to their status and conduct. The question is, why would such people who should know the exceptional ways of God want to digress downward into ways that would make them fit nicely into the darkness that they were once separated from?

The main reason people want to fit into darkness is to hide their unacceptable ways in the midst of what is considered to be normalcy. The truth of the matter is that exceptional ways call for people to hold themselves accountable as to how they perceive, respond, and conduct themselves. The problem is that due to a selfish disposition, people do not want such a responsibility. They want to be lazy when they feel like it, give in to the pagan ways of the flesh when it serves their purpose, adhere to the ways of the idolatrous world when it appears that it will pamper them, and slide by in responsibilities when no one is really looking. Selfishness is always looking for ways around authority, and desires power when it comes to making its way look superior, acceptable, and exceptional. Even though it has a high opinion of how it handles matters, it likes to hide in what it calls normalcy so that it can justify its wicked ways.[3]

Selfishness rules many people's lives. They justify it by adhering to a "good guy" principle where they do enough good deeds that they can make their selfishness feel good about itself, but they will never inconvenience themselves and go that extra mile to help someone. They will never step outside of their comfort zone to sacrifice on behalf of the betterment of something worthier or greater than they because they are content with the amount of crumbs they offer. In their mind, they "gave at the office," so what more can be expected of them? All is well in their

---

[2]   Deuteronomy 14:2; Psalm 135:4

[3]   John 3:18-21; Romans 12:2

environments, and to be challenged to step above and outside of their well-orchestrated worlds would be considered an insult or affront against them.

In studying the Bible, I can see where such an environment produces dangerous results. A collision course and a clash are inevitable. The clash will be with God and the collision course will entail some type of judgment that will strip away the quasi-environment of personal goodness that has been established. The judgment will reveal the depravity of such a state. It is such a state that causes people to become dull in relationship to God and self-sufficient in their worlds.

We see where this environment resulted in God colliding with the people of Israel as He sent judgment to slam against their quasi-environment of self-sufficiency. It happened during King David's reign. It occurred during a time of peace and prosperity for the kingdom of Israel. All looked well for this kingdom, except God was not happy with the people. The Bible does not go into any real detail as to why He was not happy, but we can conclude that maybe the people had become so self-sufficient in their prosperity that they had become non-responsive towards God. Granted, they may have been going through all of their religious motions, but their hearts were far from Him. They appeared to have their environments together, but without God holding their personal worlds together, such worlds can quickly fall apart at the seams.[4]

In 2 Samuel 24:1 we are told that God incited David to number the people. The Law required that a certain protocol be followed before the people of Israel could be numbered. The procedure required every man to actually redeem himself by paying a half of shekel of silver. Redemption was to remind the people of Israel that they were redeemed from Egypt and belonged to the Lord God Almighty. And, even though they redeemed themselves, it was to serve as a reminder that their real purpose and legacy as a people was spiritual and connected to Jehovah God. If the people of Israel failed to follow this procedure, it would result in a plague.[5]

Since God does not tempt people to do evil, we are told in 1 Chronicles 21:1 that Satan stood up against Israel and provoked, or

---

[4]   2 Samuel 24:1; Matthew 15:1-9
[5]   Exodus 30:11-16

enticed, King David to number the people. As in the times when Satan tested Job and sifted Peter, God simply removed His hedge from David and allowed Satan to entice him to do what was wrong in order to judge the people.[6] According to *"Strong's Concordance,"* "provoke" in this text implies he was actually seduced in numbering the people. It was obvious that David was greatly influenced by a wrong spirit when he numbered the people, for even his advisers around him could not reason with him. Keep in mind, David for the most part was a humble and reasonable man, but God will even use righteous leaders to humble His people. When Satan is involved in the equation, there is no ground in which you can reason with a person. There is an immovable barrier present that will keep a person from actually hearing any expressed concern or reasoning.

Some people might think it was unfair that David's action brought on the plague, but as already pointed out, God was not happy with the people of Israel. Remember, that when the people of Israel insisted on being like the rest of the nations around them by having a king, the prophet Samuel warned them of the consequences for having such a leader.[7] The people would repeatedly pay for the bad decisions made by their leaders. For this reason, people need to be morally responsible in regard to the leaders they chose to rule over them. They must make sure that leaders soberly and humbly see their positions of authority as grave responsibilities and not as platforms. We also know that God was not after David; rather, He was after the people because of their spiritual state and He used David to bring the matter to the light.

Even though God used Satan to incite David to bring about judgment on the children of Israel, God also had his man. Once David had numbered the people, he could be reasoned with from a humbled state. When King David was given a choice as to the judgment that would fall upon the people of Israel, he wisely chose to put himself and the people under God's judgment as ordained by the Law in the hope of seeking His mercy.[8]

When the angel was about to execute greater judgment on Israel, God had His man to intercede on behalf of the children of Israel. That man was King David. We see where he was repentant for bringing the

---

6   Job 1:9-12; Luke 22:31-32; James 1:13-15
7   1 Samuel 8:5-18
8   2 Samuel 24:10-14

consequences on Israel, and that he was willing to take full responsibility for his actions. Once again, we must remember that this matter was not about David. The king's action to number the people was not held against him.[9] It was about God humbling the people of Israel.

Sadly, most people do not understand the character of God. God wants to be able to bless, intervene, and prosper His people. But, if the environment of His people is contrary to His character, He cannot be in their midst, actively involved in their lives, or blessing their activities. He cannot maintain them when they are failing to keep Him the center of their lives, decisions, and activities.

As the environment becomes more indifferent toward God, He will warn, contend, and try to shake His people awake. However, if they fail to wake up and discern their spiritual condition, then He will send forth His judgment. He will use leaders or events to bring about the necessary contrast so He can bring a matter to the light by judging it.

As you study the Bible, you can actually observe the pattern that so many of God's people fall into, especially when they experience times of peace and of abundance. At such times His people actually lose their edge as they succumb to a humdrum, mediocre existence. They appear to fall into a comatose spiritual state as they ignore how the lines of righteousness are being fudged, ignored, or sacrificed along the way. This pattern is brought out in the book of Judges.

In Judges 2:2-3, the Lord reminded the children of Israel they were not to make any league with the inhabitants of the land. In fact, they were to throw down their idolatrous altars to avoid being ensnared by their gods. Sadly, in spite of all the wise warnings to remain separate from all manner of idolatry and paganism, the people of Israel came into agreement with the people of the land, falling into the popular snares of Satan.

Each time the people of Israel fell into the snare of the pagan people of the land, they found themselves being oppressed by those who they had come into agreement with. In Judges you can observe the cycle. The cycle involves five steps that caused the people to spiral downward into complete defeat before they recognized their state and begin to cry out to God. These stages were *sin, servitude, supplication, salvation,* and *silence.* These five words reveal the attitude of *rebellion,* and the consequences of

---

[9]   2 Samuel 24:18-25; 1 Kings 15:5

retribution when God actually sold them into the hands of their enemies to humble them. A call for *repentance* would go forth to the people, and upon their repentance God would once again *restore* them in order to bring them to a place of *rest*. Included in the failure of the people of Israel are apostasies that produced forms of oppressive environments and servitude which required some type of deliverance.

Apostasy begins with people's failure to recognize God's authority. They maintain a quasi state of religion by doing what is considered to be right in their own eyes. The Bible declares that all of a person's ways seem clean to him or her, but such ways could lead to death and utter spiritual destruction. These people may have evaluated that their ways were right, but God considered such ways as being perverted and strange to Him.[10]

The people of Israel began to serve the gods of the pagans as they quickly turned from the way in which their fathers walked in obedience to Jehovah God. They not only fell down in worship of these gods, but they served them in unadulterated devotion. As a result, they forsook their true God.

Once the people forsook the Lord, He delivered them into the hands of the plunderers who would despoil them. In the end, they would no longer be able to stand before their enemies, for they had become their slaves. Calamity would follow them, causing them to become greatly distressed. God then raised up judges who delivered them out of the hand of the oppressor, but in their rebellion they did not always listen to the judges as they continued to spiritually fornicate themselves with the false gods of the land. Eventually the oppression became so unbearable that they eventually cried out to God. At such a point they were ready to not only listen to the judges, but receive God's deliverance.

Can we as a nation relate to Israel's plight in Judges? We need to honestly examine the environment of our nation to understand how God would allow such wicked leadership to take center stage. Such leadership clearly reflects something about the spiritual environment of a kingdom or nation. For the children of Israel, they were often lulled to sleep by prosperity. Have Americans been lulled to sleep by the state of abundance?

In America, we have come into agreement with the concept of "political correctness." In such an environment people declare there

---

[10] Judges 17:6; 21:25; Proverbs 14:12; 16:2, 25; 21:8

is no absolute right or wrong to matters; therefore, they do that which is right in their own eyes. They have no real point of accountability or responsibility. There are no boundaries, just platforms in which they can demean, rip apart, or harass anyone who might disagree with them.

One of the many idols we have chased after in this nation is that of money. This god has allowed us to covet what other people possess, justify immoral actions to obtain it, and pursue it at any price to find happiness and obtain success. Like the gods of Egypt, this god has been greatly humbled in this nation, leaving many in precarious positions of fear, distress, and oppression.

In a sense, God has allowed our wicked leaders to sell this nation's treasures and possessions to other countries who are in direct opposition as to what we have stood for as a nation. These arrogant leaders are trying to strip us of our individuality, and extinguish the light that has set us apart as a nation as they try to bring us into step with Socialistic Europe, whose very policies are proving to be absolute failures. There are those who have been warning us and continue to warn us that we are heading down the wrong road, but how many of us listened to these initial warnings? It is only as we begin to taste the bitterness of such oppression that we are beginning to see how far away from the true light of heaven we have moved as a nation.

As we watch these wicked, godless leaders use their authority as platforms to bring us into greater oppression, there are those who are beginning to cry out to God. The question is, how many David's are there who are prepared to pay the necessary price to ensure that God's blessings are once again on this nation? What kind of price must we pay as a people and as a nation to ensure that we prepare an environment in which God can once again honor and prosper us? Granted, we can declare that we are ready to pay such a price, but the waters could become very rough and uncertain as we stand against the tidal wave that has been created by the wicked ploys and policies of the quasi environment that has been present in this nation and the visible Church.

We can only pay the price in light of what we will ultimately gain. Granted, we may lose everything, including our lives as we stand against the evil tides created by the policies of the present leadership in Washington D. C. However, we must honestly confess that in light of what is happening at the present, we have no real life. In fact, we have nothing to lose that already has not been stolen from us or is now up for grabs as these wicked leaders play dangerous games with our souls.

Do not fool yourself. These people are after our souls! They want us to sell our souls so they can do as they will with them. They want us to give up that contrast of righteousness so they can justify stomping and trampling over everything that has been considered decent and right in the past. They can use our lives for their own causes, sacrifice our souls to further their agendas, and maintain their arrogance while deeming us inferior and insignificant. This attitude justifies their actions as they build their platforms on the backs of the vulnerable and helpless.

As a people and a nation, we must count the cost. Counting the cost will not be based on the present, but in light of the future. It will not be done at the point of selfishness, but at the point of that which is honorable. It will not be done in the name of religion, but in the name of an eternal God. The Lord's goal is to be glorified by simply being in the midst of His people so that He can freely move among them and bless them from His eternal storehouse.

4

THE GOAL OF THE WICKED

Do you ever feel like a pawn in a big game of chess? The only problem is that this game of chess is being played for real as it truly represents life-and-death matters. You do not know what to trust or what will prove to be sure and real.

When Job went through his great testing, he probably felt like a pawn. He did not understand the game that seemed to be playing, but in spite of what appeared to be unfair, he still chose to trust in God. Even though his friends were falsely accusing him, he maintained or defended his ways because he understood the caliber of his character and life. He could look in the mirror and know that he had not betrayed what he knew was true and right.[1]

Man is in the middle of a big chess game that when fully unveiled, will reveal a life-and-death war. The war that is raging is between two unseen kingdoms, the kingdom of darkness and the kingdom of light. In the physical realm, we can often declare that such wars are about power, money, security, and freedom. However, it is even more black and white. The war is about the souls of men and who will ultimately reign over them.

If we are going to win this war, we must understand it. It actually finds its beginning in another conflict that took place between God and an angel named Lucifer. Lucifer lost the war and his estate as a highly regarded angel. Lucifer is known as Satan, the adversary of God. Since he lost his first estate, Satan has waged war against God. It is believed that the initial conflict is what left a big void in creation.

When God formed man to reflect His image and bring Him glory in a newly formed creation, man became Satan's most prized target. God had created a perfect environment, the Garden of Eden, in which He would be able to fellowship with man. He gave dominion over creation to the first man, Adam, to enable him to overcome all that would threaten his fined-tuned world. However, because Adam chose to rebel

---

[1]   Job 13:15

against God's authority, he lost the dominion over creation to Satan. As a result, Satan has created systems in which to take man's flesh captive, ensnare his pride, and gain the idolatrous adoration of his eyes.[2]

Satan clearly uses his world systems to enslave man in serving him. Although most people do not realize they are serving Satan, the Bible declares that he is the god of this present world or age and the power of the prince of the air. Since people cannot serve two masters at the same time, they clearly cannot serve Satan's systems and God. Those who try to serve both masters begin to resent one of the masters while they pursue the other. If they try to keep one foot in each kingdom, eventually, they will be giving lip service to the master they resent, while affectionately honoring the other one in their hearts.[3]

When the war is finally brought to the forefront, man must openly choose who he is going to serve. God often uses wicked people to bring a contrast between the two kingdoms. One kingdom represents the light of His truth, righteousness, and ways, while the other kingdom operates in the total darkness of deception, wickedness, and derisive, destructive ways. God will shine His light in the midst of the kingdom of darkness in order to give man a choice as to whom he will serve.

We know that wicked people use authority as their platform, but what is their goal? After all, they hide their real goals behind a barrage of lies and their wicked agendas under the darkness of night. They cannot afford for people to see what their real agenda is. They must create confusion and chaos while they keep people believing the image or façade in order to take them captive. They must keep them chasing after illusions of false hope while they put a destructive structure in place to bring about their wicked agendas. They must cause people to become dependant on them so that they will accept whatever crumbs they end up casting at them. They must delude people into a false reality so that they cannot see how fragile their façade or deception is. They must isolate people with hopelessness, divide them with trumped up problems, and put them to sleep with obsessive rhetoric that has no real substance to it.

Although such an environment can cause people to become restless in their souls, they often perceive they are the only ones who hold to such a perception. You can see this in the life of Elijah. In the midst

---

[2]   Genesis 1:26-27; 3:17-19; James 1:13-15; 1 John 2:15-17
[3]   Matthew 6:24; 15:7-9, 2 Corinthians 4:3-4; Ephesians 2:2

of the great idolatry of the ten tribes of Israel, the prophet felt that he was the only sane voice in the middle of insanity. The people's blatant idolatry and rebellion caused them to be pitted against God's authority. This rebellion was being manifested through the defiance that was displayed against His truth. However, God assured the prophet that there were others who had not paid homage to Baal. In fact, God stated a specific number. There were 7,000 who had not bowed to the idol.[4]

When people have been isolated by the hopelessness of darkness, and find themselves in a narrow world of depression, they cannot see how others would possess the same level of discontent. Needless to say, wicked leaders must keep such individuals in the dark. They cannot afford to have people compare notes because they would discover that those who hold to a destructive philosophy are often in the minority.

It is important for people to understand that all battles are spiritual, but they are first fought and won in the arenas of people's minds and hearts. If wicked leaders can cause people to fear their methods of intimidation, they can defuse and isolate them. If they defuse them long enough, they can gain the hearts of those who are vulnerable, uninformed, and inexperienced. By the time the majority wakes up, these leaders' goal is to have an army in place that is able to carry out their wicked agendas.

The harsh reality for both sides is that time is not on either side. The window of opportunity for those who must execute an insidious plan and those who must stand against it falls into a very limited arena. For those with a wicked agenda they must gain the minds of a generation of young people who are ignorant about their goals. For those who stand against it, they must recognize that when these wicked people begin to initially play their arrogant hand, they are the most vulnerable for defeat. Once the light comes on they must create enough chaos to keep people ignorant and confused about their goals. Once the people catch on in their initial stage of trying to gain the upper hand and band together, these wicked individuals will be forced to flee like rats for cover.

Truth at this point is the greatest advocate. Those who are wicked can only lie and falsely accuse the people who dare to expose them. This is their way of blowing smoke, throwing up dirt, and creating chaos to keep people from seeing what is really going on. It is a shell game. As

---

[4]   1 Kings 19:18

people try to follow the motion of the visible hand which is based on illusions, the unseen advancements being made with the sleight of hand are what will cause the greatest destruction. Scripture states that all these people can speak is curses.[5] Curses are motivated by hatred. However, they are lies that can set up the environment or reality that will end in destruction.

The light and transparency of truth will reveal the wicked goals and plans of such people. Once decent people see these individual's smoke screens of deception and destructive schemes, and begin to stand against them with the power of truth, the game is considered over. These rats can do nothing more than run for darkness and regroup.

The other aspect that the wicked people fail to recognize is the unseen hand that seems to thwart their plans at different points in history. Granted, their goal remains intact. The Bible refers to it as the mystery of iniquity. Obviously, there is nothing new about the goal of these people. It is the same goal as that of the god of this age, Satan, but the lies and deceptions are often repackaged with new names and titles.[6] This is the clever, subtle plan of the kingdom of darkness that allows these deluded, doomed souls to sell the philosophies and lies as a bill of goods to an unsuspecting and ignorant generation that succeeds them. Keep in mind, each new generation is subtly being conditioned, indoctrinated, and duped into believing these deadly philosophies and agendas.

The Bible tells us that God laughs at the attempts of these people to bring forth their wicked agendas. We read this summary about these people and their depraved dealings and ways in Psalms 2:1-5:

> Why do the heathen rage, and the peoples imagine a vain thing? The kings of the earth set themselves, and the rulers take counsel together, against the LORD, and against his anointed, saying, Let us break their bands asunder, and cast away their cords from us. He that sitteth in the heavens shall laugh: the Lord shall have them in derision. Then shall he speak unto them in his wrath, and vex them in his sore displeasure.

---

5   5 Psalm 10:2-12

6   John 8:44; 2 Thessalonians 2:7

It is clear that these wicked people think that if they can get rid of Israel and Christians, then they would have a utopia. The truth is these people do not know the ways of peace. Even if they managed to get rid of all those individuals whom they deem to be culprits against their ways and useless in advancing their wicked agendas, hate still drives them. The pursuit for ultimate power is still present. They cannot just let things be because they are tormented and dissatisfied. Due to their treacherous nature, eventually they will turn on each other like devouring wolves to gain supreme power.

The only thing that keeps these people from turning on each other is their common hatred for those who will not go along with their wicked schemes. They cannot stand the mirror of righteousness revealing the insane, wicked ways they are advocating. They do not realize that it is the witness of God in their midst that prevents utter destruction from falling on the world.[7] Regardless of how these individuals spout their hatred against God's people, they cannot silence or rid the world of them. However, the real rub comes because the followers of God will not agree with them that their evil is "good." These saints will not be moved from the Rock of truth. They will maintain their testimonies to ensure their ability to stand without shame and reproach before a holy, righteous God. Jesus summarized the destructive ways of the wicked in Matthew 24:22, "And except those days should be shortened, there should no flesh be saved: but for the elect's sake those days shall be shortened."

God will always have a remnant who will not forsake Him. He walks to and fro seeking to find the one individual who will create an environment of righteousness—who will not only stand for what is right but who enables Him to show Himself mighty. He is looking for that one person who could effectively stand in the gap on behalf of those who are about to taste the consequences of judgment. We see Moses and Daniel interceding on behalf of the children of Israel, Jesus on behalf of those who crucified Him, and Stephen on behalf of those who were stoning him. And finally, we have Ephesians 6:18 which tells us that, as believers, we need to pray always with all prayer and supplication in the Spirit for the saints[8]

---

[7]   2 Thessalonians 2:3-7

[8]   Numbers 14:11-20; 2 Chronicles 16:9; Ezekiel 22:30-31; Daniel 9:3-23; Luke 23:33-34; Acts 7:54-60

Can God find such people in America? Or, will it be like the days of Abraham who interceded on behalf of the wicked Sodom and Gomorrah? He actually got God down to saving these wicked cities if He could find ten righteous men in them. However, He could only find one, Lot, whom the Lord delivered out of the midst of the wickedness before He poured out His wrath upon the two cities.[9]

Perhaps it could be like the time of Habakkuk who saw the destruction of Judah. In his tender state, he wrestled before God. He questioned why God allowed Judah to reach such heights of wickedness, and why would He use even a more wicked nation such as Babylon to correct Judah. Granted, God will spare His people from His wrath, but they will not always be prevented from tasting the judgment that falls on lawless, immoral nations. As the Bible declares, the sun shines on the righteous and the unrighteous, just as the rain will fall on both.[10] In such judgment, God's people will be separated unto Him in greater measure. Some will be offered up on the altars of the world as a sacrifice, many will taste the bitter-sweetness of persecution, others will find themselves isolated and hidden away, while some will find themselves fugitives, wanderers in this world. But, like the prophet Habakkuk, they will learn what it will take to stand, withstand, and continue to stand in spite of unpleasant and overwhelming circumstances. The key to overcoming was given to Habakkuk in 2:4, "Behold, his soul which is lifted up is not upright in him: but the just shall live by his faith." Faith towards the true God of heaven is what will keep believers steadfast in their focus, anchored in hope, and will preserve them to the end.

Even though there are many claiming to be Christians, in spite of the presence of great wickedness, how many of them are doing all they can to create an environment in which God could find the type of intercession He could honor. Does the extent of our wickedness as a nation demand that the righteous Lord judge it by using leaders of nations or peoples to humble us that are considered to be worse than America?

A big consideration as to our spiritual condition in this nation rests mainly with the Church. Does the Church bring a clarity that puts up a mirror, producing a contrast between righteousness and wickedness? Or, has the professing Church become so worldly in America that there is

---

[9]   Genesis 18:17-32; 19:15-20

[10]   Matthew 5:45

no real contrast. How many in the professing Church perceive that it is failing to bring such a contrast, and are fleeing the lifeless system that expounds religious rhetoric, rather than the truth? How many are like Jonah, hiding in the hulls of their pews while wickedness and impending judgment rage against the doors of their institutions? Is the professing Church creating an environment in which the Lord can show Himself mighty? Is true repentance that leads to effective intercession taking place in the lives of His people? Such questions can only be determined by individual Christians.[11]

We must also ask ourselves whether God likes playing a chess game with Satan. The answer is no. God knows the outcome of each situation and challenge. We see where He shows long-suffering towards those who are wicked.[12] It is not His will to see people perish in their sins. His desire is to see everyone come to repentance so that He can save them from the wrath that is yet to come.

Wicked leaders cause people to mourn, for such leaders cause oppression. As a result, people desire to see such leadership change, but the moral change must occur within the people before they can be assured of moral, responsible leaders. The attitudes of people will determine the type of leaders who will rule over them. If we, as a nation, expect righteous leaders to rule over us, we must ensure a righteous environment. Such an environment begins on a personal level that is clearly maintained in the home, practiced in society, and upheld on a national level. Clearly, it is the people of the nation that set the tone of the environment. If they do not demand righteousness on a personal level, they cannot expect it on a national level. If their pursuits are pleasure, they cannot expect a leader that will take their needs seriously. If they are selfish in their agendas and inconsiderate about ensuring the common decency of others, then they cannot expect a leader who will show consideration towards them in their challenges and plight.

Likewise, if the Church is worldly, it cannot expect to possess the necessary authority to bring clarity as to what is true and right. If the Church is quick to get along with the world, it must not be surprised

---

[11]   If you would like to know more about the Church, see the author's book, *Whatever Happened to the Church*, in Volume Five of her foundational series.

[12]   2 Peter 3:9

when the world demands that it gives up whatever autonomy it may have to carry out its agendas. If the Church is self-serving it cannot be surprised when the worldly systems demand its allegiance and compliance.

It is vital that the people of America cease from living in a bubble of fantasy and turn and face the tidal wave that is upon them. This tidal wave is threatening to destroy every aspect that made this country great. Many Americans have been living in a bubble that says their country is too great to fall. However, a country is only as great as its people. And, if the people lose their edge or caliber of greatness, they cannot expect their country to remain great. It will collapse from within, for the substance of greatness that made it what it was no longer exists. It has been ebbed away by indifference and offered up on the world's altars by selfishness and the pursuit of useless pleasure.

This brings us down to the main goal of Satan and the instruments he uses to bring about the environment he desires. The goal is simple. It is all about gaining control or sovereignty over the world. Satan is in competition with God. He does not want to be accountable to Him or subject to Him. Although Satan may be the god of this world, he is still subject to God as to what he is able to do in regard to God's people and His creation.

Wicked leaders have the same goal in mind. They want to have complete sovereignty over the world. They want to control every aspect of it, dictate to every person how to think, live, and function. They want to be recognized, adored, and worshipped by their followers. They rage against any opposition. In essence, they want the known world to revolve around them. They want to be God.

The same arrogance and pursuit for godhood you see resonating with these wicked individuals can clearly be seen in Satan's attitude towards God and his pursuit for dominance in Isaiah 14:12-14. This attitude and pursuit can be traced back to the initial lie that caused Eve to transgress against the covenant in the garden in Genesis 3:4-5. That lie being that she would be as God, knowing good and evil.

Many of these wicked individuals see themselves as God. They determine what is good for themselves and what is evil in the way of any opposition. Since these people perceive themselves to be God, they fear no real consequences for their wicked ways. They are deluded by their arrogance and false sense of infallibility.

164

We see this pursuit for sovereignty raising its ugly head in the kingdom of light when Lucifer rebelled, cleverly gaining dominance over creation in the Garden of Eden. When man gave way to the enemy of God in the garden, it began an incredible battle for sovereignty that has been waged throughout the ages through different leaders' attempts to gain control of the known world. As a result, we see this battle defined by the likes of Stalin and Hitler.

The first time we see the wickedness of this plan raise its ugly head is at the tower of Babel in Genesis 11. We know, according to Genesis 10:8-10, that a man named Nimrod started the kingdom of Babel. According to *Smith's Bible Dictionary,* the name Nimrod has two meanings to it, "rebellion" or "valiant." He was the son of Cush, the grandson of Ham. We know that Ham was cursed by his father Noah. It is said of Nimrod that he began to be a mighty one in the earth. It is important to note that he was not naturally mighty, but that in some way he became mighty. In other words, he was valiant to establish an empire of rebellion against heaven itself. He was considered a mighty hunter before the Lord. The question is why would the Lord consider Nimrod if he was simply good at hunting animals?

Nimrod actually established the first known empire that extended northward along the course of the Tigris over Assyria, where he founded a second group of capitals, Nineveh, Rehoboth, Calah, and Resen. There are those who believe that the reason God took note of Nimrod is that he was mighty as far as hunting down and seducing men into following him as a means to carry out his plans to establish a one world government that would replace God. No doubt those who possibly opposed him were done away with. When you check out the "closets" of wicked leaders, you will find that they are filled with the remains of those who became dispensable as these wicked individuals strove to gain control. The skeletons hidden in their closets no doubt become a putrid stench that reaches heaven itself.

During Nimrod's time all people spoke the same language. They found a plain in the land of Shinar where they could actually build a monument to their greatness that would supposedly reach the corridors of heaven. Clearly, since these people had conquered others to rule over an empire, they were trying to make a name for themselves by creating a different platform of worship that many perceive had to do with the zodiac signs. It would be a name that would supersede any other name.

Why is this so significant? It shows great defiance in regard to God. Keep in mind that in the Ten Commandments, God stated that His people were not to have any other gods before Him, and that they were not to use His name in vain. "Name" points not only to who He is, but His character. There is only one God by name or character.[13] To try to make a name or memorial in regard to creation or oneself is an attempt to gain recognition, worship, and supremacy.

Wicked people prove to be utter fools. They may conquer men, nations, and empires, but they will never conquer God. God considered their monument in Genesis 11 and simply brought an end to their foolish attempts by confounding their language. They could no longer communicate, causing them to scatter. The ruins of the tower of Babel revealed the end results of man's attempts to become God.

We know that in this very day wicked powers are attempting to bring everyone under a one-world order of government. They are trying to create a need for a one-world economy and religious system that people will flock to in order to maintain some semblance of life. Out of this wicked agenda will come persecution against God's people. All attempts to wipe out any testimony of God will escalate.

Like all such past attempts, we as believers know the end of these people. It is recorded in the Bible in Revelation 6:12-17. We know that Jesus will one day return as King of kings and Lord of lords. When He comes back the heaven will depart as a scroll that is being rolled out. As Jesus descends from the heavens, the rulers of the earth along with those who are not prepared to meet Him, will try to hide themselves from the wrath that is about to be unleashed on the world. In fact, they will cry out for the mountains to fall on them as a means to hide them from the wrath of the Lamb of God. Even though they denied He even existed, these individuals will not only recognize who He is, but they will know their own end is at hand.

Meanwhile, what must we as believers do in these times? We must believe the Word, obey it, and walk in accordance with it. The Word tells us what to do to prepare for the time of great tribulation as the powers of darkness attempt to take ultimate rule over all of creation. We are to be ready, watching, and praying that we will be found worthy to escape the judgment of this time. We must possess our very souls in patience

---

[13]   Exodus 20:1-17; Isaiah 45:5, 14, 21-22; 46:9; Galatians 4:8

and not sell them for that which is deceptive, idolatrous, frivolous, and temporary.[14]

The question we must ask ourselves is, are we ready for our Lord? Or, will we be swept away by the tidal wave of rebellion as the wicked of the world try to establish another monument to themselves, while arrogantly declaring their godhood?

---

[14]   Matthew 24; Mark 13; Luke 21

5

COMING BACK TO CENTER

After studying authority and power, I decided that if I had a choice between the two, I would chose authority. I realized that righteous authority and power walk hand in hand. But, without proper authority, power becomes abusive and destructive.

We are seeing this destruction in the case of the leaders in our own country. We are constantly seeing positions of authority being used to further tyrannical agendas, while power is being abused to carry out wicked plans. Those who lack or improperly use authority are actually giving people vital insight into their lack of real character.

We have already considered how authority is used as a platform by those who are immoral, irresponsible, and wicked. In essence, there are actually four ways in which people can mismanage authority. Each misappropriation of authority gives each of us insight about the character of the leader or person.

When people actually <u>mishandle</u> authority, it usually reveals that such individuals are inexperienced; therefore, they lack wisdom and will prove hypocritical. These individuals cause frustration.

There are those who blatantly <u>abuse</u> authority. For those who abuse it, you will find that they are operating from the platform of arrogance. Such arrogance will always cause strife and division.

The third type of people who mismanage authority are those who <u>neglect</u> or <u>ignore</u> it. These are individuals who fail to take responsibility for their position. They become indifferent to their reality and their responsibility, which will cause chaos for those around them.

Finally, you have those who <u>overstep</u> their authority. These types of people do not really recognize or respect any authority. They have devised clever means of getting around authority or defying it. They will cause anger, fear, and oppression.

When you consider how the lack of authority affects each level of our society, you can begin to see why it proves to be destructive. For example, when authority is missing in the home, there is rebellion and frustration. When it is lacking in society, there will be lawlessness and hatred. When it is missing on the religious front, you will find apostasy.

"Apostasy" is a very interesting word. It means to fall away from the center as to what is true, pure, and right. The truth is, every aspect of society is basically going apostate. The home is falling away from moral accountability, leaving the family unprotected. Society is falling away from godly principles, leaving it open for complete failure and ruin. Religion is falling away from immovable truths, opening it up for indifference, fanaticism, and judgment.

In the book of Haggai you can see the consequences that will fall upon those who stray from the center. After seventy years of being in exile for disobedience to the Lord, the Jewish people came back to their homeland. They quickly reestablished their homes and property, while leaving the temple of God in disarray.

The temple was to represent the presence of God in their midst. However, the people preferred to establish their presence more in the land than they did God's presence among them. However, without God's presence there would be no real identification for their being, no assurance of blessings, and no real protection. Clearly, their values and agendas were wrong. Hence enters Haggai exhortation, "Consider your ways."[1]

According to *Strong's Exhaustive Bible Concordance,* "consider" in this text means coming back to center. God is the center of all matters. Without the center there is no stable foundation. There will be no stake for a person to come back to in order to get his or her bearings. There would be no means in which to examine whether an individual was on the right track or not.

Since the Jewish people had failed to start from the center, they were paying consequences. God was not blessing their activities. The reality is that everything was slipping through their fingers. They were experiencing drought, resulting in crop failure, bringing them into financial ruin and despair.[2]

When you consider apostasy, you realize that every aspect of society has fallen away from the center of that which is upright, godly, and true. As each aspect of society falls away from its particular standard,

---

[1]   Haggai 1:5, 7

[2]   Haggai 1:6

wickedness will come in like a flood to reign with a vengeance. Such wickedness will bring an unbearable spiritual drought to the souls of people.

We should not be surprised that this falling away has and continues to occur at every level. Remember that Adam not only fell away from God, but he fell into a state of separation from God into utter darkness. Adam fell into this state because he removed himself from being under the authority of God. This state has been passed down on every one of us.[3] Since we have been born into this fallen state, it would not be unnatural for each of us to find ourselves far away from what is right, godly, and true. The truth is we must come back to what we know represents the true center of man and life in order to be reestablished in what is considered to be order and sanity.

The lack of authority in any arena leaves a big gap. It leaves people unprotected, vulnerable, and ready to be preyed upon by the "wolves" of the present age. This is where the "wolves" will seize the opportunity to somehow fill that empty gap with false promises. The harsh reality is they see the vulnerability as a means to take control of the situation.

Since we have considered how people misuse authority, it is vital that we have the opposite contrast in order to consider how God intended authority to work in our lives. As already established, all authority comes from Him. He has established boundaries in which authority is to function in regard to His people in every arena of their lives.

When you consider the actual purpose behind authority, you will realize that it is meant to influence people in a right way. Those who are abusive with authority must seduce others to cover up their true intentions, flatter as a means to hide their agenda, to con in order hide their activities, and delude people into thinking it will benefit them. In a sense, these individuals must rob people of their clarity, kill any common sense in their thinking, and destroy any moral conscience that would stir them awake. The reason these people must work in such darkness is because they do not operate in reality. They lack substance because there is no integrity in their ways, and they lack credibility because there is no truth in what they say. They prove to be hypocritical because they believe they are the exception to what is just and fair, rather than subject to the

---

3   Romans 5:12

rule of common decency that calls for accountability and responsibility in relationship to others.

Once the seduction and flattery of these individuals has been lifted off the minds of people and has been replaced by reality, they will lose the power to deceive those who actually hold to the standard of common sense and decency. What started out with high hopes and innocent trust on the part of those who embraced these people's false light of promises has now turned into suspicion and opposition. What may have been considered excellent is now being regarded as foolish and destructive.

Genuine authority will always bring order to an environment. When you consider an environment that is void of real authority, you will discover chaos. In some cases it might be controlled chaos. This means that on the surface everything may appear calm, but underneath there is pressure building that will eventually cause an eruption. The fallout can prove to be extensive.

Genuine authority will bring people back to center. This means that real authority will once again be established. If authority is properly established, people will understand where they fit in the scheme of things. For example, parents who fail to display the proper authority in their homes will cause insecurity in their children because they will have no sense as to where they fit in the family unit.

Understanding where a person fits also defines what his or her responsibilities will be. Responsibilities establish conduct. From this premise individuals can be called to accountability when they fail to do their part to maintain the function of the whole.

The problem I see is that wherever genuine authority is missing, people become lost. The further they get from the center of what is right, acceptable, and true, the more lost they become. The more lost they become the more vulnerable they are to fall prey to the wolves. Authority clearly defines the boundaries as a means of protection and guidance to people. And, the responsibilities that are associated with such authority will give individuals the means to develop character and constructive habits. Such boundaries will be just and the responsibilities will prove to be necessary and honorable to ensure order.

Adam clearly removed himself out from under God's authority. From that point on Adam's world begin to turn upside down and spin out of control with problems, conflict, and sorrow. His greatest problem was that he was separated from God. He was set afloat into the dark confines of what had become Satan's world, the lion's den. His greatest conflict would be to survive without having the assurance of the intervention and protection of God. His greatest sorrow would be realized as he watched death take hold of the creation around him, realizing that all of his activity to maintain life was now vanity, useless, a waste of time and energy.

Coming back to center means coming back to God and His Word. God is a God of order. As the One who holds all authority in regard to every matter, we must come back to Him and get our lives right with Him. Until we do this, our worlds will prove to be upside down.

To get it right with God, we must obey what He has said. He has given us His Word of truth to establish the manner and ways in which people are to conduct their lives in every arena. In the home, couples are subject to His Lordship, and children are to become subject to their parents' authority as ordained by God. People are to obey the laws of the land as long as they do not prove contrary to the ways of God. In the living Church, all are to become submissive to one another as they come into line with the Head of the Church, Jesus Christ.[4]

It is clear by the fruits in our society much is out of order. As a result, people are finding themselves victims of wicked currents that are frightening and oppressive. Although such currents started out in a non-aggressive manner, they have become tidal waves pounding at the shorelines, threatening everything in their path. Praise God, many people have been awakened by the noise and the destruction taking place around them. They can now see how wickedness is eroding away every aspect of their lifestyle. Many have realized that if they do not take a stand against it, all will be taken out by the waves of destruction.

How can we stand against such waves? We must recognize our enemies. As the Apostle Paul clearly pointed out in Ephesians 6:12, we do not fight against flesh and blood, but against unseen powers. These unseen powers are what empower those who devise wickedness in their heart. Since our real enemies are unseen, we must realize that our weapons against such enemies will not be physical weapons, but a spiritual weapon.

---

[4] Acts 5:29; Romans 13:1-3; Ephesians 4:11-16; 5:21-26; 6:1-3, 5-8; Hebrews 13:17

We have been given the armor to stand against the attacks of the enemy. We have truth that will expose, righteousness that will stand, a message that will advance us, faith that will guard us against the weapons of the enemies, a helmet that will withstand any blow, and a sword that is able to put the enemy on the run. We have also been given vital access through prayer to appeal to the One who is greater than our enemies, and who will ultimately bring defeat to them.[5]

Once again, we must learn what it means to walk in authority. To walk in authority means that I stand according to the authority of the one who oversees my well-being. In order to stand in accordance to the authority of another, I must have a personal knowledge of the One who must influence my life, the way in which I must walk, and the caliber of my conduct.

As a Christian, there is only one who is responsible for my person, and that is the Lord Jesus Christ. Due to the various battles I have found myself embroiled in with the kingdom of darkness, I have learned the importance and power in standing in the authority of the Lord of lords and the King of kings. As Jesus clearly pointed out in Matthew 28:18, all power has been given to Him in heaven and in earth.

This is why the Pauline epistles are priceless. They continually speak of the reality that we are in Christ and He is in us; therefore, we stand in the authority of heaven. Such a reality should remind every believer that we not only stand in His authority, but we will withstand with His authority.

Through the years, I have grown to not only understand the authority I have with Christ and because of Him, but to appreciate the power it affords me when I am facing my enemies. In fact, I know that there is nothing the enemy can do against me unless my Lord gives permission. Even when He allows the enemy to attack, He determines the boundaries and I can be assured that it will be for my spiritual growth and benefit.

In Christ I am dead to the self-life, crucified to the world, and made alive with the Spirit of God. In Christ, I will realize the real hope in me and I can be confident of the life that resonates in me. In the end, I

---

[5]   Ephesians 6:10-18

will be emboldened to stand in assurance of the future that has been promised to me.[6]

The real challenge about the hope and victory we have in Christ is that there is only one such person. Jesus exhorted his followers to beware of accepting or receiving any other Christ but Him. Many will come claiming to be Him, but they will prove to be imposters.[7] This will be made especially evident when such people will be devoid of the authority to stand against the kingdom of darkness.

Through the years I have been made acutely aware of the ineffectiveness and the lack of power of the people who possess a false Christ. They may know the truth about a matter, but they cannot stand against the sin that may be invading their own lives or family. They may rebuke lesser powers in the kingdom of darkness with the name of Jesus, but they cannot drive back the powers of darkness in higher places, nor can they dissipate the wickedness that hangs over them.

When Jesus asked Peter about what others were saying in relationship to His identity, Peter answered that the rumors claimed he was one of the great prophets such as Elijah. Jesus then asked Peter, "But who say ye that I am?"

This is the one question that every person must ultimately answer. It is true, we can appeal to God's providence, and He might well show us mercy at different times. We might cry out to a powerful God whom we recognize as Creator, and He may intercede on our behalf in some miraculous way. After all, He is God and He will show mercy where He chooses to do so. We may acknowledge that Jesus is His only begotten Son, that His Son was indeed a good, great religious man or prophet. We might even be able to declare what Peter said when asked the question as to who he perceived Jesus to be, "Thou are the Christ, the Son of the living God."[8]

The question remains, do you really know Jesus in a personal way? Although He may hold titles, are they just words and terms that you use without any real understanding? Jesus told Peter the reason he made those declarations about Him was because it was revealed to him by the Father. It other words, Jesus' identity was not a matter of intellectual

---

[6]   Romans 6:1-10; Galatians 6:14; Colossians 1:27

[7]   Matthew 24:4-5, 23-24

[8]   Matthew 16:13-16; Romans 9:18

understanding; rather, it was a revelation from heaven that was imparted into Peter's very soul and spirit.

It is obvious that darkness is enveloping the world. There is only one true light that can penetrate this type of darkness. There is only one absolute truth that will expose its agendas and folly. There is only one way to stand in the midst of its wickedness. There is only one authority that will serve as a place of refuge, strength, and hope. That place is not a location, but a person. His name is the Lord Jesus Christ. The question is, do you know, believe, and stand in the authority of the Jesus of the Bible or do you believe and possess an imposter who will fail you in the end?

6

THE FRUIT OF AUTHORITY

As I have considered the subject of authority, I realize in some cases it appears to be illusive. We can discuss how certain titles and positions point to people in places of authority. However, such people may not possess authority. We see this in the case of Jesus and the religious leaders.

The Jewish people understood where all authority came from. In Luke 20:2 the priest and scribes asked Jesus where His authority came from. This proves that even they recognized that He possessed it. We know that God allots authority even to the kingdom of darkness. In turn, the kingdom of darkness allots power to its different ranks of spirits, demons, and followers.

The religious people of Jesus' day wanted to believe that His power came from the kingdom of darkness. This would justify their wicked attitudes and evil plans towards Him. Being quite aware of their wicked agenda to trap Him, Jesus asked them where John the Baptist received his authority. He silenced their silly attempts for they did not want to commit themselves one way or the other. After all, if they said that John's authority came from God, Jesus would have the opening to ask them why they did not believe his message and properly respond. If they said his authority came from a source other than God, they would anger the people.

If a person's authority comes from God, it will be backed by fruits that display righteousness and godliness. For most people, the issues that involve the moral aspect of the kingdom of God are not a matter of debate. If individuals are honest, they know what is right and wrong. They also know that God will not support or condone that which is contrary to all that has been deemed holy and upright.

It is interesting to consider the Apostle Paul's initial greeting to the Gentile churches versus the type of introduction given in the book of Hebrews. You realize that the Jews started from the premise of God to confirm the credibility of a matter, while the Gentiles regarded the credibility based on the title or position of someone. The Apostle Paul was always making reference to his position as an apostle or servant of God to the Gentile churches, while the book of Hebrews simply begins with God speaking through His prophets and in the last days through His Son.

When we study the religious leaders of Jesus' day, we can see that they understood that all authority came from God; however, they hid their lack of it behind titles and positions. They gave an outward appearance of their religious credibility, while abusing their positions of authority, as they tacked unrealistic demands and burdens on others that they did not personally observe. Jesus called them blind leaders in Matthew 15:14 and hypocrites and serpents in Matthew 23:14, 23, and 33.

It was for this reason that the people observed in Jesus' Sermon on the Mount that He taught as one having authority. He had credibility because He was void of hypocrisy. He not only believed what He declared as truth, He lived it.

It is important to keep in mind that authority determines the premise in which a person will approach a matter. Many people lack authority in a matter because they are trying to settle an issue in their mind in order to arrive at some premise that they can actually confidently stand upon.

The same type of authority that these people are seeking can be discovered in Esther's life. Most people know the story of Esther. She was an orphan who was raised by her uncle. When an opportunity presented itself, she was placed in the position of being queen. However, she was unsure about where she stood in relationship to her husband, the king, which placed her on shaky ground. When her uncle asked her to intercede on behalf of the people of Israel according to her position, she hesitated. She was not sure she could even make a difference.

It was not until she was ready to lose her very life to save her people that she discovered the authority she possessed. Her wisdom and actions saved her people. Esther 9:29 gives us this insight, "Then Esther the queen, the daughter of Abihail and Mordecai the Jew, wrote with all authority, to confirm this second letter of Purim." According to *Strong's Exhaustive Concordance of the Bible*, "authority" in this text points to might and strength. With all of her might and strength afforded by her position as queen she wrote the second letter in regard to the survival of her people. Clearly, her authority had been confirmed by God and established by her husband. The orphan who had appeared shy and uncertain had truly discovered her place, allowing her to stand confident in her authority.

People, who have no sure foundation, premise, or base as to what they can believe or know, will swing from one limb to the next in order to acquire some type of perspective that will create a place of authority they can trust. However, there is only one truth that will stand sure, immovable, and absolute. That truth is God and His Word. If a person does not approach a matter from that which stands sure and has been confirmed as absolute, he or she will be void of any real authority to stand. Once again, we are reminded that authority is not a platform to stand upon, but a place to stand within.

Authority is present when a person approaches a matter from a premise that has already been established as truth. Authority never operates from an arena that has not already been tested and tried. Since it is based on what is absolute, it cannot be moved from its position. It possesses the integrity that stands on tried and true principles, while it is upheld by what proves to be excellent and worthy of consideration. It knows how to conduct itself in an honorable way. In fact, it is natural for those who possess true authority to act in an honorable, respectable, and responsible way.

Scripture shows us the contrast between those who hide behind some position of authority, and those who possess it. For example, the religious leaders held positions of authority, but it is said that after the people heard Jesus teach, they realized that He possessed authority.[1] What is the difference between being in a position of authority and possessing authority? If you study the life of Jesus versus the fruits created by many of the religious leaders, it becomes quite evident as to what separates those who use authority as a platform and those who actually possess it.

If someone asked me to summarize the difference between holding a position of authority and possessing authority, in one sentence I would say that those who possess authority do so because they truly have the goods. In other words, they have what it takes to confirm their position by actually exercising authority. As I consider Jesus in light of the religious leaders of His day, it is blaringly easy to see the difference between those who simply hold positions of authority and those who have it. As Christians, we must understand the difference so we can

---

[1]   Matthew 7:29

discern between good and evil. We know that which is good possesses authority, while that which operates in the dark shadows of wickedness is devoid of real authority.

The first thing we must acknowledge about authority is that those who possess it can be clearly identified. Jesus, who actually possessed authority, stood separate from those who patted themselves on the back as they proclaimed the importance of their position. Jesus never had to make such claims. The main reason is because He never hid behind authority, He walked in it.

People who may be in positions of authority, but who do not possess it, must remind everyone else as to the positions they hold. The reason for this is because those who walk in authority do it with clarity. Jesus never went around boasting about who He was. After all, He was the Son of God, the Messiah. Therefore, it was natural for Him to walk in the authority that was allotted Him in that position.

The centurion soldier understood this particular reality.[2] As he stated, he was a man of authority. He held a position of authority, but he also understood the responsibilities of his position. He implicitly understood the chain of command and where he fit in it according to his position in the Roman army. There was no competition or debate about what his position entailed. He was a leader of a certain group of men. He understood that he not only had the position of authority over these men's welfare, but he possessed the credibility that was necessary to be an effective leader. In other words, if you are not really a leader, you will not be regarded as one. You will lack the credibility to effectively lead others.

I experienced this reality when I was in the military. There were some leaders that understood their authority, but there were others who abused their positions and caused me to want to rebel against them. In my disillusionment with their leadership, I actually tried to figure out ways of getting around their insipid and often petty rules. Sadly, their rules were often based on their prevailing attitude towards the person they were overseeing or it was inspired by how a matter personally affected them. In my book, their inconsistency and deviation from what was important brought a reproach to their rank, and disgraced the uniform.

As I considered the difference between those who were real leaders and those who played at it, I realized it was a matter of integrity and

---

[2]   Matthew 8:5-13

character. Integrity always carries that element of respect with it. It creates an environment that encourages people to discover their place and potential in the order of things.

I found this to be true when I was in the military. Those who were the truest leaders produced an environment that inspired me to do my best. Such individuals showed respect to me as a person. They did not treat me as a faceless individual that could be used for personal means, abused when refusing to placate fragile egos, and discarded for not properly playing the game.

Another important aspect of authority is that it actually leads people. Those who understand authority recognize that they are leading people. They show those whom they lead the proper respect, consideration, and honor. They are genuinely concerned for the welfare of those who are following them. They see themselves as servants who must first regard the people under them in a proper way before they can expect to lead them in a successful way. Genuine authority will create a certain loyalty that allows people to discover their potential and reach a place of excellence in their service and sacrifice.

This centurion soldier understood that by having the credentials, he could give men orders and be confident that they would carry them out. Positions of authority are considered a privilege, not a right. Privileges point to responsibilities. People show proper respect to authority by maintaining the integrity of the privilege that has been allotted to them. This proper respect is expressed through fulfilling the responsibilities that come with the positions of authority.

Genuine authority gives the liberty, as well as inspires those who are subject to it to do what is honorable and right. Such followers realize that the leader is showing good faith by entrusting them with a responsibility; therefore, it is natural for such followers to likewise show good faith in carrying it out. It is from this premise that Jesus commended that He had not seen such faith in operation as He did in the case of the centurion soldier, even among the Jewish people who believed they had somewhat of a corner on the matters of God.[3]

Jesus' authority was confirmed by those who devotedly followed Him. He showed compassion to those who sought Him out, and rebuked those in the religious realm who abused their positions of

---

[3]   Matthew 8:10

authority. Because He was who He was, and lived what He declared, He taught with authority, confirmed His credentials with miracles, and inspired people to reach their potential.

This brings us to the other aspect of authority. With the centurion soldier we see the type of attitude that must be present. The attitude is that of respect. The soldier recognized authority by respecting it. Those who are lawless have no respect for authority. If you do not respect something, you will see no need to possess it. As pointed out, lawless people are always looking for ways around established authority. They want to do their own thing and call their own shots as they justify their lawlessness. Clearly, they are fiercely independent and easily offended by those who would call for godly submission to that which is worthy, and obedience to that which is lawful and righteous.

The one element about every great leader is that they were also great followers. They understood their place and the rules of engagement. Don't get me wrong, great followers do not simply go along with the moving tides of that which proves to be wicked, self-serving leadership. They are followers by choice as to what they will adhere to. They have chosen to follow because they are in agreement with the call, agenda, or cause. They have a conviction as to the importance of a matter. In a sense, they have consecrated themselves to see themselves through to the end of a matter no matter the cost.

If so-called "leaders" sway from these basic points of agreement, those with integrity and authority will not follow, but continue on in the same manner as before. Notice those with the character of integrity are not in rebellion; they are simply staying the course. It is at such points that these individuals often become the leader. The Apostle Paul reiterated this principle when he gave this instruction in 1 Corinthians 11:1, "Be ye followers of me, even as I also am of Christ." Paul knew the real leader was Jesus. If he failed to stay the course set before him, believers were to continue to follow Jesus.

Conviction towards their responsibility is what enables this type of person to be faithful in executing the most minor details to ensure the quality of a situation. We see the faithful servant in Luke 19:17 given more authority. The Apostle Paul talked about the authority that was given to him to edify believers, not to destroy them. Such intention of honorable leadership is unlike Satan who gives his kingdom certain authority to carry out destructive agendas.[4] Here again, as saints of the Most High God, we are reminded that authority comes from above. It is measured out to the people of God according to the conviction and faithfulness that they have shown in regard to their calling and ingenuity to carry it out.

The Apostle Paul understood authority. The priests had given him the necessary authority to bind Christians to silence them. He often made reference to this fact. However, when he met Jesus on the road to Damascus in Acts 9, he changed his direction and came into agreement with the message of the Gospel. From that point on he possessed a new calling and agenda as he followed Jesus into a new life.[5]

Another fruit of authority can be seen in a person's words. I am shocked that people in authority think they can say or do anything and people will naturally follow them. However, if a person's words mean nothing, people will not believe him or her enough to follow him or her. If a person's actions do not back up his or her words, people will eventually deem such individuals as utter hypocrites.

Jesus meant what He said and said what He meant. There were no inconsistencies between what He claimed and how He lived. His words were truth, and He lived the truth. For this reason He instructed people to limit their words to a simple yes or no, for beyond such simplicity was evil.[6] To continue beyond a simple reply opens the door in which people are tempted to stretch their words in attempts to make themselves look good. These actions will cause them to commit fraud as to their intentions and will ultimately reveal that they had no real means to keep their words when circumstances proved to be trying and overwhelming.

The words we speak should be law. In other words, they are cemented in stone. We cannot be impulsive, flippant, and foolish about what we say. Our words must not be a form of idle flattery. Every word spoken must be backed up by action to faithfully carry out a matter. Every word spoken must be treated as a promise that will be kept no matter the expense, and a covenant that will not be broken no matter the circumstances. Every word spoken must first be soberly weighed, disciplined by what is real, and made realistic by action.

---

[4]   2 Corinthians 10:8; Revelation 13:2

[5]   Acts 9:14; 26:10, 12

[6]   Matthew 5:33-37

Jesus said of His words that they were spirit and life. The spirit of His words pointed to the power they have, and the life they brought forth confirmed their authority. It was for this reason that the demons trembled before Him. They knew the minute He spoke their power was broken by the authority His words carried. After all, as Creator, the worlds were framed by His words. There was no debate as to their truth nor was there any argument that could be presented against them. The demons had to come into subjection to what He said.[7]

We see where Jesus gave this same power and authority to His disciples in relationship to the demonic realm.[8] They would not be subject to the kingdom of darkness; rather, the kingdom of darkness would become subject to words spoken in Spirit and in truth.

The other aspect of Jesus' authority was that He was anointed. To be "anointed" means to be set apart to carry out a mission. In a way, it is the same as an ordination. Jesus was ordained as the Christ, the Messiah, the Promised One of God. He was anointed to carry out His heavenly commission. Luke 4:18-19 gives us insight into His earthly mission:

> The Spirit of the Lord is upon me, because he hath anointed me to preach the gospel to the poor; he hath sent me to heal the brokenhearted, to preach deliverance to the captives, and recovering of sight to the blind, to set at liberty them that are bruised, To peach the acceptable year of the Lord.

In His humanity, Jesus was empowered by the Spirit to carry out His responsibility to offer the Gospel to those who were poor in spirit. He would penetrate the very soul of man with healing, set the captive free from the tyranny of sin, do the impossible by giving sight to the blind, and do the magnificent by bringing freedom to those who have been devastated by the bruising of life. He came to bring spiritual reconciliation and restoration to mankind.

As believers, we also have been anointed by the Spirit of God to carry out our commission.[9] Clearly, we possess both the ordination from God and the power from His throne. Sadly, most Christians are not

---

[7] Luke 4:35-37; John 6:63; Colossians 1:16-17; James 2:19; Hebrews 11:3
[8] Luke 9:1
[9] 1 John 2:27

aware that they possess both the authority and power to carry out their heavenly ordination. In some cases, Christians seem to be on the outside of such authority and power as they play at being a Christian rather than walking and living as a believer.

I have struggled with why some Christians never seem to walk in authority and possess the power to be effective in their lives and high calling in Christ Jesus. As I have considered this matter, I have come to realize that the most defining aspect of the Christian life is conversion. I realize that Christians who are living on the outskirts of Christianity have never been converted to the ways of righteousness. They are holding on to their same old point of lawlessness where they are still insisting on their own ways. They do not want to give up their independence by bowing their stiff-neck in humility, kneeling in submission, and coming under the Lordship of their Redeemer and Savior. They would rather settle for the façade than possess the source of the authority of heaven. It is for this reason that they often become apostate as they fall farther and farther away from the center of righteousness and truth.

As believers, we do have the authority of heaven. We have been endowed with this authority so that we can properly walk out our lives before God, the kingdom of darkness, and those we encounter during our spiritual journey. The question is, do you possess this authority or are you on the outskirts laying claim to the benefits of the heavenly life, but not possessing the actual fruits of it that would truly identify you as a saint of the Most High God?

7

THE ORIGIN OF POWER

We have been considering the difference between authority and power. We can see how they walk hand in hand. Authority ensures the integrity of power, while power carries out the matters established by authority.

God is the ultimate authority in all matters. He alone has declared what is right, established what is acceptable, and has ordained what is required. Any matter that is attempted or accomplished outside of what He has ordained will be regarded as iniquity, and visibly rejected on the Day of Judgment.

People are forever trying to adjust, redefine, and negate what God has already established as truth. He has clearly made His character and ways known through His Word. For this reason, His Word stands as a final authority in all matters. In essence, it is law that is true, just, immutable, and eternal. Clearly, His Word not only stood sure yesterday, but stands immutable today, but will remain standing forever. Governments can try to discredit His Word, nations can try to outlaw it, religion can try to water down or change His truths, people can pervert its righteous doctrine, and man can redefine its principles, but in the end it will stand as inspired and maintained by His Spirit. His Word will ultimately bring all matters to the light for judgment.[1]

This brings us to the matter of power. The immovable authority of God's Word will be confirmed by the power to back up what has been declared. How much power is in His Word? We know that His Word is what framed the worlds. Obviously, He made the earth with His great power. However, His power will always function within the confines of His wisdom. We are also told His understanding was expressed in how He stretched out the heavens. God not only has power, but order and imagination that are manifested in a glorious, artistic way.[2]

---

[1] Psalm 119:89, 160; 1 Peter 1:23-25; 2 Peter 1:19-21

[2] Jeremiah 51:15; Hebrews 11:3

Creation clearly reveals the eternal power of the Godhead. For this reason man will have no excuse for the unbelief or contempt he shows towards God and His Word. We know that the Father designed creation, the Son formed the world according to His design, and the Holy Spirit brings distinction and life to it. Another way to put it, the Father was the architect, the Son the builder, and the Holy Spirit did the finishing touches or work on it. We not only see the creative side of the Godhead, but we see the ability, power, and handiwork of deity being complete in agreement and action.[3]

Since God is creator of all, we have no other choice but to agree with His Word that states all power belongs to Him. He exalts and He abases. He lifts up and casts down. He gives power to whomsoever He will. This perspective brings us to a confusing point for most people. If all power comes from God, why does He allot power to those who are going to use it in a wicked way? For example, He gave power to Satan and his kingdom of darkness. Satan uses the power of his kingdom to oppose God, His truth, and His servants. It is important to point out at this point that giving power has to do with God's will. He will give power to whatever vessel is available to carry out His will to bring about a desired result. If such a vessel is used in destructive ways to bring about a greater eternal purpose, so be it. Whether it is Satan sifting Peter to bring conversion or testing Job to refine his faith, or a Pharaoh who stubbornly refused to let God's people go, or a Judas Iscariot who betrayed Jesus, God allowed it. It is also clear that when a vessel is used in a dishonorable way, the Bible declares "woe" to such vessels. Regardless of the eternal purpose that is brought about by the actions of godless vessels, they will stand completely undone by the light of His truth and utterly doomed.[4]

It must be pointed out that God will never step over the will of another. For this reason, He allowed Satan and the angels who followed him to rebel. Since He holds all power, God is not threatened by the power displayed in the form of opposition. Consequences and judgment will eventually follow those in rebellion. For example, He cast those angels who left their first estate into hell, where they are still chained.

---

[3] Genesis 1:2; John 1:1-3; Romans 1:20; 1 Corinthians 8:6; Colossians 1:16-17; Hebrews 3:4-6

[4] 2 Chronicles 25:8; Job 13:15; Psalm 62:11; Matthew 26:24; Luke 22:31-32; Romans 9:14-23; 13:1-2; 2 Timothy 2:20-21

He laughs at those who are arrogant and foolish enough to believe that they will overcome Him. We know that the Lord determines the extent of wicked people's power; therefore, He sets the boundaries as to how far evil will tread into certain arenas. And, regardless of the enemy's successes, the war has already been won. It is already recorded as such. God does not lie, nor does He give false impressions as to His intentions or false promises as to what He will ultimately bring about. It is for this reason that when it came to Joseph's ordeal as a slave and a prisoner, he was able to declare that what was intended for evil by his brothers was turned around for good by God.[5]

As believers, we know and can trust that if we love the Lord, all things will work together for good and for our spiritual benefit. Granted, it may not be pleasant, but eventually, we will realize it was necessary for God to do an eternal work in us that will be completely unveiled in our inheritance. This is the glorious reality of our great God. He is who He is. And, because of who He is, He will not be stirred by that which rebels against Him. He is the Rock that cannot be moved by any contrary force or influence. He is the essence of truth that will never change, and the source of all justice that will remain sure in the end for it is eternal in nature.[6]

God is not limited in who or what He uses. Since He is all-knowing, He is not caught off guard by that which is hidden or done in the darkness of deception. This is the unique reality of who He is and how He uses His power. He may have to work around man through circumstances, but regardless of man's best attempts and the presence of the power of darkness, God will have His perfect way. And, as the righteous Judge, He will have the last say in all matters.

Every man has inherited the darkness of Adam's selfish disposition. It makes him subject to the tyranny and bondage of sin. Even though every one of us are subject to wicked powers due to sin, we have the promise of redemption that God is able to translate us from the kingdom of darkness into the kingdom of His dear Son.[7] The power that influences each of us will be determined by our heart condition. Based on such a condition God may use us for dishonorable or honorable purposes. How

---

[5]   Genesis 50:20; Romans 3:4; Hebrews 6:18; 2 Peter 2:4; Jude 6

[6]   Psalm 2:1-5; Romans 8:28

[7]   Colossians 1:13-14

He uses us as vessels will depend on our inward environment and His timing.

The vessel He uses may be a Pharaoh that will demand His intervention and judgment in a matter to bring His people to certain places of deliverance and promise. He may use vessels like Peter and Paul where He miraculously delivers and saves His people. God does not make a mistake about the vessel He uses. Instead of asking God how He could allow challenging matters to take center stage, we need to stand back and consider the vessel He is using in our lives, homes, churches, and nation. What do vessels who wield such powerful influences in our lives tell us about our own character? Do they represent judgment or blessing? Are they wicked or righteous? Clearly, the leadership on the national and religious scenes serves as a reflection of the spiritual condition of the people.

In my years of being involved with the matter of power, I have noted a few characteristics about it. The first aspect of power is that it is allotted to certain individuals to carry out a matter. Without power, people are void of ability to do anything. Granted, people may have certain strengths or qualities, but without power that comes from some point of authority such as position, or some way to influence present events with money, or an opportunity or open door, individuals have no means to accomplish or finish a matter. For example, if Obama was not President of the United States, except for his circle of like thinkers, he would still be numbered among the masses. He is not President because of his abilities, but because he was backed by those in power. No doubt money exalted him by presenting him in a certain light, while the environment in America afforded him the opportunity to be President. Take away the position, backing, and image that has been established through propaganda and Obama would be just another man in the midst of the faceless masses, void of any power.

Authority separates and distinguishes, but power exalts. For example, there are a lot of people who hold places of authority, but they do not stand out unless they are exalted by some source of power. Power not only exalts a person, but it makes him or her elite in some way. For example, strip a person of power, and he or she is rendered to being part of what the world considers to be insignificant or inferior.

The second aspect of power is that it reveals the character of those who possess it. The one area that people err in concerning God is that

God operates according to the power He possesses. It is true that God can do anything He wants to do. However, God does not operate in His power on the basis of wants, whims, moods, and impulsive notions, but according to His character, will, and purpose. Keep in mind, constructive power operates according to authority. If God stepped outside of His authority that is clearly based on His character and plan, and actually operated according to some notion, His power would become abusive. In all honesty, this world would not be here if He operated according to such unpredictable practices.

Sadly, people hold to the foolishness of their own perception of power. From the earthly or fleshly perspective there are two misconceptions people hold about power. The first one has to do with those who hold power, but are tyrannical and abusive. These misguided, arrogant individuals believe that since power has exalted them in some way that they are an exception to the rule of decency and fairness. In fact, in most cases these people see themselves as being a "god" or some type of "messiah." Because of the hardness of their heart, they cannot see that God has placed them in such a position because they were counted as being dishonorable vessels who would bring about certain results. The results could entail refining the faith and testimony of God's people and/or setting up the environment that calls for judgment. Clearly, the results will ultimately play right into the hands of God's eternal purpose. However, these dishonorable vessels stand already condemned and doomed.

The second group of people is comprised of those who hold an unrealistic view of God. They perceive that since God is all powerful, that He would naturally set things in order, answer all of their prayers, and change any unpleasant reality. It is understandable why people would hold to such a notion. In their minds if they had the power, they would be making all things right according to their ideas. They would not tolerate abuses, disrespect, or foolishness. As you can see, power can make people dictators who push their ways onto others, tyrants who use their power to gain greater power, harsh judges who can deem evil as being righteousness, and despots who have no conscience about who or what they sacrifice.

God does not do things because He has the power to do them; rather, God does things according to His immutable character and eternal plan. To rightfully understand God's power, people need to discern what such power is really saying about God's character. We are given an insight into this matter in Jesus Christ.

According to Colossians 2:9, "For in him dwelleth all the fullness of the Godhead bodily." Jesus' humanity may have veiled His deity, but stamped on every aspect of who He was and what He reflected through His teachings, work, and life was the reality and manifestation of His divine nature. Jesus had dual natures. The Apostle Paul called it the mystery of godliness. Bible teachers refer to it as, the "hypostatic union". Even though this mystery was unveiled, declared, and proclaimed to humanity twenty centuries ago, it will remain a mystery to those who refuse to receive it by faith. It is upon receiving this truth by faith, that the Holy Spirit can make it a living revelation to the spirit of man.[8]

Jesus was sent by the Father into this world with the authority of heaven. He had all of its power available to Him. In His example, we see how authority worked and power was to be used. When it came to the authority of heaven, Jesus lined Himself up to the will of the Father. He knew that outside of the Father's will the authority of heaven would become a mere platform that would serve as an affront against that which was honorable and worthy. It would thwart His plan for redemption. We are told that since Jesus could be entrusted with authority, all the power that came with His authority was given to Him in His humanity. He proved He could be entrusted with the grave matters of heaven, because He was faithful with the small details that came by way of preparation, obedience, benevolence, and righteous fervor.[9]

Romans 1:4 tells us that Jesus was declared to be the Son of God with power according to the spirit of holiness. The power was evident to confirm the identity of Jesus, and it was tempered by His mission. This power belonged to the Spirit of God. In His humanity, Jesus submitted Himself under the leading, direction, and guidance of the Holy Spirit, ensuring the integrity of all He did.[10] The fact that Jesus was led by the Spirit also confirms that even the power of heaven operates through one source or conduit. Zechariah 4:6c states, ". . . Not by might, nor by power, but by my spirit, saith the LORD of hosts."

---

[8] John 16:13; Ephesians 1:17; Philippians 2:6; 1 Timothy 3:16

[9] Matthew 28:18, Luke 16:10-12; Philippians 2:7-8 Luke 3:22; 4:1, 18; John 10:30; 17:3-5, 18, 22-23

[10] Luke 3:22; 4:1, 18; John 10:30; 17:3-5, 18, 22-23

God does not perform matters according to His might or power, but by His Spirit. The Father is not simply bringing a matter about because He is the Almighty. The Son is not doing His own bidding because He has the power at His disposal to do so. He even admitted this in Matthew 26:53-54, "Thinkest thou that I cannot now pray to my Father, and he shall presently give me more than twelve legions of angels? But how then shall the scriptures be fulfilled, that thus it must be?"

God does everything through His Spirit. The Spirit of God connects the heart of heaven with the matters of earth. The Lord's power is tempered by the gentleness of the Holy Spirit as it is imparted to others. The Father's plan is being carried out on earth according to the power of the Spirit. Jesus is being lifted up by the Spirit of truth so that He can be seen by seeking hearts and wandering souls. God's people are being emboldened by His Spirit. Nothing is done outside of the inspiration, moving, and leading of the Spirit. He moves according to divine character, inspires according to heavenly wisdom, and leads according to an eternal plan.[11]

Clearly, God's power is disciplined by who He is; therefore, He will not misuse His power on a whim or dare. He will not abuse His power by being a tyrant, nor will He adjust it to try to impress people. God's power is expressed through the moving and work of His Spirit. It is the Spirit that recreates what has been marred by sin. He is the One who separates the darkness from the light, the holy from the profane, and inspires man with wisdom from above to write and speak the oracles of God.

This brings us to the third aspect of power. There must be some type of agreement. Because Jesus was in complete subjection to the Father's authority, and in submission to the leading of the Spirit, He revealed the complete agreement that existed within the Godhead. There were no inconsistencies in what He said and did. Everything He did was according to the Father's plan and the Holy Spirit's leading. He did not skip a beat, take a detour, lag behind, or manage to get ahead of the plan. He remained in line with heaven's mission and purpose.

Without agreement there is no real power to accomplish a task. Psalm 42:7 speaks of deep calling to deep. Likeminded people are attracted to each other because they have a common ground. The greater the

---

[11]   John 16:7-13; Acts 1:6-9; Ephesians 1:17

agreement, the greater the bond or strength that is established between people. Jesus spoke of the power found in agreement in Matthew 18:20, "For where two or three are gathered together in my name, there am I in the midst of them."

Jesus also spoke of the oneness or agreement that existed between Him and the Father. Due to the agreement between them, there was confirmation to all matters that pertained to heaven. Jesus also desired to see the same agreement between His followers, stating that such unity would bring them to perfection and confirm to the world that He was sent by the Father. We are reminded that Solomon pointed out that two is better than one, for if one fails the other one is there to help him or her up. He goes on to say that two shall withstand, but a threefold cord is not quickly broken. As you understand how the Godhead works, you will realize that the Father, the Son, and the Holy Spirit work as one unit, and as His followers, we must become one Body, one living unit that functions in accordance to Jesus who serves as our head. [12]

Obviously, all power comes from God to His Son, but it is channeled through the Spirit to carry out all matters of heaven. What is not brought into the fold of heaven, will be separated for judgment. This is the final aspect of power. That which possesses the ultimate power will render power that is not in line with the purpose and plan of heaven as being judged, unacceptable, obsolete, or ineffective.

Jesus said in John 5:27 that the Father had given him authority to execute judgment. We are told that whosoever resists the power and ordinances of God, will receive judgment. Revelation 20:6 warns that those who are part of the second death will have no power over the judgment that will be pronounced upon them. And, just what is the second death? Revelation 21:8 answers this question, "But the fearful, and unbelieving, and the abominable, and murderers, and whoremongers, and sorcerers, and idolaters, and all liars, shall have their part in the lake which burneth with fire and brimstone; which is the second death."

When Jesus rose from the grave, He kept His dual nature intact. In His humanity we can see His authority as He sits on the right hand of the Father, serving in the capacity of our High Priest, ever making intercession for us. As deity, we see His power to bring about a matter to

---

[12]   Ecclesiastes 4:9-12; John 17:21-23; Ephesians 4:12-16; Colossians 1:18

completion. He serves as the Alpha, the firstborn of a new creation. He will prove to be the Omega, the last to have the final say as judge. The earth now serves as His footstool, and one day He will return to put all enemies under His feet. He will restore what was lost, exalt His servants, and set up His everlasting kingdom.[13]

Meanwhile, all prophecies concerning the closing days of the age or dispensation that we are now living in, are coming to fruition. Evil people may appear as if they are winning while they try to wear down the resolve of the saints with their incessant wicked moves, but it will be for a season. The power they possess here will give way to the ultimate power of heaven. In the end, they will taste the wicked fruits of their ways. The fruits are that of spiritual death, and the consequences and judgment which they are subject to will embrace an eternity of spiritual isolation, torment, devastation, and ruin.

We all have a choice as to how we respond to authority and what power we will ultimately give way to. All authority and power comes from above. It is vital to realize that we do not possess power that has not been allotted to us. In summation, what power we may be enjoying is not our power. Granted, our free will allows us to do as we will with it, but ultimately it will confirm our character and point of agreement. Depending on how we respond to power, it will either enable us to carry out our real responsibilities or it will give way to total judgment.

The question in the end is what have you done with the power you have been given in your life? What does it say about your character and your point of agreement?

---

[13] John 1:1-3; Acts 7:48-50; Colossians 1:15, 17; 1 Timothy 2:5; Hebrews 7:17, 23-8:1; 10:12-14; Revelation 1:5-18

8

THE PURPOSE OF POWER

It is not unusual for people to chase after some type of power. When you ask them their reason for wanting to possess power, it comes down to the desire to control their world. Such individuals have no qualms about forcing their ideas or ways upon others, regardless of what their conscience may dictate. After all, they are the ones with the power. Since they have the power, they either are a god, the messiah, or the expert as to what is right and acceptable. Therefore, in their delusion they have no reservations about insisting that others line up to their particular view of reality about something.

It is for this reason that power in the hands of the dishonorable, immature, and foolish will prove to be dangerous. To these individuals, power exalts them, thereby, giving them the license to insist on their perception. However, it is all an image that hides a house of cards and a trap door of impending judgment. If people recognize how fragile the façade is and come together to oppose it, such fragile power will quickly lose its ungodly hold and dissipate.

The problem is that people buy the image of power. When they believe the delusion being presented, they have a tendency to give up their rights in order to try to placate or keep such power at bay. In essence, they sell their souls for such things as bread, security, and so-called "peace". As people sell their individuality, they become sheep ready to be led to the slaughter by the wolves. As Judge Andrew Napolitano pointed out, the more the people of a society lose their individuality and become like sheep, the more the leadership is infiltrated by wolves. Wolves are not only predators, but they are clever animals of opportunity. They are always looking for the chance to take captive the vulnerable and bring down the unprotected. The vulnerable are represented by those who possess weak character, and the unprotected are those who do not care to know the real truth concerning a matter.

This brings us to an important aspect of understanding power. We know that power can be constructive or destructive. Clearly, God's power will prove to be constructive, while Satan's power can only delude and destroy. Therefore, how it is utilized or used will determine whether it will prove to be constructive or destructive.

There is also a third type of power which is attached to man. This power can be considered decent or wicked. When man chooses to be decent, he will prove to be well-mannered in what he does, but when he is bent on wickedness, he becomes very destructive. God's power is eternal, man's power limited and temporary, and Satan's power stands doomed. The manifestation and results of power will either confirm a matter as being righteous or end up judging it as being ineffective and condemned by the courts of heaven.

Constructive power will always be directed towards that which will bring glory to God. God's power is wielded on our behalf for the purpose of redeeming each of us from our fallen state of sin, misery, and spiritual death. It was manifested through Jesus Christ. For God so loved the world that He gave His only begotten Son as a means to save us. However, man can only be saved when he comes to the cross of Jesus and receives God's provision by faith.[1]

When it comes to man, he has the power to impact other peoples' lives. However, if his power is not being disciplined by the Spirit of God, it will prove to be self-serving, thus failing to make any real lasting impact. Granted, people may initially remember the kind acts of an individual, but they will quickly forget it as the demands of life take their attention elsewhere. The only deeds that are remembered are those loving, sacrificial acts that bring glory to God or cause great destruction, leaving untold distress in its path. Since wicked deeds will eventually be wiped from all memories and the remembrance of man's personal decency will only flicker for a short time, it is clear that the footsteps that man leaves behind in regard to his own merits and agendas will fade according to the winds of time.[2]

Destructive power will not only promote wicked agendas, but be used to destroy that which opposes it. Eventually it will cave in on itself in utter failure and judgment. Until then, it will cause great vexation to the souls of the righteous, delude the foolish with false promises, and oppress the poor in greater ways. Even though destructive power creates a tidal wave that appears to be unstoppable, it is implosive. It may leave

---

[1] John 3:16; John 1:12; Romans 10:9-10; Ephesians 2:8-9

[2] Psalm 34:16; 37:34-38; 103:14-16; 1 Peter 1:22-25

devastation in its wake, but in the end it will violently collapse in on itself as it hits the rocks of judgment and the shoreline of consequences.[3]

To properly understand power, we must understand the purpose for power being allotted to us. There is one constructive reason for God to give His people power, and that is to do what is honorable. If power is not used to do what is right, it will become lifeless, self-serving, perverted, and destructive. For example, there are people doing good things, but their intentions are dishonorable. Clearly, their good deeds are a matter of pole vaulting their dishonorable agendas or causes to the front. This is the method of those who adhere to Social Justice. In such cases, good deeds serve as a front that throws unsuspecting people off of the darkness and wickedness behind these people's real intentions.

Even though God possesses the authority as righteous Judge, His intention is to redeem people from the far reaching tentacles of sin and death. The Lord made this statement in Jeremiah 29:11, "For I know the thoughts that I think toward you, saith the LORD, thoughts of peace, and not of evil, to give you an expected end."

God uses His power to bring about His desire to save mankind. However, salvation entails deliverance from spiritual darkness. As ultimate Judge, God gives us insight as to how He secured salvation. It comes by way of pardon and redemption.

God alone holds the power to forgive or pardon sins. The Jews understood this truth. For this reason they asked Jesus in Matthew 9:6 and Mark 2:10 who gave Him the power to forgive sins. Jesus then questioned the religious opposition as to what would require greater power, the healing of the man in question or forgiving his sin. Most people would assume that the greater power would be required to heal the man in a miraculous way. However, God's power operates with the same intensity of purpose in every situation.

In order to understand the significance of this event, there are a couple of matters that must be pointed out in this specific situation. The first point we must acknowledge is that Satan also possesses a certain amount of power to heal, and man in his strength has been known to work some incredible feats as to implementing certain lifestyles and ways that are conducive to healing. With this in mind, what would exalt God's power over the power of Satan and the personal attempts of man?

---

[3]   Isaiah 57:20-21

The second point that is brought out in this situation is that only God can forgive. As the ultimate Judge of heaven and earth, He alone has the authority to remit sin or provide a pardon when it comes to His Law. No other creature, being, or entity has the power to forgive on such a level, which brings us to another fact. It takes power of authority to forgive. Sins are an affront against God's Law, covenants, and character. People who commit sins trespass into forbidden areas to partake of forbidden fruit. Even though the fruit may be pleasant up front, it possesses the seeds of death. Since contempt has been shown to God and His holy Law, it takes power to wipe clean the slate in order to satisfy the sentence of death that has been passed down on all men.

You might be saying, "Wait a minute, as believers we are to forgive." Granted, we are to forgive, but it is a responsibility. In other words, we have the responsibility to liberate ourselves spiritually by releasing the offender from making restitution for any offense committed personally against us. After all, we have no real authority or power to cause offenders to make restitution, and even if we could, it would never be enough to satisfy our prideful sense of justice because it is motivated by feelings and not subject to any real legitimate law. It is for this reason that we cannot rightfully execute any real justice; therefore, such a release ensures that no bitterness can take root in our lives, thereby, defiling us.[4]

The truth is, it takes the same power to forgive sin as it does to miraculously heal a person. However, the power of forgiveness is what exalts and distinguishes God in relationship to His power. It was in His power alone that He could bring about the means that would allot each of us a pardon. We know that Jesus took our place on the cross. With His death He satisfied the demands of God's Law that called for our very death, and with His blood He ransomed us from the tyrannical claims sin had on our lives.[5] Hebrews 9:22 tells us that without the shedding of blood there would be no remission or pardon of sins.

We know that God's redemption made way for our deliverance or salvation from the power of darkness. The power of salvation was made available in the message of the Gospel. The Gospel of Jesus declares that He died for our sins, and was put in the grave, but three days later rose to prove victorious over death. In summation, in His humanity Jesus

---

[4] Matthew 6:12, 14-15; Hebrews 10:29-31; 12:15
[5] Romans 6:23; Ephesians 1:7; 2:16-19; Colossians 1:20

became the Lamb of God that was offered on the altar of the cross as our replacement, but in His deity He broke the power of death by rising from the grave. By receiving the truth, work, and hope of the Gospel message with childlike faith, a person will be delivered from the darkness of this present world and translated into God's very kingdom.[6] Ephesians 1:19-20 gives us this insight into the power wrought by God towards those who believe the truth as to what He has done on their behalf, "And what is the exceeding greatness of his power to us-ward who believe, according to the working of his mighty power, Which he wrought in Christ when he raised him from the dead, and set him at his own right hand in the heavenly places."

The Apostle Paul actually testified of the power associated to the deliverance of God in Acts 26:18, "To open their eyes, and to turn them from darkness to light, and from the power of Satan unto God, that they may receive forgiveness of sins, and inheritance among them which are sanctified by faith that is in me."

We know that Satan's power opposes God, but man must determine what he is going to do with the strength he has been given. He must remember that all power comes from God. He alone ensures his strength, empowers him to stand against the enemy, and enables him to endure to the end. He will ultimately deliver him from his enemies as He serves as his shield and scatters those who foolishly oppose His kingdom.[7]

For the saints, there is no power to stand before their enemies or overcome them outside of God. All enemies of God will have to ultimately submit to His power. Meanwhile, as believers, we must overcome the enemy of darkness, by standing in the authority and power of God that has been made available to us through Christ Jesus. It is by being hidden in the power of God that we can be assured of victory. We will be able to endure to the end if we cling by faith to our Lord. And, when darkness attempts to overtake us, we can stand assured that its power will eventually be brought low by the penetrating power of God's light and truth.[8]

When it comes to personal strength or power, people must determine the motivation behind such power. If such power comes from any other

---

[6]   John 1:29; Romans 1:16; 1 Corinthians 15:1-4, 55-57; Hebrews 13:10

[7]   Deuteronomy 4:37; Psalm 59:11; 66:3-7

[8]   Leviticus 26:19; Deuteronomy 9:29; Esther 9:1

source other than God, such as pride, God will break it and take it away from the individual. Clearly, man must seek all power from God. In fact, all a person's strength or power must be used to properly serve God. To ensure the integrity of personal strength, a person must make sure he or she is motivated by love for God and that all he or she does on behalf of God's kingdom is inspired, disciplined, and channeled by His Spirit. As believers, we must remember at all times that all power that is not used for the sake of righteousness will end in destruction.[9]

As we can see, God allots power with a purpose in mind. Although others may abuse power for their own self-serving, wicked agendas, for Christians, the purpose for such power should not be debated or confused in any way. It must be used to glorify God and further His kingdom. As Scripture brings out in Matthew 6:13, God's kingdom, power, and glory belongs to Him. And, in the realms of eternity, the majesty of His kingdom, the unfolding of His power, and the beauty of His glory will be unveiled to those who have embraced the riches of His grace.[10]

As saints experience the eternal splendor of the many riches of His grace that enfold God's attributes and ways, they will realize that they will spend eternity discovering the depth, width, and height of God Almighty. As His authority declares, He is the all-powerful God of eternity. In such authority, He brought forth creation with His power, secured redemption by His power, and now promises salvation according to His power to all who will believe and receive His gift of eternal life.

In closing, we must ask ourselves if we have stood under the fountain of the Lord's flowing water. We must consider if we stand in the sustaining water of His authority, steeped in the powerful currents of His Spirit, and are immersed by the powerful characteristics of His eternal life. If we cannot honestly answer these questions, we need to humbly come to the altar of the cross, seeking a revelation of the powerful, penetrating light that is found in the Gospel message. It is only at the cross that we can understand the significance of His love, know His mercy, sense the flow of His grace, and experience the abundance of His everlasting life.

---

[9]   Leviticus 26:19; Deuteronomy 32:35-39

[10] Ephesians 2:7

The Dynamics
Of True
Leadership
✠

Book Three

INTRODUCTION

There are many books written about the subject of leadership. I often wonder why I would be compelled to address this subject. However, I have found myself placed in the position of leading others. As a result, I have established a goal to understand the dynamics of true leadership according to one source: The Word of God. As I have studied and meditated on the concept of leadership, I have discovered that the very characteristics and principles that determine and govern true leadership in the kingdom of God also prove to be true in the secular world as well.

Even though the world presents a different front about the subject of leadership, the truth of the matter is that the type of leadership that can impact and change the world in a constructive way also possesses the same qualities as to what Scripture identifies as being necessary in godly leadership. It is true that the world does not recognize such leadership. However, strip away the façade and veneer of the leadership the world presents from that which truly distinguishes those who lead others to greatness, and you will find the same common denominators as to attitude, character, and conduct.

The world considers leaders based on how they impact history, but true leadership must be gauged by how it impacts the character of those who follow such individuals. The truth is, any person might make some type of impact on history such as the likes of terrorists that kill the innocent to make a point or statement, but few men make a tremendous personal impact on those who follow them. True leadership will not be associated with an act that destroys but with the reality that it lives on even after its initial impact. Effective leadership continues to impact others for generations in a constructive way. It will ultimately verify and honor life-changing principles that will leave indelible footprints in the annuals of men's hearts and minds.

This book will examine what distinguishes true leadership. Perhaps you as a reader will discover you have such qualities. If so, what will you do with such a calling in a world where people desire to see such leaders step forward and take up the incredible challenges that are before us?

1

Reluctant Souls

My attempt to discover the secret of true leadership caused me to realize that the greatest leaders were those who were reluctant concerning being leaders. These individuals were content to let others lead. In many ways they never perceive themselves as being leaders. One of the reasons for this is because they have been more concerned about finishing a job, project, or mission that has already been set before them than to think in terms of leading others.

These people appear to be loners because they are so often bent on getting their present occupation or requirements completed. They see themselves in an ordinary light. In other words, they do not see anything unusual about their status or lot in life. They take seriously their personal responsibilities, display self-respect towards that which has been entrusted to them, and possess a discipline that would not let them compromise on any front. They hold themselves personally accountable to that which is excellent in all they do.

This was true for a man named Moses. The Bible tells us that Moses was raised in Pharaoh's household, but rather than choose the sins of greed and lust that were so much associated with those in power, he chose to become identified with his people who were slaves in Egypt.[1] He could have chosen the easy life that was attached to worldly prestige, but in doing so he would have sold his spiritual birthright, inheritance, and his real calling.

Moses' unwillingness to compromise caused him to walk a lonely path. He was brought low in light of worldly status. He became a shepherd in the wilderness, a profession that was considered an abomination to the society he had been groomed in.[2] His example shows us that true leaders comprise ordinary men who are often forged by the lonely ways they end up traveling. This lonely way is the result of not compromising what they know to be true and right. These individuals

---

[1]   Exodus 2:9-10; Hebrews 11:24-27

[2]   Genesis 46:34

are shaped by the howling winds of barrenness that often sweep across their very souls. Such individuals are not aware that in such loneliness they are being fine tuned to lead others through the very same terrain.

As I study the lives of various leaders, I realize that they had been forged by previous experiences to lead men down the same path they have already traveled. They must often lead others into the very jaws of despair and possible destruction. These individuals would not naturally take their leadership position; rather, extraordinary circumstances are what often require their services. It would only be at the prompting of events that these reluctant souls found themselves being swept into, or forced into the limelight as leaders for the times in which they lived.

For Moses, it was a bush burning in the wilderness. Even when Moses knew that God was calling him to lead the children of Israel out of Egypt, he still remained reluctant. He did not feel that he was equipped to do it by himself. Since Moses unenthusiastically, could not see himself as one who could eloquently represent God in the courts of Egypt, God sent his brother Aaron to serve as the voice who would supposedly present the necessary case to Pharaoh.[3]

Admittedly, I become suspicious of those who are quick to take leadership positions. I often reason that such individuals are arrogant and immature or they harbor wicked agendas that are destructive. Such individuals are seeking recognition or power. The Bible warns against putting novices in any leadership position because it will simply produce more pride in them. It also admonishes believers to not think highly of themselves for when they think they are standing, they are about to fall into the traps of temptation.[4]

The truth is, being a leader is serious business. Maturity will make a real leader reluctant to lead because of the great burden leadership carries with it, while the very process they have already been through will often make them feel weary or inept to lead. Such individuals realize that they hold the welfare of others in their hands. To lead any man in any direction must not be taken lightly. The fact is, leadership will lead men down a path of destruction and ruin, or it will challenge them to walk in the excellent ways of discovering true character in the form of endurance and sacrifice. Rest assured, following someone will cost men their souls

---

3   Exodus 3:1-4; 4:10-17
4   Romans 12:3; 1 Corinthians 10:12-13; 1 Timothy 3:6

or force them to patiently learn how to possess their souls in the ways of excellence that usually requires incredible sacrifice.

We see this seriousness of leadership resonating among the leaders of Jesus' day. Some of the leaders had their own personal agenda. They did not care for the souls that followed them, they only cared about the agendas they silently harbored behind their religious robes and appearances. They desired men to follow them, not because it constituted the real ways or righteousness of God, but because they wanted to convert them to their way of thinking as a means to maintain a religious following that could support their agenda. Jesus said of such leadership that it makes those who follow two-fold more the children of hell than their leaders. It is for this reason that the Apostle Paul admonished believers to follow him only as he followed Jesus.[5]

It is Jesus who has been distinguished as the true leader of the Living Church He died for. We are to ensure that those in front of us are truly being led by Christ. He is the One who prepares the way in which we are to walk. It is easy to take the Word of God and use it as a machete to try to cut away the obstacles before us, but it is meant to be a light that will guide our steps down an unknown path that often proves hard and dark to our personal ways and understanding.[6]

The test of true leadership and the character of those who follow will not occur when immature devotion and zeal are at the height of their emotional fervor; rather, it will come when the way becomes hard and difficult to the weary, downtrodden soul. Jesus said of the masses that many followed Him because He could feed them with bread. However, as the way became hard and difficult to grasp, as well as the pressure of possible persecution became a reality, His disciples dwindled down to 12. Finally, one betrayed Him, another denied he even knew Him, and the rest scattered when His ordeal to Calvary began to unveil itself. Jesus had to go the way of the cross alone.[7] He was the lone figure that bore the judgment of the cross upon all sin. He clearly tasted the bitterness of loneliness that comes with leadership.

This brings us to another harsh reality about true leadership. True leaders must often walk against the popular grain of the world to

5   Matthew 23:13-15, 24-29; 1 Corinthians 11:1
6   Psalm 119:105
7   Matthew 26:31-35; John 6:26-29; 6:60-71

accomplish their goal. Their path narrows with challenges, and is long and drawn out by conflict, and is hard to bear as defeat constantly nips at their resolve. It is easy to follow the tyrant and despot of each age because they offer the broad way of popularity and success.[8] They only require people to give into a mob mentality. This affords such individuals the excuse to be lawless, as well as the reason to become cruel and indifferent to others, and the platform to rage against whatever sanity might stand in their way. However, such vulnerable individuals are selling their souls to serve the wicked, unseen agendas of those who have no regard for them.

We see this hard way in the life of Moses and the descendants of Abraham. Even though the children of Israel were delivered from Egypt to possess the Promised Land, they were first led into the barren wilderness to be tempted, tested, proved, and prepared.[9] Because of Moses' process in the wilderness, he was equipped to lead them through the barren wasteland. However, the level of their character would be tested and forged by the wilderness. Sadly, a whole generation never entered the Promised Land; and, it had nothing to do with God's ability to deliver or Moses' leadership, but with the fact that many of the people of Israel did not have the necessary character to endure the testing that confronted their own souls.

At the door of every person's heart, treachery is ready to take center stage. Each of us cannot fathom that we would ever betray what we perceive to be right and honorable, but in every fallen man is the instinct to survive. When faced with the hardships that often confront the way of truth and righteousness, man will often betray that which he knows is true and right in order to live in peace with the darkness that will quickly take his soul captive. In fervor such people may declare their devotion and in zeal tout their plans, but add the narrow way of suffering due to persecution and death, allow sobriety to set in when the giants begin to stand in the narrow path of progress, and the driving, hindering forces of harsh elements of the terrain before them, and this is when man's treachery can and will take center stage.[10]

---

[8]   Matthew 7:13-14

[9]   Deuteronomy 1:19; 8:1-7

[10]   Hosea 6:7; Matthew 13:20-21; Luke 13:24

For Moses, he tasted the bitterness of treachery from those who were of his family lineage. His brother and sister turned against him in an attempt to secure his leadership position. There were times of insurrection when others from the tribe of Levi were trying to incite the weak and vulnerable to follow them down a path of rebellion. However, each time the opposition was squelched and judged by the unseen hand of providence.[11]

The narrow way will cause opposition and murmuring, suffering will cause many to slip into the shadows of obscurity, persecution will cause some to flee the battle, and harsh elements will cause others to turn back to the former comforts of their life. Granted, such people may not be able to look squarely in the mirror to confront their treacherous side, but they do have the means to justify their actions, console their conscience, declare the injustice of it all to others, and try to maintain some dignity as they point out that the task before them was impossible, a lost cause that required too high of a price.

Hence enters the last aspect about those reluctant souls who find themselves thrust into leadership. These individuals must possess the necessary resolve to walk into the very throes of hell if necessary to see a matter through to the end. If they must go it alone, they will do so because there will be nothing of worth left behind them and nothing of value will remain once tainted and ravaged by the present circumstances. True leaders are always keenly aware that they are most likely walking towards their demise.

For many true leaders, death is not an enemy to avoid or flee from but a destiny to embrace. They cannot imagine walking any other path. They have the hindsight to recognize the life they once lived is all but gone, and they have the presence of mind to realize that the life that is presently taking center stage is not worth living according to the tidal wave of darkness that is causing everything to be slammed against the rocks of utter destruction. They also have the foresight to see that the only hope for any real quality of life rests on the other side of the great gulf of despair, destruction, and ruin that is before them.

These reluctant souls count the cost.[12] The cost has nothing to do with material possessions or worldly prestige; rather, the real cost has

---

[11] Numbers 12; 16

[12] Luke 14:28-33

to do with something that is not tangible or for sale. It has to do with personal character that ensures self-respect, hope that will not settle for that which does not allow or demand excellence, and a way of life that speaks of that which represents quality and purpose.

When the children of Israel followed Moses out of Egypt, they went through a baptism. "Baptism" represents death to the old in order to embrace the new. It is a type of door that people must choose to walk through in order to pursue the promises that have been set before them. Once a person enters through the door, there is no turning back. The old must become dead to them in order to endure the preparation that will ultimately lead them to a new life of redemption, liberty, and satisfaction. However, what lay between the baptism of the Red Sea and the Promised Land was the graveyard of the great wilderness. When there is death, it will be naturally followed by a grave. [13]

For the children of Israel, the Red Sea represented the door of baptism, but for Jesus a manger represented His door that ushered Him from the glories of heaven into the barren wilderness of the world. Jesus spoke of counting the cost that would lead Him to His death on the cross. He was forever facing His demise and a tomb, knowing that it would provide the way for you and me to find everlasting life that would prove satisfying to the longing soul.

Reluctant souls are often content to live in the shadows of greatness. They are happy to settle for a simple life where hard work and initiative has the liberty to produce what is honorable and worthwhile. They never look for a platform of greatness, but they will not sit idly by when they perceive that that which is truly worthy and great as being threatened by the tyrants and despots of the world.

Today many are looking to the limelight to find that one leader who possesses the quality of greatness. However, the real leaders are not to be found in the popular limelight of the world. Perhaps it is time to look behind the limelight into the shadows, but in doing so we, as individuals, must consider if we are prepared, willing, and worthy to follow such a leader. Leaders are meant to lead the people. Although they may be willing to ride into hell and taste the harsh reality of death while leading others, they know that nothing will be accomplish unless those following them are willing to dig deep into their own personal character and pay

---

[13]   Romans 6:3-10; 1 Corinthians 10:1-13

whatever price is necessary to ensure the integrity of that which is worthy for the sake of something greater than themselves. Such character ensures that future generations will benefit from the legacy that such leadership leaves in its indelible wake.

2

Courageous Souls

There is an incredible awareness of weariness and insufficiency that comes with true leadership. The battles often seem endless, the way to victory long, unforgiving, and formidable, and the destination unreachable. For this reason true leadership requires the reluctant soul to take courage in what he or she knows to be true and right in spite of weary opposition and insufficient resources.

Presented in a pure form, history can give us insight into the courage that such men had to nurture in the face of great obstacles before them. Notice, courage is not something that one naturally will have in the face of great testing. Courage starts with a choice that must be developed through action in order for it to come to any real fruition in a person's life.

In many cases courage is nothing more than flinging off the hindrance of personal fear, uncertainty, and doubts in order to risk all as a means to possibly experience or witness what seems impossible. In every battle the giants are real, the iron chariots cruel, and the enemy formidable. There are no guarantees that such courage will ever be successful, noticed, or rewarded. Surely, there have always been courageous acts through the years, but such acts do not constitute courageous souls.

At such times when there is fervor, patriotism, or experience behind acts of loyalty it is noble to present one's life to such causes. In such situations people have the possibility of receiving great honor or recognition which will produce heroes. However, dying for an unpopular cause that is considered useless or lost is another matter altogether. Very few fight a battle that they think they will ultimately lose. Yet, it is in the face of such battles that unlikely heroes victoriously emerge.

For the great leaders of the past, one thing often distinguishes them. It appeared as if the battle before them was already a lost cause. The army may have been too great, the obstacles too many, and the terrain impossible to conquer. The Apostle Paul expressed it best when he stated in Romans 5:6-8, "For when we were yet without strength, in due time

Christ died for the ungodly. For scarcely for a righteous man will one die: yet peradventure for a good man some would even dare to die. But God commendedth his love towards us, in that, while we were yet sinners, Christ died for us."

We often harbor romantic notions about war. We want to choose our war, the place of battle, and the type of sacrifice we make. We want to be assured that the war is already in the bag, the battle already won, and the sacrifice visible enough for all to admire. We want to come out with scars, but not deep wounds. We want to come out wearing badges of courage, and not the nightmares of defeat.

The truth is, that the greatness of character is never unveiled or forged in one's life unless it is in light of utter defeat. True heroes do not emerge because all is going their way, they emerge because defeat is all around them and they refuse to accept the verdict. They do not see the overwhelming circumstances engulfing them; rather, they sense a compelling urgency to push past the obvious to salvage what is worthy or honorable in the midst of the wreckage of destruction and ruin. They do not see the ravages of war, but the destination before them. Nor do they hear or take note of the evidence of the outcome around them, for they only can hear the desperate cries of comrades, the moans of the wounded, and the last breath of the dying. True leaders never take pleasure in the sacrifices of others from either side; rather, their main goal is to make a matter beneficial in the end for everyone who has been involved in the conflict. Although there will be sacrifices and losses in any conflict, when the righteous remain standing, that which is excellent will rise out of the ashes of defeat.

This brings us to another aspect of true leaders, when the chips are down they are the ones who prove to be courageous souls. It is not that these individuals lack fear, rather, they perceive that the way of what was is closed and the present way will destroy what is if they do not stand; therefore, they must continue to march forward even when every weapon is pointed at them. They refuse to retreat unless they intend to fight again. They will refuse to stand still because they have already decided to actively stand for what is right, and they will march on even when the battle seems lost. The individual knows that only by going forward can the way open for him or her to advance.

There are three such examples of this type of leadership in the Bible. It is interesting to follow the lives of these three men. Their history varies, but the mark of their leadership is quite clear and decisive. The men I make reference to are Joshua, Caleb, and Jonathan.

If you could ask these men what made them the great leaders that they were, their answers would probably vary. One might say it was the influence of men such as Moses. Perhaps, the other one might say it was the circumstances that allowed him to discover the essence of greatness in the midst of rebellion and defeat. Maybe the third one would admit it was the lack of greatness during his time that forced him to take the high road of excellence and risk it, not only to discover greatness, but to ensure that it was given the necessary opportunity to come forth in an environment of defeat and hopelessness.

When you study these men's lives, you can find one constant denominator that truly ties them together. That common denominator was their dependency on God. The real substance behind courage for true leaders is faith in something greater and more worthy than themselves. Such courage in this text is best summarized as having the faith to let go of the familiar to allow the impossible to take place.

These men understood their limitations, but they also believed and knew the God of the impossible. They knew that if He was for them, who could be against them. They did not walk in their own strength, but learned to depend on the strength of their great Deliverer to do the impossible. They understood that the strong hand of Providence needed to be on their side if they were to accomplish the task before them.

Studying the spiritual aspect of people often proves to leave much to speculation. We often see the fruits or outcome of such people, and not the steps or process that brought them to places where their lives in God were developed to a stage of spiritual maturity and integrity. The reason for this is because spiritual maturity is developed in the secret place of obscurity. Every person must discover this place for him or herself. Clearly, each person must personally seek for and find this place as the path varies for each individual. Therefore, these secret places are not meant to be observed by others so they can devise some method or formula to follow.

Admittedly, the one who gives us a bit of insight into this secret place is Joshua. Joshua is a good example of someone who stands in the shadow of greatness. He was a companion or minister to Moses. Moses served as his mentor and ordained Joshua to lead the children of Israel into their first battle in the wilderness. We are told that when Moses went up into the mountain to meet with God, Joshua went with him. Even though there probably was some point where Joshua had to stop and simply wait for Moses, we know that he was as close as he could get to the reality of God. Keep in mind that on the formidable mountain of Sinai, God's holiness caused the darkness of separation as it engulfed the mountain. The naked eye could not see what was taking place between Moses and God.[1]

No doubt Joshua's closeness to Moses' interaction and life before God greatly influenced him. It appears that he waited for Moses on that mountain, meaning that he also waited for forty days and nights. As a result, Joshua was separated from and not part of the idolatry that took place among the children of Israel during the time of testing and waiting.

Clearly, the children of Israel's loyalty and confidence towards the God who delivered them proved fickle. For them, the waiting became too unbearable. Ultimately, they failed the test. While Joshua was waiting somewhere on the mount, the children of Israel were dancing around an idolatrous altar, honoring a golden calf.[2]

Another interesting aspect of Joshua' spiritual life was brought out when God judged the children of Israel for their idolatry. When he came down from Mount Sinai after interceding on their behalf, Moses took the tent of meeting outside of the camp for it was defiled by sin. Moses had to make atonement for the children of Israel after judgment was executed on many by the Levites.

Some of the people remained within the camp, while others ventured outside of the camp to draw near to the tent. Moses entered the tent to meet with God face to face. When the presence of God came down on the tent, some were content to worship Him from a distance, but when it came to Joshua, the young man remained in the tent even when Moses returned to the camp.[3] Once again, we must note that Joshua was not content to remain at a distance or even somewhat close to God, he wanted to be where God's presence was and he wanted to be close to those who knew Him on a personal level. To me, these small

---

[1]   Exodus 17:8-13; 24:13

[2]   Exodus 32:15-19

[3]   Exodus 33:1-11

glimpses into Joshua's life speak volumes as to the type of spiritual life he developed before God.

The wilderness points to the test of character, but it is in waiting that preparation takes place. The Apostle Paul clarified the test of character in this way, "And not only so, but we glory in tribulations also, knowing that tribulation worketh patience; and patience, experience; and experience, hope" (Romans 5:3-4). It is at the point of waiting on the Lord that many will go back to what they formerly knew. For the children of Israel, they went back to idolatry, worshipping the creation rather than the Creator.

The trial of trusting God will test the resolve of man to do what he knows is right regardless of the unknown that is taking place around him. Those who choose the way of faith towards God will refuse to look back, knowing that they have been set free from the many entanglements of idolatry, death, and destruction. As these individuals resolve to do right in times of uncertainty, they will begin to temper their inner self with what they know to be true and honorable. Such tempering is a form of discipline that only occurs when these individuals learn to wait in the midst of the unknown rather than revolt in utter fear and speculation. In such times of tempering, such people learn to possess their souls in patience, ultimately experiencing hope that comes with assurance and peace.[4] Such assurance is based on the character of God and the peace represents a person coming to rest in the knowledge that regardless of what happens, he or she is still in the right place as far as God is concerned.

The Apostle Peter talks about the trials of our faith.[5] Will I trust God with the unknown? Can I trust God when everything seems contrary to what I know? Will I wait even though it feels like eternity, or will I give in to my fears and vain imaginations?

Joshua probably had no idea that he would be the one who would ultimately lead the children of Israel into the Promised Land. Moses may have been prepared to lead the children of Israel through the wilderness, but Joshua would be prepared to lead them into the Promised Land. Moses represented deliverance from the old, but Joshua's leadership pointed to possessing the new. It was in the grave of the wilderness that

---

[4]   Luke 21:19
[5]   1 Peter 1:6-9

the children of Israel would have to shed the old ways of slavery in order to be prepared to embrace the new ways that required them to become one people, a peculiar or special nation in the midst of paganism and idolatry.

It took two years at Mount Sinai to establish the tabernacle and religious life among the Jewish people. No doubt people of Joshua's caliber were being firmly established on, in, and with the reality of Jehovah God. When it was time to enter into the promises of God, twelve men were sent to spy out the land. When the twelve men returned, they could agree with God's evaluation of the land, it was a land of abundance, but their perspective as to whether they were able to possess it was mixed.[6]

Here we are reminded that whether we possess all that God has for us will come down to what we emphasize. Many of the spies emphasized the military power of the kingdoms in the Promised Land, while only two men emphasized the mighty power of God. In light of personal strength ten men fainted and gave in to fear. In light of the power of God, two men took courage and firmly stood on the greatness of God to do the impossible. We know those two men were Joshua and Caleb.

The results were devastating to those who would not take courage in God and believe that the One who provided in the wilderness would also prepare the way of victory to possess that which was promised. Every great and wise leader will not delude themselves about the obstacles and resistance that is before them, but they will have the faith to take courage in the providence of the One who is greater than all the armies that stand between them and their objective. They will understand that that which is excellent is superior to that which may be greater in numbers and strength, but will always prove inferior when it comes to character, principles, and ultimate objective. True leaders are willing to ignore the false presentations of the inferior to ensure the excellent, knowing that the nominal leads to that which is empty, substandard, and unsatisfying

This brings us to the harsh reality of inferior or wicked leadership. The character flaws and lack of faith of the fearful ten spies caused others to melt into a puddle of fear, unbelief, and rebellion. If it were not for Moses' intercession, God would have wiped out the whole lot of them except for Moses' family and start over. Instead of wiping them out,

---

[6]   Numbers 10:11-14; 13:26-33

God pronounced that a whole generation would never enter into the Promised Land except for Joshua and Caleb. This meant everyone over the age of 20 would die in the wilderness and never see the fruition of God's promise fulfilled.[7]

Fear, unbelief, and rebellion carry the seeds of death. Those who give way to the type of leadership that encourages such reaction will die in the barren wilderness of vanity. Like Cain, they will wander in the world as fugitives from one mark of despair to another mark until the breath of the earth subsides in their earthly tabernacle and their bodies are put in a lifeless grave to return to dust.

The children of Israel wandered out in the wilderness for forty years. A few men and a new generation had to be sojourners in the wilderness before they could enter into the promises of God. Their status in the wilderness was the product of the sin of unbelief. The question remained. When tested, would they give in to unbelief or would they trust God and follow a new leader into the Promised Land?

Most of us know the answer to that question. The new generation did enter the Promised Land under Joshua's leadership. However, we need to realize that Joshua did not consider himself sufficient enough to lead them into the place God had promised them. We see the Lord speaking to Joshua, He gave the same exhortation in the first chapter of Joshua three times: "Be strong and of good courage." The Lord was not saying to Him be strong in your own power, but be strong in what he knew Jehovah God had already established. He was not saying to Joshua take courage in his abilities; rather, take courage in what the Lord had already promised and verified to him.

Strength comes from believing God's words, while courage comes from trusting God's faithful character to bring forth a matter that He has clearly promised. It is for these reasons that the Apostle Paul made this statement, "Not that we are sufficient of ourselves to think any thing as of ourselves, but our sufficiency is of God" (2 Corinthians 3:5).

True leaders are realistic about their abilities. They know that all leadership will reveal their personal character and wisdom. They have no real abilities unless they find favor with those they lead, gain respect of those who will follow, develop wisdom that possesses honor and

---

[7]   Numbers 14:1-24

discretion, and most of all have a reliance and faith in the God who is able to do the impossible.

Joshua maintained this reliance on God through his life. In leadership he started with God, and when he finally was able to relinquish his responsibilities as the military leader of Israel, he gave this exhortation to the people:

> Now therefore, fear the LORD, and serve him in sincerity and in truth: and put away the gods which your fathers served on the other side of the flood, and in Egypt; and serve ye the LORD. And if it seem evil unto you to serve the LORD, choose you this day whom ye will serve; whether the gods which your fathers served that were on the other side of the flood, or the gods of the Amorites, in whose land ye dwell: but as for me and my house, we will serve the LORD (Joshua 24:14-15).

Joshua pointed out that the God we serve will determine the quality of our character. Today many are worshipping the creation rather than the Creator.[8] Such people are humanistic to the core and prove to be amoral, self-serving, and indifferent in regard to the plight of others, and socialistic in their philosophies. Such individuals may tout many different titles, but the one thing for sure is that there is a great division between those who serve the God of heaven and those who hide behind the present age of gods promoted by immoral, liberal, political correctness.

This is another aspect of true leadership, it must have the substance to unite an army or nation according to that which is true and honorable. In the wilderness, Joshua was prepared to become a military leader that would lead an army, as well as a nation, into the Promised Land to possess the land. Caleb and Jonathan would prove to be fearless soldiers who were not afraid of taking the high ground even in the midst of impossible odds. Their example would spur on others to unite and follow their example to victory. Obviously, great leaders will inspire others to greatness.

---

[8]   Romans 1:20-28; Colossians 2:8

Caleb has always been an interesting man to study. He was a natural leader, but his leadership qualities had been developed in the wilderness, tempered by patience, and proven in light of his faith. Even though Caleb was part of an army, he was willing to fight his enemies in order to gain his inheritance without any assistance. He knew that God was on his side, and did not fear the enemies before him.[9]

Caleb came to Joshua and reminded Joshua that he was not one of the spies who caused his brethren to faint. As a result, he was guaranteed that he would inherit his inheritance. He also pointed out that he had wholly followed the Lord. This clearly speaks of the secret behind his spiritual life and character. He also presented his case that he was as strong as ever. He asked Joshua to give him the mountain where the dreaded Anakim resided. These people had fortified cities that were considered great. They clearly presented a challenge, but as Caleb declared in complete assurance of God's ability to keep His promises, ". . . if so be the LORD will be with me, then I shall be able to drive them out, as the LORD said" (Joshua 14:12c).

We see this same fervor in Caleb's daughter and his nephew Othniel. Caleb put forth the challenge that whoever smote and conquered Debir, he would give that man his daughter, Achsah, in marriage. Othniel took him up on the challenge. True leaders expect that which is excellent from themselves, but they also expect it from others. Othniel's excellent qualities also came out when he became the first judge of Israel. We see where this distinction also became apparent in Caleb's daughter, Achsah. She did not settle for a nominal or partial inheritance when it came to the matter of water. Water was greatly prized in this area. She wanted to possess the blessing of having the upper and lower springs.[10]

Jonathan was another man of excellent character. The son of King Saul and in line of the crown, he was willing to trust in God to do the impossible. The one aspect of character that stands out in Jonathan's example is that righteousness must be personally chosen. The only way to choose honorable character is to choose to go the way of excellence. This requires faith that will risk it all in order to give God the means to show Himself mighty.

---

[9] Joshua 14:6-15
[10] Joshua 15:16-19; Judges 3:8-11

We see Jonathan choosing honorable character in the midst of weak leadership. His father, Saul proved to be weak in leadership. Weak leadership is the result of a person giving way to personal character flaws, rather than going the way of excellence. Here are some of the reasons leaders succumb to weakness:

1) They lack faith in God.
2) They are afraid of losing present position.
3) They are unwilling to make the hard decisions that may require sacrifice and end in failure.
4) They have not learned temperance during their times of waiting.

King Saul did not trust God. In the end he disobeyed Him, losing the throne for his descendants. We see where God instructed the prophet and judge of Israel, Samuel, to anoint another to be king of Israel. We know that David would be anointed as the next king.[11]

Meanwhile, Saul became more and more indecisive in his life. The only thing he could make up his mind about was that David represented a threat to his claim on the throne and had to be done away with. It was during the indecisive times of Saul's life that Jonathan would prove to be a voice of courage, inspiration, reasoning, and discretion.

In one incident, where the army of Israel was at an impasse with the Philistines, Jonathan went alone with his armor-bearer to check out the Philistine garrison at a place called Michmash. It was at that time that Jonathan decided to challenge the Philistines. If they answered in a certain way, he would know the Lord was giving him the necessary permission to take on the enemy. As the story goes, we know that Jonathan challenged the Philistines and met with victory, causing the Philistines to flee and the army of Israel to pursue them.[12]

Great leaders know how to give God permission to be God in a matter. Jonathan had an unseen life with God outside of the weak, indecisive leadership of his father. Most real leaders are not waiting on others to lead when there is a stalemate or some type of action is required; rather, they are waiting on God to show them the way in which they must walk. Once the way is revealed, they become fearless. It is such

---

[11] 1 Samuel 13:8-14; 15:16-26
[12] 1 Samuel 13:15-14:23

leadership that will always inspire others to greatness regardless of the obstacles.

The other aspect of Jonathan's character is his willingness to give way to what was established by God. He knew that the ways and plans of God were honorable and would ultimately prove worthy. He was willing to give way to death because of an impulsive, unrealistic vow his father made. He prophetically recognized that God's choice for king was not him, but David. He was willing to concede all claims to the throne as the first-born of Saul and give way to David. Like John the Baptist, he realized that he would have to decrease for the chosen king to increase. He was willing to accept his fate in light of David's true calling and destiny as king of Israel.[13]

We can have much debate about what constitutes great leaders, but the Bible is very clear about leadership that exemplifies the type of character that will make an impact on souls.

Can you see yourself as the ten spies that fainted in the face of challenges before them, or as Joshua, Caleb, and Jonathan? Only you can properly determine what category you fit in.

---

[13] 1 Samuel 14:27-45; 20; 23:17-18; John 3:27-36

3

UNCERTAIN SOULS

Solomon made this observation in Ecclesiastes 10:7, "I have seen servants upon horses, and princes walking like servants upon the earth." It was clear to Solomon that the world was upside down by how it considered matters. As a result, those who are princes are often in a servant's status, while those who serve every type of master the world has to offer are treated like princes.

We clearly see this in the present leadership of the world we live in. Something is often terribly amiss among many of those who are in positions of power. Their greatest quality is that of arrogance. Their most outstanding feature is not character, but the vanity and rhetoric of words that completely reveal their lack of integrity. For the most part they claim to be leaders, but they have to create confusion and insanity around them in order to lead. They either have to seduce people into their confusing worlds of insanity, or bully them because they lack any real substance that would distinguish them as being noteworthy leaders. They are brutish and lawless in their pursuits and are void of true wisdom or discretion to constructively lead. They are impressed with who they think they are, deluded by what they say, are ridiculous in their claims, and fools in their philosophies. Their eyes are hard with the glint of indifference, their hearts made cold by hate towards that which would dare oppose them, and their platforms of exaltation from which they declare the heights of their greatness are constructed by the ruined, destroyed reputations and lives of those they have sacrificed along the way. In a sense, they cover the stench of their wicked feats with false promises, but if such promises are ever secured, it will be at the expense of the ignorant, vulnerable, and weak.

The truth is, these leaders have never really paid the price that comes with true leadership. For some, they have been groomed by the ruthless to serve as puppets to cover up dark, hidden activities and agendas of death and destruction. For those who are outwardly brutish, they will prove to be bullies who have ruthlessly taken the reins over the lawless after proving to be more shrewd or clever in their feats than the previous leader.

When one considers leadership, can we really label those who present a dark picture of tyranny and despotism as leaders? Clearly, such individuals prove to be nothing more than imposters who have robbed, killed, and destroyed to be in their positions. What distinguishes a true leader? Is it a person who first must deceive to entangle followers into some destructive web or is it an individual who simple leads others into arenas of what is excellent, honorable, and true?

In the Bible it is easy to answer such a question. Those who proved to be tyrannical despots were always brought down in utter disgrace, while those who led with honorable distinction were regarded in an admirable way.

This brings us to the attitude that real leaders display—that of meekness. "Meekness" in this text does not point to timidity but to temperance. Such temperance means that the person's strength is being channeled or tempered by that which is honorable and worthy. For godly leaders it means that their strength is being tempered by the Spirit of the living God. They are simply giving way to that which is honorable to ensure that their conduct will be disciplined and channeled in a way that ensures excellence in what they do.

When I have considered those leaders who display meek souls, I realize that the premise they often started from was uncertainty. The environment they were in caused personal hesitation for them when it came to taking the leadership position. In many cases, they had no sense as to their purpose. In some situations, it seemed that what was considered possible now seemed impossible; and, what was regarded as victorious in the past appeared to lay in utter defeat and hopelessness. There appeared to be no absolutes in the present environment, and what once was considered great had been replaced by that which was inferior. From all appearances the "bad" guy was winning and evidence of the "good" guy was obscured by the darkness of bondage and despair.

For one man by the name of Gideon this was the reality that surrounded him. He had heard of God's greatness, but the environment in which he existed implied that the oppressive ways of the Midianites appeared to prove to be more powerful than the ways of God. These wicked people had prevailed against the people of Israel, causing them to become slaves in their own land. No matter what the Israelites did, the Midianites were there to benefit from their labor. The people of Israel had become greatly impoverished in their oppression as many hid in dens, caves, and strongholds.[1]

When the children of Israel began to cry out to the Lord about their oppression, He sent a prophet. The prophet brought an indictment against the people of Israel. God had delivered them from Egypt, but instead of maintaining their liberty and way of life in God, they began to worship the false gods of the nations around them. As a result, Jehovah God delivered His own people into the hands of those who influenced such idolatrous worship. In their captivity the people of Israel were tasting the bitterness of their idolatrous, foolish ways. Clearly, they needed a leader who would deliver them from the oppression of the Midianites and the consequences of their foolishness.

Even though Jehovah God brought an indictment against the people of Israel, His desire was to show them mercy and grace by once again raising up a leader. But, what man in the midst of such idolatry was willing to take the necessary responsibility to lead a fickle, idolatrous people into opposition against those who had taken them captive?

God knew of such a man. He was the man who threshed wheat by the winepress as a means to hide it from the Midianites. From all appearances Gideon did not appear to be a courageous man. However, God does not judge a man according to his appearance or outward actions.[2] He considers a person in light of his or her heart and potential. Consider the greeting the angel of the LORD gave this man, "The LORD is with thee, thou mighty man of valor" (Judges 6:12b).

God saw the potential of Gideon. Needless to say, Gideon had no clue as to his potential. He was an uncertain soul as he wrestled with the whys behind Israel's present state. This is clearly brought out in his response to the greeting of the heavenly messenger when he asked if the Lord was with the people of Israel, then why had all this terrible fate befallen them? Gideon went on to boldly ask where were the miracles which were witnessed by their fathers, as well as the deliverance that they had experienced in the past.

It is important to note how the messenger declared that the Lord was with Gideon, not the people of Israel. He was the one being singled out as the person who would emerge from the darkness of idolatry to serve

---

[1]   Judges 6-7
[2]   1 Samuel 16:7

as God's means of delivering the people of Israel from the consequences brought on by their rebellious ways.

Interestingly, if you consider Gideon's questions, you see a man who was wrestling with the aspect of his faith in regard to his Creator. Clearly, he was considering and meditating on Jehovah God. His faith might have been at a crossroads or it could have been in crisis, but he had not walked away from the faith that had been delivered to his fathers. In his confusion he may have been uncertain, but his soul was still open to embrace the greatness of God.

Gideon's heart meditations and willingness to boldly ask the questions put him in the position of becoming part of the solution. Have you ever noticed that most people do not care to ask the simple questions or ponder the reasons why something is in the state that it is? As noted, many of the people of Israel were hiding from the problem, while Gideon was trying to still function in spite of the problem. In uncertainty, courage is initially unveiled when individuals begin to boldly ask the questions.

The reason that few people ask the questions is because they are waiting for someone to miraculously step on the scene and deliver them in their plight. As I have discovered in the past, if I take personal interest in a matter, it is usually because I am ready to address it in some way. This means I have to somehow become identified to it by understanding the real problem with the intent of confronting it. Granted, I may be uncertain about how I am able to confront it, but if I never ask the questions as a means to come to an understanding as to why something exists in its present state, I will never be ready to avail myself to become part of the solution.

Another reason people do no ask the necessary questions is that once they know the answers, they do not want to be held accountable for failing to act. The reality is we prefer to hide in the dark dens of fear, the caves of personal ignorance, and in some form of wishful thinking or false hope. In such a state, we are content to wait in some stronghold for someone to save us from the fate we have often brought upon ourselves in our rebellious and lawless ways of transgression and iniquity.

In God's kingdom, when an individual humbly seeks God to answer hidden questions of the heart, it provides the opportunity for the Lord to step on the scene and reveal the answers. God is always looking to and fro, searching for that one person who is open to honestly consider the why's of a matter.[3] God does not need a great army to deliver His people. He only needs one willing soul to avail him or herself to stand in the gap. Ezekiel 22:30 summarizes God's search in this way, "And I sought for a man among them, that should make up the hedge and stand in the gap before me for the land, that I should not destroy it; but I found none."

Before Gideon could lead the way of deliverance, God had to answer his questions as to why He was remaining silent. At the core of Israel's oppression was idolatry. The Lord warned people that if they did not eliminate the idolatrous, pagan people from among them, then these individuals would become snares that would entrap them. Entrapment is bondage or slavery. However, the people did not take God seriously. They did not rid the land of all foreign gods or pagan ways. As a result, they were being constantly entrapped into the kingdom of darkness. Their own logic would blind them to the trap as they considered such matters as being insignificant. However, such environments cause people to become spiritually dull.

People equate problems with uncomfortable environments, when the real problem is always spiritual. As in the case of the children of Israel, the problem was not that they were in bondage to the Midianites; rather, the problem came down to who they were serving. They were serving idols. The unholy mixture between their rich history of Jehovah God and idolatry had caused them to become amoral. We are told in Judges 17:6 and 21:25 that they did what was right in their own eyes. After all, there was no real sharpness as to what was right or wrong based on their amoral view. Because of their view, the standard of Jehovah God was being redefined or removed, and in such a quasi religious environment man could define a matter according to whatever self-serving religious notion he might adopt along the way.

Scripture is clear, there is no other God before the true God of heaven or beside Him. He alone is God. Since He alone is God, He is a jealous God who will not tolerate sharing the worship or devotion of men with that which is not deity. Clearly, idolatry will strip or demote God in people's minds. The Lord will not be in competition for the hearts and minds of His people with any other idols. He will always turn His people over to the lifeless, pagan, destructive ways of their idols. In the end, they will learn how lifeless, dead, and useless such gods prove to be when they

---

[3]   2 Chronicles 16:9

need deliverance from their enemies. They would also learn how their desperate cries to their idols for deliverance would go unheeded, as their need for intervention would end in despair, and their enslavement would become unbearable in the midst of great hopelessness.[4]

Great leaders have often had to be great reformers like King Hezekiah and King Josiah. King Hezekiah had to throw open the doors of the temple after his father had closed them in preference to blatant idolatry. He had to reestablish the witness (temple) and the priests of God. It was only after the standard and witness of God was once again established in the midst of the people that they began to experience miraculous deliverance from their enemies.[5]

King Josiah also came to power when idolatry had caused much of the children of Israel's way of life to run amuck. God was ready to bring judgment upon His people. However, King Josiah's tender heart towards the Lord, along with his zeal and willingness to tear down idolatrous altars and images, burn the bones of idolatrous priests, repair the house of God, read His Law, and seek His face as to what needed to be done in restitution for the people's grave transgression and lawlessness before the Lord, stayed God's judgment until after his death.[6]

Such leaders must have their spiritual bearings established regardless of the idolatrous, pagan environment they may live in, or they will be unable to address that which often enslaves the minds and hearts of men. As Ezekiel pointed out, real idolatry occurs in the hidden secret chambers of the heart and in the high places of man's imagination. The Apostle Paul stated that the real strongholds are found within the imagination where such strongholds have been erected against the true knowledge of God.[7]

When we consider Gideon, he first had to address the real reason for the people of Israel's bondage. It was idolatry. God instructed Gideon to cut down the idols and erect an altar to Him. Upon that altar he was to take a bullock seven years old and offer it on the altar as a burnt offering. This is very significant. The bullock did not necessarily represent the first fruits. Perhaps it is because the Midianites always took the best for

4   Exodus 20:1-7; Isaiah 45:5, 14, 18, 21-22, 46:9; 48:12

5   2 Kings 18-19; 2 Chronicles 29:1-31:21

6   2 Chronicles 34:1-35:19

7   Ezekiel 8:3-18; 14:3-11

themselves, but it did represent the amount of time that the children of Israel had been oppressed by the Midianites. God may have not been the children of Israel's first choice, but He would be their only choice when it came to deliverance. To offer a bullock also pointed to the fact that it would personally cost the family of Gideon. After all, that bullock could have been used for food that no doubt was becoming quite scarce.

The bullock was to be offered as a burnt offering. A burnt offering points to consecration. In other words it designates identification and ownership. It was being offered up to Jehovah God. Although unseen, He is the owner and redeemer of the people of Israel. The victorious battle that was about to ensue would be solely accredited to God and not any idol. There would be no debate as to who delivered the Israelites from their unpleasant predicament.

Gideon took ten of his servants by night and destroyed the altar of Baal and cut down the idol's images, erected an altar to God, and offered up the burnt offering. The fact that Gideon did it at night made him appear cowardly. The truth is, a good leader discerns how to fight a battle. Such a leader will never be driven by an impulsive desire to be exalted or make his advancement known by the enemy. The leader will determine if sniping action is effective or a frontal attack is necessary. Good leaders know when to retreat to fight another day and when to advance to gain back the territory that has been lost. Clearly, Gideon was showing discretion as to the most effective strategy in dealing with the idolatry.

Even though idolatry had allowed the children of Israel to be taken captive, the people were still holding to Baal. This was made obvious when the people of his village arose the next day and found the altar and images erected to their idol in ruin. They wanted to kill the culprit who brought their miserable idol down in utter defeat. However, Gideon's father showed wisdom when he challenged the men that if Baal is god let him speak for himself, as well as save himself. We know that no idol can speak for itself, let alone save itself. If an idol cannot plead his cause how can he plead the cause of men? If he cannot save himself, how can he save man?

An idol's identity has been construed in the imagination of man and empowered by the darkness, superstition, deception, and lies of the heart. The attractive lies are always the same in each age. Idols promise to bring security, happiness, and purpose to a person's life.

Gideon's example reveals to us that the idea that any God will do is erroneous. There is only one God who is able to truly save man from that which enslaves him. For this reason idolatry is what creates the greatest bondage in man. He is left unprotected and vulnerable to that which is tyrannical. He has no authority, power, or hope to change his plight. He will find himself impoverished by what he worships, left empty by that which proves to have no life, and hopeless by that which has no substance or value. He will eat what little fruits of his labor remain in utter despair as he tastes the bitter injustice of it all. His cries will fall on deaf ears, lifeless forms, and stone hearts. It will become obvious that idols cannot save people from being entangled and taken captive by the tyrants of the world.

Every age has their idols that will test the hearts of men. America is no exception. The idols may not be carved images, but they exist, and like those in Egypt during the children of Israel's enslavement, every idol was eventually exposed and brought to ruin. We have witnessed the ruin of our idols from money, greed, power, entertainment, sports pleasure, man-made religion, and so forth. Each idol may have drawn our attention away from God in order to receive exaltation and adoration, but each has proven to be ineffective in pleading its cause or saving us from the grave darkness encroaching into our lives. Even though we may rage against slavery, we must concede that our particular idol could never save us from the enslavement of the tyrannical designs of the greedy, power-hungry tyrants. These idols could never preserve what is sacred, and the only way we will maintain any sanity and keep our bearings is by coming back to the basics and center of the godly principles this nation was founded upon. We must call out to the God whose hand was upon those who maintained that His providence and sovereignty had to be present to ensure blessing and prosperity.

Man's heart will always be tested by the idols of his particular age. The test will reveal his source of life, reliance, and hope. In many cases, it will make known what man worships, as well as what part of creation he puts his trust in to save him. For some, it is a form, face, or image emerging from some part of God's creation. For others it is money, power, or prestige that is part of the world's systems. However, none of these sources have any real life or ability to save man from the unseen forces of darkness, the insidious power of wicked governments, and the brute, intimidating force of the tyrants and despots of the world.

Once God was exalted and the idol brought down, Gideon could be given his marching orders. We see in Scripture that there were 22,000 men willing to follow Gideon into battle. But, God wanted to prove a point. When God is involved in the personal affairs of man, great armies or formidable weapons do not win battles. The battle belongs to God. God whittled the army down to a mere 300 men. Victory would clearly establish the real Victor in the confrontation with the Midianites.

It is interesting as to the type of men and tools God used to display His power and victory in regard to the Midianites. The men who were chosen were the ones who showed they were alert to their environment by using their hand to scoop up the water to drink, while those who bent over and lapped it up like a dog were more focused on the task than the environment. All good soldiers are always alert and sensitive to their surroundings.

The tools that were used to win the battle proved to be practical and insignificant in light of the task. There were trumpets that would be used to call the soldiers to battle, as well as declaration of victory. There were also the empty pitchers that would be broken, causing confusion for the Midianites, and lamps that were ready to give an appearance of power and distinction as they gave off light in the darkness.

Most of us know the story of Gideon, but how many of us consider what really made this man distinct in his time. The answer was his faith. Was his faith strong and unusual? That answer is no! He was an uncertain soul, but he chose to ponder the why's, consider the possibilities, ask bold questions, ensure God was behind the plan, and then obeyed in light of the uncertainties and impossible odds before him. He was ordinary in every way, but what made his situation extraordinary was God using the ordinary and the unlikely to show Himself mighty on behalf of the fearful and undeserving.

Did Gideon bring reformation to Israel? It is hard to say how many people came back to Jehovah God after the victory over the Midianites. But, there is one thing for sure, Gideon brought reformation to his own life and most likely to his family, community, and the men who followed him into victory. God always has His remnant of people who will never bow their knees to the Baals of their age. They may be hidden away by the darkness of slavery and poverty, but their hearts remain steadfast towards God even though they live in insane times. Like Gideon, they may be threshing behind the winepress, but their spiritual search always lead them back to the reality of the one true God. In silence they may have to cleave to past victories of God, ponder the possibilities of God in light of the present, and trust that regardless of the circumstances, in the end, Jehovah will ultimately be exalted as the only true God of heaven and earth.

4

HONORABLE SOULS

Proverbs 14:34 states that, "Righteousness exalteth a nation but sin is a reproach to any people." We are living in the days when it appears as if evil is winning in every arena. In such a time, we enter the time of woes, where the wicked are calling good, evil and evil, good. This is when the wicked justify their assault against the righteous and their rebellion against their Creator. In this environment, God's anger will take center stage as He stretches forth His hand and lifts up an ensign to bring judgment and destruction to devour such individuals with a holy fire. In the end, the memory of these individuals will eventually be wiped from before the face of the righteous God and His servants forever. As the Bible declares, the wicked will never inherit the land.[1]

In such times of insanity, those who are righteous begin to taste the bitter reproach that is brought on by the sin that is invading their nation in the form of wicked leadership. Sin will cause vexation in their souls, contrition to their spirits, and despair in their environment. Times such as these drive righteous people to their knees in repentance and intercession.

What determines the quality of leadership that will pass through, as well as survive, the fires of judgment and the wrath of a holy God? As I have studied leadership according to Scripture and the secular world, I have noticed four types of leadership emerging at different points in time. This is how I grade the different levels of headship. They are excellent, mediocre, ineffective, and wicked. For example, if I were to grade the presidents that I have been able to observe in my lifetime according to this scale, I would consider President Ronald Reagan as an excellent leader, both George Brushes as mediocre leaders, Bill Clinton as an ineffective leader, and Obama as a wicked leader.

This brings us to the question as to what separates and defines each of these leaders. To answer this question we must go back to the Scriptures. Scripture clearly shows us that the quality of leadership will

---

[1]   Isaiah 5:18-26

be determined by the leader's heart condition. For example, to bring a Scriptural comparison I would grade the following kings in this way: David was an excellent leader, Uzziah a mediocre king, Rehoboam an ineffective king, and Ahaz and Amon wicked leaders.

As you study each of these leaders, the Bible reveals aspects of their character. Character is simply the manifestation of the heart condition. The heart condition determines how leaders walk before the Lord in regard to those they are overseeing. This is what we are told about the heart condition and walk of the four types of leaders. For example, David walked according to the integrity of his heart. He was an honorable soul in all that he did in light of his relationship to God. This did not mean that he did not prove to be human for he was and had bouts of failure due to the weakness of his flesh and the lapse of his moral character. But, as you will note, other kings were somewhat compared to King David as to the quality of their leadership. This is also true for our day. Present presidents are often being compared to Ronald Reagan's quality of leadership as a means to define their character and the effectiveness of their leadership to properly guide this nation.[2]

King David was a great leader in so many ways. He had learned what it meant to face predators in the strength of the Lord as a shepherd tending his sheep. He was prepared to victoriously face a giant on the battlefield and walk a line of integrity when a jealous king became his enemy without cause. When he realized that King Saul was trying to kill him, he did not try to cause division in the ranks of his soldiers; rather, he separated himself from the environment to let God handle the matter. He attracted a ragtag army of men who proved valiant on the battlefield. He was the sharpest when in battle, for he understood that without God no battle, no matter how small or great, could be won.

David had a heart after God. The reality of the heart after God is that as a man he could be reasoned with concerning sin, broken by the reality of sin, and restored by God from a place of true repentance and humility.[3] David was very human, but he was also always pliable when it came to God. He knew what it meant to be in right standing with God, as well as what it meant to get right with God, and be right before Him. It is obvious that righteousness points to those who possess an honorable

---

2   1 Kings 9:4 2 Chronicles 28:1-4

3   1 Samuel 13:14; Psalm 51

soul towards God. "Honor" implies that the character of a person will prove trustworthy and excellent in all of his or her ways.

Possessing such ways is the secret of all great leadership. The quality of leadership will always be based on a man's relationship with God. If man's heart is complacent towards God, his leadership will prove to be mediocre at best. If man's heart is fickle and fleshly before God, his leadership will prove to be ineffective. If man is wicked, he will find himself coming into opposition with God, signaling utter defeat.

As we follow the kings, we can see this reality being played out on the screen of history. When it comes to Uzziah, also known as Azariah, there were aspects of his reign that revealed acceptable character. It is said of him that he did right according to his father, Amaziah. When you study Amaziah's life you will see that he started off doing that which was right in the sight of the Lord, yet not like David. He clearly addressed idolatry and the abominations in the society. He was somewhat of a reformer. He started off with zeal but fizzled out. In other words, he compromised in some ways, rendering his reign to be mediocre at best. As you study Amaziah's life, he greatly compromised at the end of his life. We are told that his heart became lifted up in pride, preventing him from hearing warnings that led to defeat.

There is nothing that will make a person more stiff-neck towards God than a proud heart that refuses to be broken by God's displeasure towards sin. Not only did King Amaziah subject Judah to defeat, but he caused much of the glory represented by the temple to be taken away from the people of Judah in disgrace. From this point on the glory of the people remained tarnished up to Judah's demise as a kingdom.[4]

As you observe the kings, you will see that the weaknesses of character that existed in the fathers were often passed down to their sons, which caused a mixture that produced mediocre results. This was true for King Uzziah. He greatly displayed his father's weakness of a prideful heart when he intruded into the priesthood. Although this king was accredited with great innovations, he also reigned in total isolation. When he trespassed into the priesthood, he came out a leper and had to be separated from the rest of society until his death.[5]

---

4   2 Kings 14:3-14
5   2 Kings 15:1-7; 2 Chronicles 26:1-21

As I especially consider the second President Brush, I can see a man who had much integrity, but there was something that proved to be amiss in his administration. He seemed to start out right, but then he made a wrong turn and began to intrude into arenas that the Bible clearly states are off limits. The main arena I am talking about is Israel. The Bible is clear that no man must try to divide the land of Israel or determine the fate of Jerusalem.[6] It was obvious that those who compromise righteousness are often motivated by unrighteous agendas. Whether such agendas are personal, national, or international, they lack true righteousness before the Lord to stand against the tide of wickedness. In the end, such individuals will end up with mediocre leadership accomplishments at best, or find God fighting against them at worst. Such leadership will become tarnished as it begins to be swallowed up by one problem after another.

You can see the same pattern in both of the Brushes' presidencies; however, the end results are brought into sharper focus in the son's leadership. During President George W. Brush's term in office we witnessed some of the greatest devastations happening to this nation on a larger scale from 9-11 to Katrina to name a few. However, he would not listen to or heed the warnings of those who understood prophecy concerning the matter of Israel.[7] Even though he kept this nation from another terrorist attack and brought some integrity and moral correctness back to the White House and the presidency, he left the office without his glory intact. Although President Brush took consolation that in the end history would clarify his presidency in a more positive light, he still failed to understand it does not matter how history ultimately sees one's leadership; rather, it is how God will ultimately define it in light of His Word.

The fruit of President George W. Brush's leadership is what the people of this nation were left to partake of as a nation. As a nation, his mediocre leadership left the people's resolve compromised, causing them to be open to predators in greedy pursuit of power. Without the decisiveness that comes with righteous leadership, people are open to

---

6   Genesis 12:1-8; 15; 17:1-21; Ezekiel 48; Zechariah 12:2-3

7   If you would like to study the Scriptural warnings in light of history and see the affect that American policies towards Israel had on this nation, see the book, "EYE TO EYE", by William Koenig.

seduction that will always promise some type of change from mediocre leadership to something different. The truth is people can only reside in a limbo or mediocre place for so long before they become unsettled in their souls. However, the difference that is often presented to people in such a state, as made apparent in this nation, will prove to be wicked, and it will end up stripping the nation of its already fading glory.

The next type of leadership was exemplified by Rehoboam. Rehoboam was the son of Solomon. Scripture shows us that Solomon started off in a right way but because of his love for idolatrous wives, he forsook God. His moral deviation not only caused a split in his relationship with God, but it caused a crack in the kingdom of Israel that later resulted in ten tribes splitting off from Judah and Benjamin under his son's rule, Rehoboam. Jesus warned that a house divided against itself will not stand.[8]

Although there was an attempt on the part of King Jehoshaphat to reunite the kingdoms into one kingdom, God's judgment to bring a separation between the tribes could not be reversed. One of the main reasons is because the ten tribes of Israel went the way of idolatry and never came back to center in regard to Jehovah. As you study the ten tribes from this point, you will see the epitome of wicked leadership taking center stage and the destruction it would eventually end in for the kings and the people.

Even though King Jehoshaphat was a follower of Jehovah God, he tried to bring the holy and the unholy together, causing devastating affects that almost cost him his life, as well as bring financial failure on some of his attempts in regard to trade. It would also morally profane his family lineage. Due to this unholy agreement, many of his descendants went the way of Baalim. In the end, a power struggle ensured that cost the lives of most of his descendants who were in line to be king. The one descendant who did survive the purging became an ineffective, morally inept leader at the end of his life to such a point that he was not even buried in the sepulchers of the kings.[9]

We clearly can see that any unholy agreement will produce mediocre leadership. As you study Solomon's life, you can see the devastating affects of moral deviation and unholy agreement upon people and

---

[8] 1 Kings 11:1-13; Matthew 12:25

[9] 2 Chronicles 17-24

nations. As rulers and people deviate from the center of what is right, moral, and truthful, they become unreceptive and indifferent towards the matters of God. In fact, when a contrast of righteousness is brought before such individuals, they can become quite insulted and mocking towards it. For God to bring such a person back to center as to what is true, He must greatly chastise him or her. We can observe this in the case of the leaders who fall into this category. We see where the Lord stirred up adversaries against Solomon to correct him in his deviation.[10]

As you follow a ruler's life who is plagued by moral deviation, you can see that it renders him or her ineffective as a leader. Such a ruler will often be consumed by one scandal after another. In the end, the leader will not have the necessary credibility to lead others. His or her character and acts will always be tainted or brought into question as to intentions and truthfulness. People will not take such an individual seriously as his or her name or leadership becomes a byword or joke that will end in some form of mocking.

The problem with moral deviation is that it can become more predominate in the generations that follow. It has been interesting to note how this digression manifests itself in regard to the different dynasties that ruled in Israel. In the case of the Northern Tribe of Israel (the ten tribes), you can actually follow the departure of these leaders from righteousness. What is interesting is that God allows such digression up to the third or fourth generation. If each leader becomes increasingly morally depraved, while causing the people to become more morally bankrupt without any correction, God's chastisement of such leaders along the way will end in judgment. In such judgment He actually brings a complete separation or end to the rule of that particular family or line. We can see this in the case of the rule of King Jehu, in the descendants of the priest Eli, in the life of Rehoboam, and eventually with the royal lineage of David.

In the case of Judah, we see where God raised up kings who proved to be reformers at different intervals to stay the inevitable judgment upon the wicked ways of Judah and her leadership, but nevertheless, a pattern clearly emerged. Under the prophet Jeremiah, it was declared that no one of the lineage traced back to Solomon would ever again sit on the throne after the wicked reign of King Jeconiah. Although, Jesus

---

[10]   1 Kings 11:14-40

was named in this royal lineage in Matthew 1 to prove He would be rightfully in line with the throne of David, Joseph was not His biological father. His mother's lineage, which was traced in Luke 3, went back to Nathan, Solomon's brother.[11]

We can follow Rehoboam's leadership and see how ineffective he became. Even though his father, Solomon, was considered one of the wisest men, his son proved to be foolish. Instead of listening to wise leaders, he listened to upstarts like himself who simply fed his ego, causing the split within the kingdom of Israel between the tribes.

Scriptures tells us his foolishness did not stop with losing a great portion of the kingdom. We are told that he forsook the Law of the Lord and took all of Israel with him. Since God had made a covenant with King David, the Lord chastised this young fool by using Egypt. Egypt came in and took away the treasures of the house of the Lord. Reheboam did repent, but in the process of his foolishness, Judah lost her initial glory. Instead of the house of God being represented by gold, Rehoboam had to settle for bronze.[12]

Solomon's heart may have been turned away from God by foreign wives, but in Rehoboam the religious environment translated or produced a man who was not prepared in his heart to seek the Lord. As a result he did evil.

We see that Rehoboam's son, Abijah walked in all of the sins of his father, proving his heart was not perfect before the Lord. He only reigned for three years. However, Abijah's son Asa, who represented the fourth generation from Solomon, did what was right before the Lord. We are told that his heart was perfect with the LORD all his days. As a result, he reigned forty one years.[13]

As you follow these kings, you can see where King Amaziah did what was right in the sight of the Lord, but not with a perfect heart. We see where later on this king falls into idolatry and is defeated by the ten tribes of Israel. His son, Uzziah is made king. Uzziah did what was right in the sight of the Lord according to the ways of his father, Amaziah. In other words, his heart was not perfect towards the Lord either. As a

---

[11]   1 Samuel 2:27-36 (refer to 1 Samuel 22:6-23; 1 Kings 1:7; 2:26-27); 2 Kings 9:1-13; 10:30; Jeremiah 22:28-30; Matthew 1:11-12

[12]   1 Kings 14:21-31; 2 Chronicles 10-16

[13]   1 Kings 15:1-15; 2 Chronicles 12:14; 16:13

result, he arrogantly intruded into the priesthood and became a leper who remained shut away until his death.[14]

Uzziah brought many positive changes to Judah's quality of living, but his mediocre leadership was followed by his son, Jotham. Jotham also did what was right according to his father, Uzziah, except he did not enter into the temple. We are told that this king did do mightily before the Lord because he prepared his ways before Him.[15] Notice he prepared his ways, not his heart. Perhaps he had a certain fear of God due to the consequences his father paid for his prideful indiscretion, and recognized that it was beneficial to have God on his side even though his heart might have not been totally consecrated unto Him. The reality is that not much more is written about this king, as it was in the case of his grandson, Hezekiah and future descendant King Josiah. Both kings brought reformation to God's people.

Ahaz followed Jothan. This brings us to the fourth generation of kings in this particular grouping. The imperfect ways of the former kings ended with a wicked king that walked in the idolatrous ways of the kings of Israel. He led Judah into idolatry, closed the doors of the temple, and sought the support of other kingdoms when being chastised by God. It was clear that this wicked king had no intention of repenting. He clearly proved to be an utter fool.[16]

Wickedness not only shows itself to be defiant towards God, it refuses to humble itself to seek God when He is trying to rein in such a person from walking in destructive ways in order to bring instruction and restoration. This wicked man only reigned 16 years, but Judah was left as prey to her enemies. This is a harsh reality that comes with wicked leadership. The people have no real protection as long as such a leader has the reins.

Ahaz was followed by Hezekiah. Hezekiah was not cut from the same cloth as his father. He did that which was right in the sight of the Lord, according to all that David, had done. This king was a great reformer. He turned Judah back to Jehovah God. Granted, there are some things he did not do right, but in the end he got it right.

---

[14] 2 Chronicles 25:1-3, 14-27; 26:4-5, 16-21; 27:2
[15] 2 Kings 15:32-38; 2 Chronicles 27
[16] 2 Chronicles 28; 29:3

Hezekiah brought worship of Jehovah God back into the midst of the people. He opened the doors of the temple, called the priests back to their duties, and reestablished the identity of the Jewish people by conducting the Passover. As a result, this king would be able to stand before his enemies, withstand them, and remain standing when all looked hopeless. The secret to his success was no secret. He turned to God as his true helper and deliverer. In his right standing with God, he was able to effectively seek Him to intervene on his behalf.[17]

There was a point in Hezekiah's life where he did not accept God's will, and his heart did become lifted up in pride. His examples need to bring some sobriety to us as to how we look at God's will, as well as take heed as to the condition of our hearts. God's will was that Hezekiah get his house in order because his life was to come to an end. Hezekiah prayed and God extended his life for fifteen more years. Sadly, in that fifteen years, a son was born to the king by the name of Manasseh. He began to reign at the age of 12, and his reign lasted fifty-five years.[18]

Manasseh turned out to be a despot. He brought every kind of evil, abominable practice imaginable into the midst of Judah. The Lord's prophets rebuked him, but the king and the people refused to listen and take heed to the rebuke. Irreversible judgment was pronounced on Judah. In other words, God would eventually carry out the judgment. However, God made a covenant with King David that He would not ignore.[19]

As a result, the Lord humbled the arrogant, idolatrous king in such a way that Manasseh did come back to center, staying God's judgment for a season upon the land of Judah. However, Manasseh's son, Amon, followed in the evil ways of his father, proving to be an utter fool. His reign only lasted two years, when he was killed by his servants in his own house.[20]

In the third generation, Manasseh's grandson, Josiah proved to be a reformer. He actually carried out a prophecy that was given to the first king of the kingdom of Israel, Jeroboam.[21] As a result, God stayed the

---

[17] 2 Chronicles 29-31
[18] 2 Chronicles 32:24-25; 33:1-2
[19] 2 Chronicles 33:2-20
[20] 2 Chronicles 33:21-25
[21] I Kings 13:1-2; 2 Chronicles 34-35:19

irreversible judgment pronounced against Manasseh during Josiah's lifetime. Although Josiah proved to be very human before his death, he still was considered a righteous king. After Josiah's death, God begin to greatly humble Judah resulting in its demise as a kingdom.

What can we learn from historical Biblical examples? We can learn that every great leader understands that if God's providence is not recognized and adhered to, they will fail as leaders. Whether they fail to establish the right example, maintain the right ways, and ensure righteousness in character and deed, they will not only fail as leaders, but they will fail those they lead.

Great leaders ensure that a right environment is present to benefit those they lead. They cannot leave those they lead in a mediocre state. For example, King David made sure that Solomon had all the materials needed along with the format to build the house of God. He had gone to great lengths to establish every aspect of the house of God and the duties of the priests to ensure that it would run smoothly. His instruction to Solomon was, "Do it!"[22] David knew that, for the people of Israel to remain great, God had to be in their midst. His providence had to be evident and His approval obvious.

The second great lesson we must note is that God will intervene, stay judgment, and show mercy for the sake of righteous people. Due to Abraham's intercession, God would have saved Sodom and Gomorrah if He could have found ten righteous men in the midst of these two cities. Instead he delivered Lot and his family out of Sodom.[23] Because of His covenant with David, He refrained from destroying Solomon's lineage. And, in relationship to the present, for the sake of Christ, He shows long-suffering so that people can come to repentance.[24]

As we face some of the darkest times the world has ever known, we must consider if there are those who stand righteous before God, which allows Him the necessary environment or opening to intervene, stay judgment, and show mercy upon us as a nation. I sometimes shake in my shoes when I think of Ezekiel 22:30-31,

---

[22]   1 Chronicles 22:1-28:10

[23]   Genesis 18:17-19:29

[24]   2 Peter 3:9

And I sought for a man among them, that should make up the hedge, and stand in the gap before me for the land, that I should not destroy it: but I found none. Therefore have I poured out mine indignation upon them; I have consumed them with the fire of my wrath: their own way have I recompensed upon their heads, saith the Lord.

Will God be able to find such a person in these days in regard to our nation? Let us hope so, let us humbly make ourselves available like Job so we can maintain or defend our ways before God, knowing that we stand righteous before Him.[25] As a result, we can be assured that the Lord will have an opportunity to intervene, stay judgment, and show mercy, even when the wickedness around us seems to be at the height of its glory.

---

[25] Job 13:15

5

HUMBLED SOULS

Regardless of how the world portrays leadership, the truest expression of it is not one of self-confidence; rather it is one of self-awareness. When I speak of self-awareness, I am not speaking of introspection that often proves morbid and ineffective, and ends in a state of nirvana. Such a state is simply a dead-end where emptiness echoes of vanity and is devoid of purpose and real direction. Rather, I speak of self-awareness that understands the weakness that is inherent in every person. This self-awareness has to do with the inability to accomplish even what would appear to be the most menial task without some type of intervention outside of self.

Self-awareness causes us to honestly admit when something is too great, too important, or too wondrous to imagine being accomplished without intervention, the proper inspiration, and knowledge of how to bring it about. It is the type of self-awareness that allows each of us the freedom to be rendered into a humble soul that seeks sources outside personal limited strength. In humility such a soul will have the freedom to admit personal needs, fears, uncertainties, and inabilities.

Some people would consider humility and honest evaluation as a sign of weakness. Granted, we do not always have to admit such matters to others, but we do need to confess them first to ourselves. We need to recognize our need to seek intervention from one who is greater and more capable. Once we are honest with ourselves, then we need to admit such needs and inabilities to God with the intent to seek His help.

Such a state of honest evaluation is the essence of the humble soul. Such a person is realistic and aware as to his or her real state of being needful and inept. Ultimately, this type of place or position will provide a platform where great things can be accomplished by God through a person's life.

In the last chapter Solomon's life was briefly considered in light of how one can slide into digression in his or her spiritual life. However, when Solomon initially began his journey into manhood as a king, he started from the state of humility. We are told that he loved the Lord and walked in the statues as his father, King David. As a result, we see the fruit of his love and obedience. He was a humbled soul who willingly admitted to God that he did not have what it would take to rightfully reign over such a kingdom as Israel.[1]

Solomon was tender towards God. His awareness made him realistic about the task before him. He did not perceive that he had the wisdom, experience, or maturity to accomplish such a feat as rightfully ruling over God's people. He recognized he was needful of intervention, of something outside of himself. He clearly needed help to properly reign over those whom he had been entrusted with.

Keep in mind, there are no real instructions that come with such a responsibility. All the education in the world will not prepare a person to lead or rule over others. Solomon understood being in such a position did not imply or guarantee he could properly do justice as a leader.

In Solomon's humbled state, the Lord told him to ask what he would and He would give it to him. As we consider Solomon's loving, tender state towards God, we would have to admit that he presented a clean slate for God to write upon. In summation, he could be entrusted with having his heart in the right place to receive such an open-ended invitation. This is made clear by what he asked God for, "Give therefore thy servant an understanding heart to judge thy people, that I may discern between good and bad: for who is able to judge this thy so great people" (1 Kings 3:9)?

Solomon was asking for wisdom to reign over God's people. It is man's tendency to ask for things for himself, not to ask for that which would ensure the integrity of what has been entrusted to him. Wisdom is summarized by knowledge that has been put into application. Such wisdom is actually experienced and proves itself to be effective. It is not just any knowledge that has been applied; rather, it is functional knowledge that consistently works because it is based on what is true and right.

Most people operate from a premise of knowledge that has never been tested or tried. This type of knowledge can only puff up those immature and inexperience individuals who see themselves as being wise in their conceits towards the matters of life.[2] Such knowledge may look

---

[1]   1 Kings 3:3, 7-10
[2]   Romans 12:16; 1 Corinthians 8:1-3

good on paper and sound logical to those who are inexperienced, but once put into practice it proves to be anything but functional. In most cases, such knowledge lacks practical sense. Instead of being simple or practical, it proves to be unrealistic, perverted, confusing, complicated, and will often prove to be utter foolishness.

Scripture describes two types of wisdom: The wisdom from above and the earthly, sensual, devilish wisdom of the world. The wisdom of the world produces jealousies, strife, confusion, and every evil work. However, the wisdom from above results in righteousness and peace. It is pure, peaceful, gentle, easy to reason with, full of mercy and good fruits, not partial, and devoid of hypocrisy.[3]

Wisdom from above is an incredible gift from God that will benefit those who encounter it. For the woman who was about to lose her son because of the selfishness and jealousy of another woman, it proved to be a blessing when her son was properly restored to her by King Solomon according to wise judgment. For others, they will find themselves attracted to the simplicity and beauty of such wisdom. Like the Queen of Sheba, some will travel from afar to hear the nuggets that such insight contains.[4] The queen saw that Solomon possessed such wisdom and described it in this way:

> Happy are thy men, happy are these thy servants, which stand continually before thee, and that hear thy wisdom. Blessed be the LORD thy God, which delighted in thee, to set thee on the throne of Israel: because the LORD loved Israel for ever, therefore made he thee king, to do judgment and justice (1 Kings 10:8-9).

We see where a good leader is a wise leader. Such a leader does not have to exert brutish force or power over others, for most needy souls will be attracted to the justice of such a person's wisdom. In this type of wisdom, leaders will fear God for they will dread displeasing or profaning Him. Wise leaders will also realize that the people must be able to respect and trust their motives, intent, and ways if they are going to gain their loyalty.

---

[3]   James 3:13-18
[4]   1 Kings 3:16-28; 10:1-10

Followers, who are able to trust the leader's wisdom, will have confidence in the way in which they are called to walk. If a leader does not possess the means to attract or gain the loyalty of those who follow him or her, such individuals will not see the need to die for such a leader. Wisdom from above also brings glory to God. Mere man is simply the vessel through which the Lord imparts His wisdom, but it must be allowed to flow out to benefit and attract others to what is true and right.

Solomon understood the importance of this wisdom and the need to impart it to, or share it, with others. When you read his books, Proverbs and Ecclesiastes, you can see how much heavenly wisdom should be desired and sought after. The first eight chapters of Proverbs were basically dedicated to the virtues and fruits of wisdom that will keep people from the destruction and foolish ways of sin, while the rest of the book brings a contrast as to how the nuggets and promises of wisdom enrich the lives of those who seek after it, live by it, and allow it to discipline and determine personal attitudes and conduct.

In the book of Ecclesiastes wisdom serves as the great teacher that will bring one to true and right conclusions about the matters of life. Solomon clearly revealed the vanity promoted by the world in light of the foolishness of the perception behind what it values. Ultimately, true wisdom will bring people to sound conclusions about the matters of God and life. Consider the conclusion that Solomon's wisdom brought him to, "Let us hear the conclusion of the whole matter: Fear God, and keep his commandments: for this is the whole duty of man. For God shall bring every work into judgment, with every secret thing, whether it be good, or whether it be evil" (Ecclesiastes 12:13-14).

God not only gave Solomon an understanding heart in which to discern and rightfully judge the people, but he would possess insight and wisdom that no mere man would ever come close to possessing who lived before or after him; that is, except one man. That man was not a mere man; rather, He was the Son of God, the essence of complete heavenly wisdom in bodily form. Jesus made this statement about Himself, "The queen of the south shall rise up in the judgment with this generation, and shall condemn it: for she came from the uttermost parts of the earth to hear the wisdom of Solomon; and, behold, a greater than Solomon is here" (Matthew 12:42).

It takes pure wisdom to recognize heavenly wisdom and to embrace it with the disposition of a child. Otherwise such wisdom will elude those who are deluded by their so-called "conceits". The Apostle Paul stated that God has placed each of us as believers in the essence of wisdom, when He placed us in Christ Jesus. In other words, Jesus serves as our source and example of true wisdom.[5] There is no real wisdom to be sought outside of Him.

God also entrusted Solomon with riches and honor.[6] Riches and honor can serve as a big test to most people. However, with real wisdom a person would know how to best utilize both without them becoming the main focus or pursuit of the individual. As pointed out in Scripture and confirmed in the practical world, a fool is quickly parted from riches, and to bestow any type of honor upon such an individual will ultimately reveal how foolish, tyrannical, and treacherous he or she can be.

James pointed out a person is devoid of that which is needful because he or she does not ask for it. It takes a self-awareness of the foolishness that is bound in our hearts to realize how needful we are of the wisdom that comes from above. We are so limited by what we do not know and cannot see. We need wisdom from outside of our personal calculations and conclusions to know that we only know in part and can only see from a restricted plane.[7]

I cannot tell you how much I have asked God for His wisdom about all matters. I may have knowledge of something but if I do not know how to put it to practical use, it will prove to be of no real benefit to anyone. I am not content to strut around with arrogant, impractical knowledge that I pride myself in because I believe it will work when needed. I want to be able to effectively use knowledge, knowing full well it will work. I do not want to be top heavy in my understanding of something; rather, I desire to be fair, just, and practical in my judgments and applications in order to accomplish something. I am not concerned that my knowledge may prove to be flawed; rather, my greatest fear is that I hold to knowledge that in the end will prove to be foolish and silly, and regarded as being ridiculous, useless, and a waste of time.

---

5 1 Corinthians 1:30
6 1 King 3:13
7 Proverbs 22:15; 1 Corinthians 13:8-12; James 4:1-3

It is important at this time to point out that Solomon not only was a tender soul before God, he was a concerned soul. It was obvious that he cared about the people of Israel. If you have no real concern for those you have been entrusted with, you will not care about whether you are able to do right by them. Obviously, Solomon wanted to be a good leader who desired to do right by and for the people by being just in his judgments.

Solomon understood to do right by others, he would have to be given the means to properly rule over them. It would become obvious to his subjects that Solomon possessed the necessary wisdom that could be trusted to make sound judgments.

Sound judgments bring much needed security to people. They do not have to worry that they will be provoked, taken advantage of, or taste the bitterness that comes out of those who prove to be wicked, biased, or unfair in their judgments. In fact, there is nothing more disheartening and oppressive than an environment where justice proves to be nothing more than abusive power on the part of those who are despots in their way of thinking and being.

It is interesting to observe the leadership of despots. The reality is that in many cases those who are close confidents to such people may enjoy privilege and power or share the same ideology. However, there is no respect or common decency among them. Treachery looms around every corner, while the masses simply follow out of fear. Leaders who have to con or bully others to gain a following will prove to be nothing more than imposters. They will demonstrate that they are tyrants, instruments of Satan who will sacrifice the masses for selfish agendas. Eventually, such leaders will meet the fate of a fool.

The question is what happened to Solomon? How can a wise man be rendered into a state of ineffectiveness and foolishness? How can a man recognize that his end will prove vanity unless he learns what his real purpose and duty is in relationship to God? How can one of the wisest men lose his way?

The answer lies in what the Lord told Solomon at the very beginning, "And if thou wilt walk in my ways, to keep my statues and my commandments, as thy father David did walk, then I will lengthen thy days (1 Kings 3:14)" It means nothing if you start out right and finish wrong. Solomon had to keep walking in the ways of righteousness to finish the path established by God.

Wisdom may ensure that you make sound judgments, but righteousness ensures that you keep on the right path. Solomon's affections were turned from God to foreign, idolatrous women. As a result, he ceased to remain tender in his heart towards God. We are told that God became angry with Solomon and after a couple of warnings pronounced judgment that he would divide the kingdom and give ten tribes to another person. He also chastised him by stirring up people against him.[8]

Obviously, Solomon became more obstinate and unreasonable towards the Lord. He would not allow himself to be corrected in his foolish ways. Therefore, consequences were pronounced and chastening became the byproduct.

When you study the lives of those who started out right, but ended wrong, you realize they forgot who they were in the first place. They forgot their humble beginnings. In essence, they forgot that they started out being needful of God's intervention.[9] Their hearts became lifted up in some way, causing them to be set up for a fall. As such people become increasingly independent from God, they become more dependent on their personal strength and the ways of the world.

For Solomon, he became self-sufficient in the glory of his riches. He collected the things of the world including wives, horses, and chariots. In his collection of things and unholy agreement with foreign women, his disobedience and worldly emphasis caused him to drift away from the center of what was true and right.

God knew down the line that the people would prefer a king to His rule. He knew as Creator that unless certain precautions were taken by the king, that power and riches would cause matters to become tainted and perverted, snaring the king into destructive traps. As a result, the Lord put some very decisive instructions in the Law concerning how a king was to conduct himself and the affairs of Israel. We find these instructions in Deuteronomy 17:14-20.

King David pretty much stuck to the instructions found in the Law. For example, David actually hamstrung most of the chariot horses.[10] The kings were not to multiply horses and wives unto themselves as a

---

8   1 Kings 11:1-14
9   Zechariah 4:10; 2 Peter 1:8-9
10   2 Samuel 8:4

means to compete with or make agreement with the foreign nations. Even though Solomon was just in his judgments, he became lustful and worldly in his attitude and conduct. In his riches he did become self-sufficient and in his unholy agreements, his heart was turned away from God. He was no longer interested in being honorable and righteous, but with simply being comfortable in his world.

Humble souls will remain true to their origins and allegiance regardless of the power allotted them. One such humble soul that remembered her small beginnings was a woman named Esther. Esther was an orphan, but her Jewish uncle, Mordecai, took responsibility for her well-being. When the opportunity became available for beautiful women from all over the kingdom to present themselves for the purpose of being queen, her uncle encouraged her to avail herself. Obviously, he saw her beauty and potential to have a better way of life.

These two individuals would have no idea how their actions would later result in the salvation of the Jewish people. If you consider Esther's character and conduct, she accepted the wise instructions of others. Have you ever noticed how people who are arrogant will not receive wise advice? They refuse to be wrong or admit they do not know or understand a matter. People like Esther are not gullible souls, but they are realistic individuals who are aware of their need for wise counsel when they do not completely understand a matter or how to bring it about.

Humble souls are able to receive wise instruction. Whether the instructions were directly inspired from above or came through a wise individual, they recognize the instructions being as such, and would humbly receive and obey them.

We can see this in the case of a man named Barak. Barak was a military leader during the days of judges. At the time Deborah served as the judge over Israel. Barak submitted himself to Deborah's wise, prophetic judgments.[11] As a result, he is often put down by preachers and teachers who are plagued by a fragile ego that clearly sits on a pinnacle in their lives of so-called "manly arrogance".

Barak realized that Deborah was not only a wise judge, but she was truly a woman who could hear from God. He wanted her with him in the battle and was not interested in what vessel or way God communicated

---

[11]   Judges 4:6-11

His wisdom. He was only interested in the fact that God was the source and instruction behind such wisdom. Barak proved to be a humble soul, and as a result was accredited with conquering kingdoms.[12]

This is the reality of humble souls. In the case of Esther, her beauty and demeanor clearly captured the attention and preference of the king. When she discovered the evil plans of a leader to extinguish the Jewish people, she recognized that she was in her particular place as queen so that she could offer up her life if necessary to save them. Even though fear gripped her soul at first, her uncle reminded her of her insignificant beginnings. Due to her tenderness, she stepped up to the challenge, ready to risk it all for the sake of her people. She would make the declaration that if she perished, so be it.[13]

Humble souls must insist on godly wisdom to always ensure the integrity of their humility. In other words, they can always be reasoned with at the point of what is true and right.

Esther interceded on behalf of her people and they were saved. Today, the Jewish people commemorate her intervention and leadership with the celebration of Purim.

Humble souls are willing souls. They are willing to see the wisdom, purpose, and necessity of a situation or action and become a willing vessel to be used regardless of the consequences. In fact, what you see evident in such tender souls is a child-like faith that simply trusts the wisdom and character of those around it.

This brings us to the next humble soul, Mary, the mother of the man, Christ Jesus. Mary was quite aware of who she was, a simple handmaiden who also needed a Savior. However, God could intrude into her life and entrust her with the very glory of heaven, the prize every man should possess, the Savior of the world. She was not only entrusted with wisdom from above, but with wisdom in bodily form.

What a precious soul Mary must have possessed to be entrusted with the Messiah. You can get glimpses into her spirit and soul and her heart attitude when you read about her response to the angel's proclamation in Luke 1:38 and her prayer in Luke 1:46-55. She clearly had child-like faith to accept the angel, Gabriel, and his message. The humility she showed was made evident when she, in so many words declared, "So be

---

[12]   Hebrews 11:32-33
[13]   Esther 4:5-17

it!" She put her fate in the sweet hand of Providence. She did not press past the point of how she could be with child without the natural order of things happening. She simply accepted that it was not impossible for God to bring about the miraculous.

Perhaps there are those who would consider Mary and ask, "Where is the leadership?" Her leadership came by way of her example. She humbled herself before God and took on a burden that was ordained before the foundation of the world. As she submitted to the burden, she came into subjection to heavenly wisdom and intervention with great sincerity and grace. This is the example of leadership. It must be able to recognize authority and submit to the burden and duty of what has been deemed necessary, important, and worthy. In the end, the person will not bring glory to self, but glory to that which he or she has submitted to. It is in true submission that God can exalt such an example for others to consider and follow, as He uses the vessel in a magnificent way to carry out His purpose.

We know that Mary pondered some of the events that surrounded Jesus.[14] Wise souls know how to ponder the matters of God. They will remember what has been said, what has been done, and what is coming.

Pondering souls seek understanding of a matter. Such understanding is not about gaining knowledge, but gaining the ability to be wise when such matters come to fruition. A wise and willing soul desires to be a prepared soul. Such a soul does not want to be caught off guard and prove to be unfaithful. Mary experienced joy in being entrusted with God's precious Son. However, she was forewarned that a sword would pierce her very spirit when the precious gift of God hung on a cross.[15]

Only a parent who has suffered the loss of a child would know what Mary possibly experienced on that terrible day when she witnessed her Son being led to His death. However, only God could truly identify with her when it came to Jesus dying on a cross. Only God could have felt how deep that sword pierced her very soul and spirit when the very heart of Jesus was broken on behalf of mankind. Truly, they shared the precious revelation of who He was and what He came to accomplish—to save lost, undeserving, rebellious mankind, those who were more apt to mock and reject Him than embrace Him.

---

[14]   Luke 2:19

[15]   Luke 2:34-35

Jesus not only came to save those who believed, but those who would yet believe. He did not come for those who perceived themselves to be righteous, He came for those who knew they were sinners, doomed in their helpless state of sin and death. He even knowingly died for the despots who would ultimately reject Him in their hearts. The Apostle Paul summarized it in this way in Romans 5:6-8,

> For when we were yet without strength, in due time Christ died for the ungodly. For scarcely for a righteous man will one die: yet peradventure for a good man some would even dare to die. But God commendeth his love toward us, in that, while we were yet sinners, Christ died for us.

Do you have a humble soul that will prove to be willing to respond to God, prepared to meet Him, and would your soul be considered precious to Him? Do you possess the type of soul that would allow Him to carry out His eternal plan in and through your life?

6

PASSIONATE SOULS

When I consider real leaders in the Bible in relationship to the kingdom of God, I think of the prophets. Often sole figures who appeared to be loners, radical, and strangers to the world around them, they were in many ways regarded as anything but leaders. One would reason that to be a leader, you must have followers.

People can be leaders in different ways. As already eluded to, the greatest type of leadership is one that leads through example. Those who lead through example are not looking back to see who is following them. The fact that such leaders are sole figures is what often makes them unique in leadership. They are not looking for followers nor are they interested in gaining notoriety.

You can see this in the lives of the prophets of God. The main reason for their attitude was that there was a fiery, burning passion in their souls. This fire was not a matter of good causes or religious convictions that made them unique in their walk; rather, it was a passion for God and the message He entrusted to them. These individuals could do no less but speak with the message they were given. The message not only had a fire behind it, but no doubt it was a message with an attitude.

We see that such passion could stir people to respond to the message being spoken in some way. Those who were stirred up because they knew the message to be true, could not but help respond to it with either obedience or service.

However, such messages could also stir up the wrath of those who were enemies of God and truth. The reality of such passionate souls is that they brought contrast between light and darkness. Such contrast would literally fling hearers into the valley of decision.[1] The hearers could not remain on the fence of indecision. They could not hide in the shadows of dead religion or in the midst of lifeless rituals that lacked substance.

---

[1]   Joel 3:14

Studying the prophets of God allowed me to see into the fierceness that so often separates greatness from that which is mediocre. These men were firebrands of something that could not be easily defined because it was regarded as being radical and often diametrically opposed to what was acceptable, normal, and sane according to the world's estimation.

The leadership the prophets brought to God's kingdom clearly marked the type of leadership that was forged by the hand of God. As you consider these men, they were reluctant souls who had to look beyond human frailties to see that greatness originated with God's estimation of a matter. In many ways these firebrands began from a premise of uncertainty, only to find courage in the message or mission that was given to them. They were indeed humble souls who were awed that a mighty God would even consider them in regard to ministering His affairs.

It was only in light of God, and the fact that they were entrusted with a heavenly message that had an air of urgency to it, that they were empowered with a fierce attitude that would not be quieted by opposition, persecution, or the threat of death. They had to obey what they knew was true, proclaim the message that was burning in their very souls, and maintain their spiritual center by keeping their spiritual bearings.

As I have considered those who possessed passionate souls, I have realized how much aflame the fire burned in their inner being. They could not let go of what they sensed or knew. Perhaps the fuse that lit such a fire varied, but nevertheless the fire was present.

There was a combination that served as the fuse for the firebrands. It was the message, but what set the message ablaze with a fiery passion and urgency was the Spirit of God. The message could be two-fold—that of forthtelling (preaching) and foretelling (predicting future events). These individuals were not fortune tellers. Granted, they proclaimed messages in light of future events. However, these messages admonished, warned, and contended with people based on the type of environment their spiritual lives were producing, not only for themselves, but in regard to future generations.

To me, the first real preacher or prophet who stood out was Noah. We do not have much detail about him, but we know he was a preacher of righteousness.[2] We can safely conclude that his preaching came in two forms: words and actions. No doubt as people asked him what he was doing when building an ark, his answer had to be a proclamation of the judgment that was about to come upon the world. He would have been both forthtelling and foretelling.

As the ark was being constructed, it served as an indictment against the people. Surely there was a plague of skepticism and unbelief present in the onlookers as they possibly mocked any mention of pending or future judgment that was foreign to their understanding.[3] Knowing human nature, these individuals probably scoffed at the so-called "foolishness" of building such an object. However, Noah would not be deterred. His mission was clear, his vision set, and his actions decisive and obedient.

The Bible tells us that because Noah walked with God in the midst of a wicked generation, he found favor. For Noah, grace meant deliverance for him and his family from the judgment that was about to come upon the face of the earth. He had believed God concerning what He showed him, even though it was foreign to his understanding or past experiences. In dread of failing God he obeyed and built an ark. Scripture states that Noah's righteousness is what ultimately brought judgment upon the earth.[4] He was truly a man who brought the contrast of righteousness in the midst of that which was grossly evil. There was no excuse for man to be lost in judgment. What Noah revealed about man is that he often refuses to believe God, thereby, becoming lost to His means of saving him.

True leaders often walk contrary to what most people are willing to accept or believe. For this reason such leaders are often mocked and persecuted. The message they refuse to compromise will prove to be sharp against the foolishness of man's reality, revealing his unbelief towards God and his rebellion against what is true and right.

Another aspect about prophets is that they also served as judges. They would judge or discern the wickedness or righteousness of a matter. For example, judges such as Deborah and Samuel were people who clearly represented the voice of God to the people. We are actually

---

[2]   2 Peter 2:5

[3]   Hebrews 11:7

[4]   Genesis 6:8-9; Hebrews 11:7; 2 Peter 2:5

given an insight into this before Samuel heard the voice of the Lord and became one of His prophets. 1 Samuel 3:1 tells us, "And the child Samuel ministered unto the LORD before Eli. And the word of the LORD was precious in those days; there was no open vision." It is also interesting to note that after four hundred years of silence between the Old and New Testaments, the first one to emerge on the scene was the one who was referred to as the voice crying in the wilderness. We know the voice belonged to John the Baptist.[5]

There is much that we can learn from the examples of these firebrands. Take the prophetess and judge, Deborah. She was a wise trustworthy judge. The people actually came to her for judgment. She was the wife of Lapidoth.[6] According to *Smith's Bible Dictionary*, his name means "torches." Was he the one who often lit her fire with encouragement so she could carry and maintain the torch of truth and justice in Israel?

Can you imagine being a husband of such a woman? The humble military leader, Barak, insisted that she come with him into battle, but her husband had to allow it. He would have to be "comfortable in his own skin" to allow her to be who she was in light of her calling and life before the Lord. This means he most likely was not apt to give way to a fragile ego that could not and would not concede to God. He had to recognize and accept that his wife was who God ordained her to be. In summation, Lapidoth had to be an honorable man in order to avoid thwarting, opposing, or standing in the way of his wife's calling.

For many of God's people the greatest opposition takes place in their own homes. Spouses are often made uncomfortable or brought to a place of complete opposition against their mates because of the calling of God upon their lives. They have to know or be comfortable with who they are before they can comfortably let their spouses fulfill their excellent calling in God.

Deborah led the people of Israel during difficult times. They were being greatly oppressed. Her fame and trustworthy judgments had to be known from afar because people sought her out as to her judgment on matters. We see where she called Barak and asked him whether or not the Lord had commanded him to go and confront the enemy. She

---

[5] Judges 4:4-9; 1 Samuel 3:8; Matthew 3:1-3
[6] Judges 4:4

was forthtelling as she reproved him for not obeying. When she warned Barak that a woman would be accredited for taking down the actual opposing leader of the Canaanites, she was foretelling. The fact that what she predicted came true confirmed she was a true prophetess.[7]

True leaders are not interested in gaining a following, nor are they caught up with confirming their calling. They know who they are and understand what they must do. We see this in the case of Samuel. He not only served as a judge and prophet, but he was a priest as well. He traveled from place to place according to the Lord's directions. He would serve as the last judge to reside over the people of Israel before they insisted on having a king so they could be like the pagan nations around them.[8] Do we not have the same scenario today where people want us to be like the European nations?

When will people learn that the distinction that is often lost is that which is honorable, excellent, and worthy of consideration. I have to admit, I have never seen where people who maintained pagan ways were asked to give up their practices by the world. On the other hand, it appears as if those with wicked agendas do all they can to put away that which is honorable. Distinction that sets people apart has to do with excellent character and honorable practices. Such distinction is necessary if people are going to remain true to who they are individually and as a nation.

Samuel had been trained from an early age about the matters of God. He first heard the Lord's voice when he was young and tender serving Eli the priest. He foretold future events concerning Eli's priesthood before he forthtold the people's consequences for wanting a king to rule over them rather than God. The Lord was with Samuel. It was said of his character that he did not let any word he spoke fall to the ground. In other words, he meant what he said, and said what he meant. If he stated the Lord said something, the people could believe him. He personally identified with the people's sin by mourning their rebellion towards God. He contended with King Saul in his foolishness. Through it all he maintained the integrity and excellence of his calling and position.[9]

---

[7] Deuteronomy 18:20-22; Judges 4:6-9, 19-22

[8] 1 Samuel 8:19-22

[9] 1 Samuel 3:1, 7-21; 8:5-22; 12:2-5; 13:8-14; 15:12-35

True leaders not only rightfully judge, but they have the capacity to see down the road. They cannot be limited by the present situation for much of their message has to do with the fruits that will come forth in the future. If their vision is limited by the present, then they will not know how to lead the people. Without any vision or revelation the people will perish.[10]

We are reminded that integrity is an individual decision or choice. Even if individuals grow up around impeccable character, they can still prove to be scoundrels in the end. People's natural tendency is to go down the path of least resistance. However, real leaders will choose the path of personal discipline, responsibility, and accountability. They will choose the way that challenges them the most, a lifestyle that often does not afford them any excess luxury to partake of frivolous appetites and activities, and standards of excellence that will hold them responsible and accountable to what is true and right.

This leads me to the prophet in 1 Kings 13. I refer to him as, "the unknown prophet" because Scripture does not give us his name. He was sent by God to pronounce judgment on the idolatrous leadership and practices of the newly formed Northern Kingdom of Israel. He was given specific instructions by God to go strait to Bethel and cry against the idolatrous altar located there. Can you imagine the possible passion he had as he proclaimed judgment against the altar? In fact, he prophesied that a person from the house of David by the name of Josiah would burn the bones of men upon it, which, as we know, came true decades later.[11]

God always confirms His word with some type of unmistakable sign. This prophet's message was verified by a sign. However, the prophet's mission was not completed. He was instructed to return to Judah another way. He obeyed the Lord's instructions to a point, but made one small error, he stopped to rest under a tree. It was there that temptation caught up to him and lured him into taking an understandable detour. Judgment was pronounced on him that he would not make it back to Judah.

God's handling of the unknown prophet reveals how serious a matter it is when it comes to obeying all of His instructions. Real leaders understand the need to properly finish the course. This is the only way to ensure that the mission is completed.

---

[10]   Proverbs 29:18

[11]   2 Kings 23:4-20

The unknown prophet shows us that even those who are passionate can be lured away by temptation directed at their weak flesh. Such temptation is meant to thwart their mission in some way. We can see that such a prophet as Elijah had to contend with the weakness of his flesh when he least expected it. Even after he experienced great victory at Mount Carmel, fear cast this prophet into a pit of despair, causing him to take a detour as he ran away from confronting it.[12]

In spite of the detour, God met the prophet. He was not through with him. Elijah had to get his spiritual bearings. He witnessed God's great power, but he still had to hear that small still voice of the Spirit to be reminded of what his mission was. The mission required him to hear the voice of God, be directed by His Spirit, and speak forth the message regardless of the idolatrous environment. He did not have to worry about how others received it. He did not have to single-handedly take on the wicked kingdoms of the likes of Ahab and Jezebel. He just had to speak the message burning in his soul and obey the instructions he was given. He had to stand at the place of the crossroads of indecision where men often stand between two opinions as to who or what to serve.[13]

The prophet Joel described this crossroad of decision in this way, "Multitudes, multitudes in the valley of decision: for the day of the LORD is near in the valley of decision" (Joel 3:14). Because of indecision towards God, many people are suffering from spiritual famine. Amos describes this famine occurs because people are not hearing the Word of God.[14] Even though Americans have many Bibles, people do not have the ability to properly hear or receive the Word in the right way. Their spirits are suffering from malnutrition and their souls are becoming lean and weak from worldly sin and compromise.

After volunteering his service to the Lord, Isaiah actually was warned about the condition that many people had succumbed to due to their spiritual state in Isaiah 6:9-10.

> And he said, Go, and tell this people, Hear ye indeed, but understand not; and see ye indeed, but perceive not. Make the heart of this people fat, and make their ears heavy, and

---

[12] 1 Kings 19:2-4
[13] 1 Kings 18:21; 19:11-14
[14] Amos 8:11-12

shut t heir eyes; least they see with their eyes, and hear with their ears, and understand with their heart, and convert, and be healed.

The Old Testament prophets prove to be an unusual breed. Like Elijah and Elisha they were entrusted with a mantle. This mantle distinguished not only their prophetic office, but their authority to represent God and the power to see a matter through to the end. We can especially observe this in Elisha's life.[15]

Due to Elisha's persistence, he received a double portion when the mantle of Elijah fell upon him after the great prophet was translated. Elisha was not willing to settle for less. For Elijah, the mantle empowered him to pronounce unpopular messages. In the case of Elisha he walked away from the life he lived to prepare himself to live totally consecrated unto the Lord for His use and service.

Elisha would not accept any disrespect towards his authority as a prophet. When young men from Bethel mocked him, he cursed them in the name of the Lord. It is written that two she-bears came out of the woods and tore the foolish young men apart.[16] It is one thing to mock the person and another thing altogether to show disrespect towards that which has been separated unto God. Without the proper respect, people will not even give a person the time of day, let alone listen to what he or she has to say in regard to the Word of the Lord. Disrespect towards the matters of God must not be tolerated.

These godly men had to be committed to the calling of God upon their lives. They never knew what they would encounter or have to endure to deliver the message and finish the course.

There are those who perceive or fancy themselves to be mouthpieces of God. However, if they had to endure the challenges that come with such a position, they would not see it in such an immature, unrealistic way. Such a calling does not make for a glamorous life. Most people are unreceptive towards God's message and mock anything that sets such an individual apart.

Even though prophets were to be watchmen over the souls of men, they were rarely received and often met with persecution. We know that

---

[15]   1 Kings 19:13-14, 19; 2 Kings 2:1-15

[16]   2 Kings 2:23-24

Isaiah was warned that people would not hear or see what he was saying. Jeremiah was told not to be afraid of the faces of those he delivered the messages to, but to remember that he was serving as the Lord's mouthpiece and the Lord would be with him to deliver him. Ezekiel was told that he was a watchman who needed to warn the people of the judgment that was about to come upon them. However, they would not heed the warnings, but, if he failed to warn them, their blood would be upon his hands.[17]

At times these prophets were told to do unusual things. Jeremiah was told to hide a girdle, and then retrieve it. Ezekiel was instructed to lay on both his left and right side to reinforce a point as to the length of the people of Israel's rebellion. Hosea was told to marry a prostitute.[18]

In many ways, these people suffered some type of loss. For Jeremiah, he was told not to marry and Ezekiel was instructed not to mourn the death of his wife.[19] Many prophets were tortured and some martyred. No doubt these men needed the passion of the Spirit to not only endure to the end, but to carry out God's instructions.

These stout-hearted individuals needed an exemplary spirit. Such a spirit is best represented by the prophet Daniel. It is said of him that he had an excellent spirit. This man's conduct was exemplary and consistent. He had purposed in his heart to do it God's way at a vulnerable and challenging time in his life, and he never betrayed it. He was not willing to compromise any aspect of his life even if it meant being eaten by the lions. He was set in his heart when it came to the matters of God, firm in his devotion, and unwavering in his conduct.[20]

The truth of the matter is that the world is not worthy to witness such a passionate commitment from unwavering souls. Most people prefer what we call "pillow prophets." These are the popular prophets who will tell people what they want to hear. Like a good story teller, they will lull people to sleep with fables that will please the flesh and tickle the ears. Their messages will allow such individuals to comfortably lay down in their cesspool of sin and unbelief as they slide closer and closer

---

[17]   Isaiah 6:9; Jeremiah 1:7-10; Ezekiel 3:17-21; James 5:20

[18]   Jeremiah 13:1-7: Ezekiel 4:4-8; Hosea 1:2

[19]   Jeremiah 16:2-4; Ezekiel 24:15-18

[20]   Daniel 1:8; 6:3-28

to the abyss of hell in blissful ignorance that all is indeed not well with their worlds.

It is for these reasons that these rare firebrands are sent forth by God. They will cut through the spiritual dullness of people's souls and penetrate their darkness with the distinct light of God's truth in hopes of pulling someone out of the fires of destruction.

Today, these prophets and their messages have established an incredible foundation that cannot be moved. It is upon this foundation that we believers have the opportunity to construct our spiritual lives. It is because of their prophecies that we can be sure of what God has promised us, entrusted to us, and what He will bring forth in us in the present age we live in and in the world yet to come.[21]

---

[21]   Ephesians 4:11-13; 2 Peter 1:19-21

7

ENDURING SOULS

Jesus made this statement about the leadership of the world, "Ye know that the princes of the Gentiles exercise dominion over them, and they that are great exercise authority over them" (Matthew 20:25). Then He goes on to say that such practice will not hold true for those who are leaders in the kingdom of God. Whosoever will be considered great among those who follow Him, must be a servant of all.

It is because the world is upside down that many leaders fail to recognize their position of leadership. In the world's mind how can people exercise dominion over others unless they are strong and powerful? How can they exercise authority over others unless they have the means to carry out, either by flattery or brute force, what was ordained?

Yet, Jesus made it clear that true leadership is not based on how much power a person can exert, or how much authority he or she might claim. Acceptable leadership is based on greatness, but such greatness is measured by one's service to God and others.

Clearly, in God's kingdom we have been shown that greatness is not measured by how much we can persuade or exert pressure on someone; rather, it is measured by gentleness that has been tempered by the Spirit of God. We have learned that it is not those who perceive they are leaders who prove to be great in such leadership positions; instead, it is those individuals who are reluctant, uncertain, and humbled to be in places of leadership that often prove to be great leaders. These unassuming people are inspired by a passion to do what is necessary and would consider it dishonorable and disgraceful if they failed to fulfill their reasonable service or obligations. In many ways, such individuals are willing to sacrifice all that they have for a matter that they consider to be worthy and greater in vision than their present reality.

These are the qualities that make up such souls who find themselves often thrust into leadership positions because of the times they live in. They often feel they are born out of season. In other words, they cannot imagine that they were meant to shine at this time. They perceive that perhaps another time or age would allow them the environment to somehow function in a greater capacity. Clearly, in their present environment they feel inept, unequipped, and insignificant to take on the task before them. But, they also know they cannot ignore that which has been branded on their inner souls. They cannot deny what is at hand. They did not design the matter or times in which they were born and lived. They cannot ignore the task which calls for their intervention. In their minds it is not a matter of fate, but of a destiny that they cannot and would not deny or ignore. To do so would be a denial of all that is real, good, important, and honorable. In essence, it would deny the very existence of God's providence that rests upon all matters.

This brings us to the next example of leadership in Scripture. Our first introduction to this individual begins with Gabriel, the angel who seems associated with delivering messages that directly involve the Jewish people. He announces in the temple to the elderly Zacharias that his prayers, and the prayers of his wife, Elisabeth, were about to be answered.[1]

And, what did their prayers entail? To have a child. However, like Abraham and Sarah of old, it seemed impossible for them to have a child. Elisabeth had been barren and appeared to be past such a season in her life for such a blessed event to take place. But, to God miracles are not an abnormal matter; rather, it was the way things were to be done to confirm, reinforce, and bring into focus the matters of eternity.

It is important to point out that God was not simply answering the prayers of this couple, but it was all part of His plan and timing. It was only proper that the child of Zacharias and Elisabeth be enveloped and associated with the miraculous. He had, after all, been prophesied. He would not only come forth out of a womb considered barren and of past season, but he would also come forth out of the barren wilderness of humanity into the midst of that which was lifeless and had been held captive to the darkness of the world. He would come forth after 400 years of silence from heaven. He would come forth as a voice that would be distinct, loud, and clear. The part he was to play in God's plan of redemption was of the uttermost importance. He was to prepare the Jewish people for the long-awaited Messiah.

---

[1] Luke 1:5-25

His name would also be important. Due to Zacharias's unbelief towards the message of Gabriel, he was struck dumb. His wife would be given the name of the child. No doubt his very name would be revealed to her heart as she meditated on the wonder of it all. The child's name would be the first word out of Zacharias's mouth after months of silence. This miraculous child who would bring great joy to his parents, hope to the wandering souls around him, and who was born out of season apart from man's will and capacity, would be called, "John."

According to *Smith's Bible Dictionary,* the name "John" is the same name as "Johanan," a contraction of "Jehohanan." "Johanan" means "the gift or grace of God" or "Jehovah's gift" John would no doubt prove to be an unexpected gift from God to his parents. Since he was somewhat "born out of season," he would also prove to be a matter of God's incredible grace.

God was not only about to give Zacharias and Elisabeth a gift from heaven, but He was about to show His favor by injecting the very gift of His only begotten Son into the midst of humanity. John would be the one who would come out of the wilderness preparing and introducing this gift of God. In fact, it would be in his mother's womb that John's calling and destiny would begin to take shape. It would be from the confines of the womb that he would not only verify or point to Jesus, but he would be anointed to fulfill His calling and sealed to his destiny by the Holy Ghost.[2]

Most people are content to live their lives on the plateau or plains of normalcy. However, greatness comes from outside of normalcy. Few realize that in every season or age, extraordinary events require or afford man to step outside of such normalcy to discover how God can take the nominal and impact both the physical and unseen worlds.

The Bible is clear that we are each predestinated to be conformed to the heavenly in the midst of the nominal.[3] Clearly, we are to take on something that is eternal in order to impact the age we live in. We do not realize that we have been born according to a designated season and time. Such a realization should cause us to ponder that perhaps we have been entrusted with a certain "destiny" besides the one we have settled into. We must be open to discover it.

---

[2]   Luke 1:39-45

[3]   Romans 8:29

We must understand that such destiny will never be found in normalcy; rather, it will come from outside of such an environment. It must be interjected into our being and plans. However, for such an interjection to occur, we must be prepared for the hand of providence to intrude into our nominal times when least expected. It will not seem normal, logical, and the way things should function. It is an intrusion that signifies or puts a mark on the extraordinary matter at hand.

As servants of God, we must not think such an intrusion is abrasive, unfair, and insignificant. We must not show contempt for it because we simply want to live life on the plateaus of comfort and convenience. We must recognize that even though our lives, or the affect we may have on such times, may start out as a small pebble cast into the water of humanity, God can take the small ripple it produces and turn it into a wave that will indeed affect the present terrain of the world we live in. The truth is, we do not, nor are we, always intended to know the affect such a ripple will have on the shoreline of people's lives, but God knows the destiny of such ripples. He has ordained each one according to His foreknowledge. After all, it was His intrusion according to an eternal plan that started the ripple affect with John the Baptist's conception.

This brings us back to John. He was anointed and sealed in the womb, but he would be prepared in the barren wilderness. There would be nothing normal about his existence. We do not know anything about his life after his conception and baptism in his mother's womb or during his formative years, but we do get a sense of him when he appears on the scene 30 years later.

Although he could have served as a priest in Herod's extravagant temple, wearing priestly clothing, his attire was made of camel's hair, his loins defined by a leather belt, and his food was locusts and honey. From the womb John was ordained to be a Nazarite. The vow of a Nazarite meant he could not cut his hair, drink wine nor strong drink, nor have any association with even the products that were associated with any fermentation. Such fermentation was related to the effects of sin or defilement. If John was to be drunk with anything, it was to be with the fullness of God's Spirit.[4] Nazarites were dedicated to God, consecrated to avail themselves to serve Him, and set apart to be distinguished by their devotion and their service to Jehovah.

---

4   Numbers 6:1-8; Matthew 1:4; 1 Corinthians 5:7-8; Ephesians 5:18-19

John would be the one who would connect the old with the new. His camel's hair raiment was worn by the prophets of old. His voice crying out of the wilderness would point to the fire and urgency of the message he had been entrusted with. It would identify him to his prophetical office that was predicted by Malachi. Malachi 3:2 gave us insight into this man's passion and impact, "But who may abide the day of his coming? And who shall stand when he appeareth? For he is like a refiner's fire, and like fuller's soap."

Malachi 4:5 states that this prophet would have a ministry like Elijah. Jesus brought this up in Matthew 11:13-14. Obviously, the Jewish people were actually looking for Elijah, not one who was like Elijah. To this day, some Orthodox Jewish homes keep an empty chair at their table to welcome Elijah. In their minds he is still to come. However, he came to prepare the way for the Messiah. He stood ablaze amidst dead religion and declared that an axe would be put to the roots of the tree. He called people to repentance that would be alive with works that would verify a complete change in their disposition, attitude, and ways.

John's uncut hair would identify him to his form of consecration. Clearly, he had been totally consecrated to God and sanctified by God to carry out a very important mission. His food would classify his training ground. Obviously, he ate the physical food found in the barren wilderness of preparation, but he was nurtured on the Word of God. His voice would be distinct, his warning of forthtelling and foretelling would display that cutting edge that would leave no doubt or room to debate, speculate, or for wishful thinking. He would bring the old together with the new. He would connect the dots as he pointed to the Messiah, the one who would be the fulfillment of the old covenant established in prophesy and the Law, as well as become the unfolding of the new covenant that would be brought forth through His sacrifice as God's Passover Lamb.

To try to capture the appearance of John is something that has been done by the best attempts of Hollywood. But, could we begin to imagine what this man may have looked liked when he hit the scene and landed in the midst of the drum beat of the pomp and circumstance that was present? You had the self-righteous religious camps of the Jewish priests and Levites and the governmental ranks of Caesar. Both camps were co-existing in a quasi state that often hid dirty politics between the two groups. This was quite obvious in how both sides handled Jesus the night before His crucifixion. He became a hot potato that was often thrown back and forth as each side tried to outmaneuver the other. Their co-existence would present a picture of a false peace as both sides placated each other with chess moves to balance the fragile power that could easily cave in or erupt like a volcano at any time.

In such a state, the sheep have a tendency to become unsettled in their souls. There is a false sense of security that brings no real stability or confidence. The meal being served up has no substance or lasting qualities to it. The voices that are being heard are self-serving and have no mark of eternity to them. In the empty vacuum left by such environments there are what we refer to as the "restless natives" that are ready to strike and cause an insurrection against the insane and senseless environment that is present.

In such an environment a voice is heard coming out of the wilderness. This voice has been set afire by the Spirit of the Living God, and prepared in the wilderness of obscurity. After 400 years of silence from heaven, this voice appeared to arise out of the ashes of conflict during a time of spiritual drought of grave proportions. The voice is calling man to repentance for the kingdom of heaven was coming near to him.[5]

How can people recognize the Messiah unless they are turned in repentance from their lifeless practices, compromising worldly ways, and empty pursuits? It is for this reason that John instructed people to bring forth fruits worthy of repentance.[6] People must cease to peer into the darkness brought on by the age they live in, and turn to the light to face the living God in repentance and brokenness. They must be able to see that which has caused brokenness to their lives, their relationships, and that sever their spiritual connection with God. They must see in order for reconciliation and restoration to take place.

Hence, came the voice, ready to proclaim and reinforce the message that was burning in John's bosom. To reinforce the message, he would baptize in the wilderness, and preach repentance for the remission of sins.[7] The point of identification that people had truly repented would also be identified to his person and work. The identification would be

---

[5] Matthew 3:1-3

[6] Luke 3:3-14

[7] Mark 1:3-5

baptism, where a person's sins were symbolically being remitted or washed away in the water of baptism. John would also be distinguished by the act of water baptism. He would be best known as John the Baptist. He would also be the one who would baptize the Messiah to suffice righteous requirements.

However, water baptism was not just a physical symbol, it was an example of how a person's very life needed to change. There had to be a point of total immersion into what God had ordained. There had to be evidence of a complete inward change towards the matters of God. There had to be separation from the old in order to embrace the new, to ensure that heaven's mission would not fail.

The preaching of repentance and the symbol of baptism was John's way of preparing people to recognize their Promised Messiah. He would simply point Him out. If John was a man of pride he would have taken advantage of people's ignorance and vulnerability. He would also have accepted their conclusions or speculations that he was the Messiah.[8]

John the Baptist made it quite clear that he was not the Messiah; rather, he was the voice that was to come first. Clearly, John knew who he was, understood his mission, and was quite content in obeying God. John was a true servant of both God and man.

Subsequently, this brings us to what made John the Baptist great in the kingdom of God. Remember, Jesus stipulated that the greatest among His followers, would be considered the least among them. Their greatness would not be distinguished by how many people followed them, but what caliber of servant they proved to be in relationship to the kingdom of God.

In John the Baptist's life we see what real greatness entailed. It involves regression. Many people were attracted to this firebrand's ways and message. But, John did not come to stand out in the crowd, lead people to some great religious pinnacle, or be known as some great pastor or preacher. He came to point man to the Messiah, while regressing from the spotlight. He came to point to, direct, and declare the "Anointed One" to everyone who would hear. He came to give way to the One who needed to become people's all-consuming reality. This reality would invade man's vision, heart, and mind with light, hope, and salvation. This was John's mission. He was not confused about it. Even though his

---

8   Mark 1:7; Luke 3:15-18

soul was constantly being consumed by his mission, he would not sway from the path ordained by his destiny. He had endured the preparation of obscurity and the harsh elements of the wilderness. No doubt he was aware that his time to fulfill his destiny would be short. Meanwhile, his life would burn with great intensity to light the way for others, until the unveiling of the greater light of the Messiah, which would not only signify completion of his mission, but would completely overshadow it.

When the light of the Promised Messiah lit up the countryside, John the Baptist would be content to take the back seat. He described himself as the best man to the bridegroom.[9] He was there to assist the bridegroom in any way he could. In summation, he was there to make the occasion of God's visitation and intrusion into history a matter of great importance as he made sure that the spotlight would come to rest on the Son of God. He would gladly recede into the background, rejoicing with the bridegroom, knowing his calling and purpose was being fulfilled. The Promised One who was truly worthy of all consideration would ultimately be honored, exalted, and worshipped by those who made up His bride. John the Baptist even summarized this regression when he made this statement in John 3:30, "He must increase, but I must decrease."

Most people who have any knowledge of the Bible know what happened to John the Baptist. Since he was a firebrand, he would not be silent about sin, the judgment to come, and about the times in which he lived. He called sin, sin, even when it came to the powerful leaders of the Roman Empire. He stepped on toes with the truth. Even though he brought some fear to the hearts of people such as Herod, he also spurned utter contempt by others such as Herod's wife.

John the Baptist was not the head of the body or the church that would rise out of the travailing that was wrought on a cross. He was the best man, the servant who came for a time to prepare for a specific occasion in order to give way to the One who was worthy. His leadership was powerful, but he had to decrease while the head of the Body, the Church, became the center focus. We know that John the Baptist would lose his head to the despots of the world after his mission was completed, but his example would forever be lifted up in the inspired and prophetical Word of God. He would actually be eulogized by the

---

[9] John 3:28-29

bridegroom, the Son of the Living God. We read this eulogy in Matthew 11:1-19.

It would benefit us well if we consider what Jesus said about John. We are given much insight into greatness when it comes to the kingdom of God. To understand the significance of greatness in God's eyes, we must once again recognize that our whole mission is not to be great, but to honor that which is worthy and great.

Greatness only becomes a reality when a person is identified to it. John the Baptist was only made great because of the mission he was entrusted with. Granted he carried out the mission and endured to the end, but he knew that what he was doing was his destiny. Obviously, the greatness did not rest in who he was, but in the message and the calling that was bestowed upon his life by the very hand of God. Clearly, John the Baptist never started out to be great, and was glad to recede when that which was worthy was unveiled and exalted.

It is also important to point out that even though John the Baptist was a prophet, he never did any miracles. What made him stand apart was the message. It was inspired to reach into the souls of men, cut away the dross from people's ears, become a salve to their eyes, and reach into their very depths with hope and purpose. It was to cause them to hear the warnings of where they were going, to see where they had to go, and be receptive to receive what had been ordained for their lives from before the foundation of the world.

At his eulogy, Jesus asked the people who did they go out to the wilderness to see? Was it some reed that was shaking in the air according to the fickle winds of the world, or did they go to see one who spoke the truth with the authority of heaven and in the power of the Spirit? Did they see a man who came from kingly houses, whose clothes spoke of the riches of the world and the façade of religious righteousness, or did they see a servant who was prepared in obscurity and wore the mantle of a prophet? It is from this premise that Jesus made this statement, "Verily I say unto you, Among them that are born of women there hath not risen a greater than John the Baptist: notwithstanding, he that is least in the kingdom of heaven is greater than he" (Matthew 11:11).

Once again, in the kingdom of heaven, we are reminded that anyone can be greater than those who have gone on before him or her. However, greatness is measured by how abased individuals become in their souls before God and in their service to others. Jesus even admitted that those who followed Him could end up witnessing greater works.[10] This statement, of course, is in relationship to the empowerment of the Holy Spirit upon the many-membered Church sent forth by Jesus Christ with the message of salvation and hope to the lost and downtrodden souls.

There has been criticism from some towards John the Baptist. Jesus' eulogy was given after John sent some of his disciples to question Jesus' identity. However, I do not believe this was unbelief on John the Baptist's part. My take on this was that in light of facing his own death, John wanted the necessary assurance that he had completed his mission. A precious soul such as his would not be content to let go of this present world until he or she was assured that his or her mission was completed.

Jesus told John the Baptist's disciples to go back and tell him what they had heard as far as His teachings and what they had seen as far as the miracles. However, there was something else that was said that in the right context might also have confirmed that not only had John the Baptist completed his mission, but it was successful. John the Baptist would have understood the meaning behind this statement that is greatly misunderstood today.

Let us consider what was said in regard to John the Baptist's ministry. "And from the days of John the Baptist until now the kingdom of heaven suffereth violence, and the violent take it by force" (Matthew 11:12). Most people interpret this Scripture as seizing upon the kingdom of heaven by force, but John the Baptist never used any such force. In their book about the difficult words of Jesus, authors David Bivin and Roy Blizzard explained that this was actually an idiom. It had to do with a shepherd putting his sheep in a pen overnight. He would block most of the pen with rocks and put someone in charge to block the opening for the night as a means to guard the sheep. By morning the sheep would be restless and pushing against the sides of the pen to get out to water and pasture. When the one who blocked the entrance stepped out of the narrow opening to let the sheep out, they would almost violently knock the walls down. Clearly, John the Baptist created such a hunger and thirst in the flock of God that when he stepped aside for the Messiah, it caused them to break forth from the pens that held them captive to pursue, not only the life that awaited them, but the Shepherd who would lead them to the pastures of God's will and the living Waters of the Spirit.

---

[10]   John 5:20

John the Baptist had indeed proved to be an enduring, trustworthy soul when it came to the matters of God. His willingness to recognize greatness and give way to it proved the character of his person. His life may have only shined forth for a short period of time, but his character would endure to the end and continues to endure as an example of true greatness in the kingdom of heaven.

8

Unlikely Souls

We have been considering the type of soul who will, in unexpected ways, emerge as a great leader. The one common denominator between many of these individuals is that they are considered unlikely souls in regard to acceptable leadership according to the world's standards. They may be considered insignificant and from all appearances have no real ability, worldly means, or points of attraction that would be able to influence others. In many cases, such individuals are not in positions to wield any real influence. They appear hidden away or oppressed by the events around them, or in humble positions and lonely places that imply that they have been born out of season in relationship to the times they live in. In essence, they appear to be the odd man out or the odd duck that will never fit in the scheme of things.

The question is what do true candidates who would be deemed as possible leaders by God look like? We know from Scripture that God looks at the heart, but what is He looking for in regard to disposition, attitude, conduct, capabilities, and strength? Surprisingly, God laid out the criteria He is looking for in such a person. The Apostle Paul described such an individual in 1 Corinthians 1:18-28.

Before we can get into the criteria of what such a creature looks like, we must understand the premise and perspective within which these criteria are being presented. The Apostle Paul presents the criteria of greatness in light of how people perceive and react in relationship to the Gospel.

The simple message of the cross where Jesus died for our sins, and where His body was buried in a silent grave for three days and nights, only to rise up in resurrection power in a glorified body, seems either impossible or too ridiculous for people of various ages to receive as truth. Such a message seems insignificant and out of touch with the particular challenges of each age. However, it is the memorandum that was established by God. It is the challenging proclamation that shakes each age regardless of the times in which people live. It is a message that cannot be silenced by the greatest attempts of religion to refute or replace it and the world's attempts to disqualify it.

As the Apostle Paul pointed out, there are two premises in which most people will perceive the message of heaven, along with all of its implications. The first premise that many people will consider the Gospel from is their religious understanding and traditions. This was true for the Jews. They regarded all spiritual matters according to their religious perspective and various traditions. Their reaction towards the preaching of the cross became a stumbling block to them. They thought it to be absurd, but they could not get around it. They had sought the signs that were to identify the Promised One, but even though such signs followed the man known as Jesus of Nazareth, these unbelieving souls would not accept the claims that He was the Son of God.

These leaders also would not accept the challenge Jesus clearly posed to the fragile power they held in the age in which they lived. Instead of establishing their religious kingdom, He advocated another kingdom. Rather than ushering in the national sovereignty of Israel, He died on the cross. No matter how they debated it in the courts of the synagogues or in the outer courts of the temple, the exigent reality of Jesus never went away. Due to the witness of His resurrection, the proclamation of the Gospel seemed to crop up in unlikely places, posing a real challenge to their religious kingdom.

The second type of reaction towards the Gospel came from those who considered themselves intellectual, rational souls. During Paul's day such people fell into the category of the Greeks. The Greeks took great pride in their intellectual ability to question, rationalize, philosophize, and seek the deep insights in regard to life and the matters that affected the world they lived in. They had erected many gods to explain the unexplained. The problem with such exercise was that these gods were no different than mere man in his appetites, emotional makeup, and handling of the matters of life.

Even though Greeks sought wisdom about the matters of life, they could not discern true wisdom. They often viewed the wisdom of heaven as being foolishness. They would scoff at it with great scorn.

The Jews were forever trying to silence the truth about Jesus, but the Greeks were deeming it as being beneath their consideration. Even though the Greeks had done much to explain the unseen, they often humanized any concept of God and deified man in some way. In so many ways man stood equal with any concept of God, producing myths about God. This handling of the Gospel was their way of deeming it as too stupid to regard, and completely impertinent in light of what they considered to be great knowledge.

These are the two attitudes that the Apostle Paul often confronted when it came to the preaching of the Gospel. As Paul clearly declared in Romans 1:16, the Gospel was and is the power of God unto salvation. However, neither group was open to the Gospel, thereby, negating or doing away with its ability to penetrate the darkness of their souls with the truth of God's glorious provision.

It is from the premise of these two attitudes that we gain God's perspective. The Jews could not properly debate the Gospel, while the power of the Gospel often revealed that the Greeks were the ones who proved to be foolish in their attitude towards it. As we consider God's perspective of the Gospel, we see that God was pleased to use what was considered foolish by those of the religious and intellectual worlds to proclaim salvation to those who were open to believe. These individuals were receptive to the message of heaven that was simple and pure. It had the capacity to actually ring true in their spirits, thereby, inspiring the faith that allowed them to receive eternal life.

It is at this point that God brings an indictment against the foolish evaluation of these two groups. It is His evaluation that reveals the criteria in regard to those who He would use in the scheme of things to bring forth His kingdom. When you consider His criteria, you will see how He uses the unlikely souls to serve as those who would lead others to His kingdom in search of truth, hope, and salvation.

God's first indictment is that He uses what is considered foolishness by the world to actually reveal His wisdom. He takes what is considered as weakness by the arrogant to show His strength that is clearly established through righteousness. Obviously, God uses that which is unlikely and unacceptable to the world to show Himself to those who are truly seeking Him. It is His way of bringing a clear contrast between the world and His character, ways, and kingdom. It is for this reason that we are reminded that the poor in spirit will inherit the kingdom of God and the pure in heart will see Him.[1]

---

[1] Matthew 5:3, 8

Let us consider this contrast. The Apostle Paul reminded the Corinthians of their calling. He wanted them to note that those who were being called and used by God were not considered wise by the world, nor did they possess any real means to influence others. They did not hold noble positions in light of birth and heritage. This was His way to confound the wise of the world by using what appeared insignificant and weak.

God clearly chose the base things of the world. "Base" has to do with the unknown. Such people would not be regarded as having anything to offer. However, it is the base things which God is able to exalt to a place of significance. In such exaltation it is not the instrument or vessel that will receive the glory, but the One who is showing Himself mighty through such an insignificant creature.[2] Keep in mind that most creatures who see themselves as being the least and are considered base have no idea that they are being used in such a glorious way. It is for this reason that God uses them.

When you consider Moses, you see how God hid him away in an ark as a baby until the right person came along to properly exalt him in an unlikely way. However, Moses would find himself born out of season when the people of Israel were not ready to recognize or receive his leadership. He was once again hidden away in the wilderness, where he lived the simple life of a shepherd.[3]

In the eyes of the Egyptians, the position of being a shepherd was considered a despised position.[4] In other words, it was an abomination, a position of contempt. Talk about being debased and despised in relationship to being raised in the courts of Pharaoh. As a shepherd, Moses would be least esteemed in the eyes of the Egyptians, unknown by the people of Israel, and set at naught by his lonely status in the wilderness. Who would have ever guessed that this man at the age of 80 would be called out of the wilderness to fulfill his destiny as the shepherd and giver of the Law of the nation of Israel?

Consider Gideon. He did not seem like any real leader. His activities were often done in secret for fear of Israel's enemies. He appeared to hold

---

[2] Luke 18:14
[3] Exodus 2:1-15
[4] Genesis 46:34

no real significance to anyone of his community. How many would have suspected that he would lead a small army to tremendous victory?

When you think of the orphan, Esther, hidden away by her status among many, who would have thought that she would ever be queen? What about Mary, a handmaiden who held no real position in her community or in the eyes of the world? Who would have ever suspected that God would choose her to be the mother of the Messiah? Let us not forget Joseph, a carpenter. How many would have guessed that he would be entrusted to raise the Son of God in such a lowly position?

What about King David? He started out as a mere shepherd, hidden away among the sheep. As a shepherd, he knew how to face the lion and bring down a bear, but his feats were never published in the countryside. He was considered arrogant by his brother and foolish for wanting to face Goliath. Until then he was not even considered at all. He was an unlikely soul, regarded insignificant by those who passed him by, as well as being held in utter contempt by his enemy, Goliath. Even after his victory over the giant, he was content to be a shepherd.[5]

When you consider those who made up what I consider to be David's motley army, you have an unlikely assortment of men. Granted, some of the army was made up of David's relatives, but we are told that the men who followed him sought him out because they were in distress, in debt, and discontented. In many ways they were wanderers, failures, fugitives, and out of sorts with the present situation.[6] However, some of these men proved to be courageous, honorable, and sacrificial in their allegiance and service to David.

Another unlikely candidate was a man named Nehemiah. He was a simple cup-bearer to the king in Shushan. Granted, he was the first front line of defense in protecting the king when it came to poisoning the king through food or drink. Clearly, the king had to have an impeccable trust in this man's character to entrust his life to him, but who would have thought a cup-bearer would lead in the rebuilding of the walls of Jerusalem while enemies clamored and threatened to destroy and thwart all attempts to finish the project. It was Nehemiah who instructed the men of Israel to hold a sword in one hand and a hammer in the other.[7]

---

[5]   1 Samuel 17:28-58

[6]   1 Samuel 22:1-2

[7]   Nehemiah 2:2-8; 4:17-18

This brings us to the next group of unlikely candidates in God's kingdom of God: the disciples of Jesus. The world's concept is to look for great men. The reason for this is because it is great men that make the world appear great. For example, consider how athletes make a particular sport or event desirable and great to the masses. People pay to see the athlete they admire most or the team that has earned their loyalty. It is the idea of greatness that makes the things and activities of the world attractive and great to the onlooker. The world rewards such greatness with titles and trophies, but without displays of greatness there would be no real attractions to entangle people into a false idea of what constitutes real accomplishments of importance. Without the greatness or distinction of people in certain arenas, the world would have no contrast or means to offer the masses any form of prominence that could be found and admired by them.

It is for this reason that God's perspective is contrary to the world's idea of greatness. It has already been alluded to as to why God would choose such unlikely people to be leaders in His kingdom. The Apostle Paul clearly verified that no man will glory in the Lord's presence about fleshly accomplishments, nor would he ever be able to complete with God's incredible majesty on any front.[8] Therefore, the world thinks of those the Lord uses as being base and despises those whom He exalts for the contrast they bring to the world.

Those who are great in God's kingdom will not agree with the world's idea of greatness and will not be impressed with who the world chooses to call great. Let's face it, very few people the world exalts display any real integrity or character. Such individuals often prove to be foolish in their dealings, hypocritical in their presentations, and undesirable in their lifestyles. As someone once observed, morality sees further than the intellect touted by the world or the abilities of mere man.

When you consider the disciples of Jesus, they certainly would fit the criteria of being considered foolish and base by the world. We know that due to the contrast and challenge they posed to the Jewish and Roman leaders, they became despised on different fronts. Who would have thought that an assortment of men who were unknown or unaccepted by the world, for the most part, would become Jesus' disciples? Consider Jesus' disciples. Some were known as insignificant fishermen, another,

---

[8]   1 Corinthians 1:29-31

a despised tax-collector, and there was one who belonged to a group of zealots who refused any compromising ground when it came to the Law of Moses. However, these insignificant men would be used to turn the world upside down. Granted, a couple of the men were willing to follow Jesus, even to their demise; but, even among such bravery and their best intentions, when tested, they proved to be cowards. For Peter, he not only followed Jesus afar off in His darkest time, but he denied he even knew Him. For Thomas, he doubted that Jesus rose from the grave even though his comrades declared they had seen Him.[9]

You can also see those who had a passion in them like the Sons of Thunder, James and John. They wanted to call fire down from heaven on the Samaritans because they would not regard Jesus in a proper manner. However, Jesus rebuked them for being in the wrong spirit.[10]

Among these men you can see great zeal, as well as great fear. You can see men who were willing to forsake all, but failed to believe that they were safely in the providence of God's hand of protection and His will when confronted with the buffeting storms of life. Here were men who witnessed great miracles, but when their precious leader died on the cross, they did not believe in a great deliverance. Here were men who heard of great promises, but hid in darkness and unbelief when the fulfillment of the greatest promise was unveiled to women at an empty tomb.

These men were a dichotomy. They were fickle in so many ways, inconsistent, and unsure. In some ways they faced their lack. On one occasion they asked the Lord to teach them to pray. They occasionally displayed humility as they came to places of awe and worship before Jesus, only to squabble over which one of them would be considered great in the kingdom of God. They knew that the Lord regarded the poor, insignificant, and despised, and yet they quietly wondered why Jesus would give any real consideration to a Samaritan woman at a well. There were times when they were even transparent about the fact that they were unsure of their own character, like the night Jesus was betrayed. When He told them that one of them would betray Him, they all asked if they would turn out to be the culprit. Even though at times they displayed commendable loyalty to Jesus, they also revealed their

9   Matthew 26:31-35, 56; John 11:14-16; 20:19-29; Acts 17:6
10   Luke 9:51-56

human side when they scattered in the night during Jesus' ordeal that led up to Calvary.

What one word could describe Jesus' disciples? It would be the word "ordinary." Greatness can only be realized in light of what the world considers to be ordinary. What makes the ordinary great is when the extraordinary is accomplished through that which is considered commonplace. No one expects something of significance to ever come out of the ordinary. After all, it is what it is. It does not stand out, nor does it make a mark. It is not regarded as to whether it fits or does not fit in the scheme of things. It is just there, functioning like so much of the grind that takes place in the world.

God took these ordinary men and caused the world they lived in to take note of them, as many stumbled over them. Although poor in the sight of men, they were rich in faith.[11] Peter said it best to the lame beggar outside of the temple, "Silver and gold have I none: but such as I have give I thee: In the name of Jesus Christ of Nazareth, rise up and walk" (Acts 3:6b). Miracles followed these men of faith, confirming their message of the Gospel, as well as their faith in the One who they upheld and declared to be the Messiah, the Promised One, the Son of God.

The followers of Jesus caused a response wherever they went. After Pentecost, they talked in unknown tongues in order to proclaim the Gospel message among the many foreigners that were present with convincing authority and undisputable power. When the religious leaders considered Peter and John, they saw unlearned, ignorant men, yet they had to take note that they had been with Jesus.[12]

The followers of Jesus' distinction rest in the fact that they truly had been impacted by His life and teachings, and that they also had been anointed by His powerful Spirit to proclaim the Gospel. Although this message was simple, it challenged the fragile world of the religious and exposed the foolishness of the age they lived in, while becoming a source of hope to the ordinary person. The other part that became undeniable was even though these ordinary men once were considered too ignorant or insignificant to take seriously, they could not be moved away from their mission of proclaiming the Gospel no matter how much the intellectuals and religious debated, threatened, or persecuted them.

---

[11]   James 2:5
[12]   Acts 2:1-21; 4:13

What can we learn about greatness in God's kingdom from these ordinary men? God seeks out and uses such a person. The reason why is because ordinary men realize that greatness is not measured by the vessel, but by the impact something leaves. The ordinary man never perceives that he has reached a pinnacle of religious or intellectual greatness or belongs to an elite group that has a corner on a matter. In fact, such ordinary individuals have nothing to lose and possibly everything to gain if they step outside of the nominal boundaries allotted to them by society to expose themselves to the extraordinary. It is from such a premise that these individuals are able to embrace that which has been cut out of a different cloth. In fact, they might gain that which is impossible if they are willing to leave the ordinary status behind in order to embrace what is marked by the excellent ways of that which is truly outstanding.

The ordinary man accepts a higher calling. It is not a matter of changing his status; rather, it is a matter of discovering his purpose and fulfilling his destiny. It is not a matter of doing that which is extraordinary, it is a matter of discovering what his life can be if he is willing to risk it all to explore the possibilities of that which has been stamped into his being by something greater than he. And, it is not just a matter of fulfilling some type of destiny, but experiencing the excellent ways in which such a destiny will be fulfilled through him for the glory of that which is eternal, unseen, and unchangeable.

These ordinary men were always walking towards their demise. In the end, some would forever fade from historical accounts to remain unknown for the most part. No doubt their names and deeds are recorded in another book, while the impact they left would be noted in the very corridors of heaven. In the case of others, their lives, letters, and deeds would be recorded in the Bible, while some would go on to become legends time could never erase.

When it comes to the kingdom of God, greatness is always born out of the ordinary. It never begins from that which is already considered great by the world, but from that which is considered foolish, base, and despised. It is from this premise that real greatness is realized.

It is hard to find real hope in the world. However, if Christians grasp this simple truth about greatness, it can bring great hope to their souls and expectation to their spirits. It can cause them to realize that so much of the world we live in banks on people accepting the ordinary rather than exposing themselves to and pursuing the extraordinary. It is from this premise the ordinary person dares to believe that the impossible can take place in his or her life, the incredible can be realized in his or her journey, and the excellent can be obtained in a world that attempts to minimize his or her potential for the type of greatness God regards and advocates, by simply labeling it "ordinary."

9

RELENTLESS SOULS

When we think of great leaders, we think of those who have accomplished great feats or victories. However, there are many people who were not necessarily on what we consider the right side of a matter such as in the case of military conflicts. But, in light of history these individuals were and are still considered to be great leaders. Perhaps these people did possess some incredible abilities in the area of displaying a military mind in which to devise incredible strategies. However, these same individuals are not always widely known except to those who study such matters.

If you consider some of the generals who fought in the Civil War, you find men who were not only considered great leaders on the Confederate side, but they were also great men. To think these men gave their lives up for a lost or questionable cause, such as to maintain slavery is absurd. The truth is for many of the men in the Confederacy the issue was not about slavery, but state's sovereignty. The right for people to govern themselves at the state level was a moral and ethical matter of the utmost importance to some of these men. After all, such a concept went back to the fuse that lit the passionate fires that were fanned into a blaze in the Revolutionary War.

So much of our history appears black and white, but it is not. Many people will not choose a side that casts shadows or darkness on their character. They will not die for causes that are not regarded as honorable and decent. What many people fail to realize is that many great people die on both sides when conflict arises. If you could question them about the whys, you would discover that they were fighting for something that would have been considered noble and honorable indeed.

It is for this reason that the tyrants and despots of the world must find the right cause in order to convince the masses to fight. Whether it is legit or not is immaterial to them. They are simply trying to stir up the masses, whether it be in the name of rights, religious purposes, or patriotism, to convince those who are influential that it is the honorable thing to do before the masses will respond. The masses will turn a deaf ear to any rhetoric or call that is void of purpose. They will not see any value or need to pledge their allegiance to a cause that is questionable or foolish. Even despots know that initially it is better to lead the masses who are loyal to a cause than to bully and create an environment of fear and oppression where people are being forced against their will to follow self-serving agendas.

Due to the nature of the beast, we know that under a despot an environment of fear and oppression will eventually emerge to keep the masses in order. But, the initial goal of such a wicked individual will be to first gain the allegiance of the masses to carry out his or her plan to create an environment that will allow terror to ultimately reign with a deadly iron fist.

This is the harsh reality of how easy mankind can be led down the path of destruction. We are basically sheep ready to be led away by some cause to a slaughterhouse for the wicked causes of a few. It is true, noble, and honorable causes can also produce loyalty, but those who lead in such causes are few and far between. The truth is that the dark ways of tyranny are always working under the cover of darkness. Such darkness produces treachery where fear ends up being the driving force behind the masses. No one is able to trust anyone. People end up constantly looking over their shoulders.

People must clearly own a cause to be loyal to it. It must seize their heart, not just their soul. It must be honorable for them to pledge their loyalty and worthy for them to give their lives. This is the creatures we are. Our logic deems that only fools would die for lost or dishonorable causes.

As I watch events play out on the TV screen, I can see where the masses are being stirred up by different camps. Each camp seems to present what many would consider "honorable causes." However, for the masses to make sure they are not being led as sheep to the slaughter by fools, they must stop, back up, and educate themselves as to the real issues behind the cause and the character of those who are leading the charge. They must examine their own lives and attitudes. They must consider whether they are mean spirited and looking for a fight to express pent up anger or frustration. They must be honest about the fruits such motives and causes are producing in regard to their own lives. They must consider where it is leading them. This is necessary if they are going to properly determine if the side they are on is presenting a true picture as to what is at stake. The truth is, despots need followers to carry out wicked and insane agendas. Such individuals couldn't care less about their followers and will not have any qualms about sacrificing them to obtain what is dishonorable, wicked, and destructive.

This brings us to the reality that great leaders have what I refer to as a relentless soul. It is a soul that will not relent or relinquish what it knows to be true and right. We see this relentless soul in the Apostle Paul.

The Apostle Paul is an interesting man to study. If ever a man found himself initially advocating and pursuing with such tenacity what appeared to him a right and honorable cause, only to discover he was on the wrong side, it was this man. In his mind, he believed the new religious belief of "The Way" was a complete affront to what he held dear to his heart as a devout Jew. There was no way that this new religious movement that was associated with some man named Jesus, could ever be tolerated by any sane, committed Jew. It had to be snuffed out before it could become a destructive cancer that would enslave the hearts and minds of the weak and simple. Even though his most respected teacher, Gamaliel wisely advised the religious council to let Peter and John alone, stating that if their work was of men, it would come to nothing, but if it be of God, they would not overthrow it and end up discovering that they were even fighting against God, Paul still took it on himself to wipe out the newfound faith.[1]

He was certain in his mind that he was on the right side of God. Let's face it, most people will not fight or commit themselves to something that would be considered a "wrong side." However, the despots of the world know that if they can convince others that their side is right, then it will become right in the minds of such individuals regardless of whether it is or is not. Proverbs warns man that in spite of his ways appearing to be clean and right, the spirit can be wrong and the end results destructive.[2]

Paul, whose initial name was Saul, entered the scene when the first martyr of the newfound faith was being offered up by the religious people. He held the coats of those who stoned a man whose very words had cut to the very depths of their being. Instead of recognizing it as

---

[1]   Acts 5:33-39; 21:40-22:4
[2]   Proverbs 14:12; 16:2, 25

conviction, the crowd flew into a rage. They picked up stones in the name of religion and stoned a righteous, Holy Spirit-filled man. Since they were blinded by the darkness of their own souls, they could not see what the martyr witnessed—that the Son of God was standing up to receive him into glory.[3]

No doubt it proved a magnificent time for the first martyr of the Church, Stephen, as he asked the Lord to forgive these poor misguided souls just before he entered into glory. But, for those who foolishly let blind rage rule, darkness invaded their souls in greater ways. The man, Saul was no different. He felt that their murderous actions were justified. In fact, he chose to pick up the so-called "torch". He would root out such a "contemptible," "blasphemous" belief from their midst.[4]

It was not until the light of Christ penetrated his dark soul that he realized how wrong he was.[5] The main reason people hate being wrong is because it proves to be a very humbling experience. To be wrong produces a very uncomfortable state. In such a situation people must face their guilt, be accountable for the shame it has wrought, take responsibility for the wrong it has done against others, and, if possible, take whatever necessary actions to right it. It is for this reason that people often refuse, and in some cases resolve that they will never be found wrong. Sadly, such people either go into self-delusion that sets them up to fall into utter ruin, into stifling fear that at any moment their fragile reality will cave in, or become so stiff-necked that they will prove a matter to be right regardless of how wrong it may be.

The ironic aspect of Paul's decision to rid the world of this "wicked blasphemous belief," was the very means that the Lord used to scatter His followers throughout the world. In essence, the new Church was forced out of its comfort zone by Paul's actions so that it would fulfill its commission to preach the Gospel throughout the known world. We have been told that what was intended for evil, can be turned around for good.[6] It was as though Paul was fulfilling his very calling before he was saved, by causing the spread of the message he was trying to silence for good.

---

[3]   Acts 7:54-60

[4]   Acts 8:1-4

[5]   Acts 9:1-16

[6]   Genesis 50:20

Until the light of Christ finally penetrated through Paul's darkness, no amount of logic could have stopped his relentless pursuit. It was the light of Christ that revealed how wrong Paul was. Here was a man who had been versed in prophecies that looked forward to the coming of the Messiah. When the Messiah came, this religious zealot did not even recognize who He was. His soul was so darkened by self-righteousness that it never dawned on him to think outside of his religious box and examine the evidence. Even though he was looking for the Messiah, he was not really expecting Him or he would have recognized that Jesus fit all the criteria of the Promised One. In essence, he believed, yet he did not believe. In summation, he believed the promise, but had no expectation of seeing it come to fruition. Paul had the zeal, but not the vision. As a result, he was blindsided.

The reason people are blindsided is because they are not looking in the right place, nor are they expecting to see something. Perhaps, they are assuming that they clearly see the matter in front of them; therefore, they do not have to take any further action to look beyond their present range of vision.

The light of Jesus revealed the darkness of Paul's soul and caused him to repent. He was not only brought to a standstill in relationship to his passionate pursuit, but it completely changed his attitude and momentum towards Jesus Christ. Now everything would be directed towards Him. Paul would take his zeal and passion and pursue Jesus. In fact, he would become a relentless soul in possessing Him.

Meanwhile, we must consider how a man who perceived himself to be absolutely right, be so very wrong? Paul explained the significance of his spiritual plight in 1 Timothy 1:12-16. He admitted that he was a blasphemer and persecutor of those who followed Jesus. However, he did it in ignorance. Ignorance is the main reason why many find themselves on the wrong side. The Bible clearly tells us there is none that do right, no not one.[7] It is hard for most people to realize that once brought to the light, much of their understanding and activities would prove them wrong.

We often wonder why people cannot see how wrong they are, but their darkness keeps them from seeing. The problem is not that such individuals are incapable of seeing, it is because they often refuse to see.

---

[7]   Romans 3:12

They have been conditioned or indoctrinated into their way of thinking. As a result, it is far more comfortable to prefer their particular darkness, than face the prospect of changing it. Clearly, such darkness covers their rebellion and will keep their conceit and foolishness from being exposed. Granted, there are those who delude themselves about their understanding, but most people are quite comfortable in their particular box.

According to Paul's confession in 1 Timothy 1:12-16, his ignorance about Jesus caused him to become a chief or leader in his sinful cause to rid the world of the testimony of Christ. The Apostle Paul was behind in his understanding, which caused him to be totally blindsided by the truth. It amazed me that he had not been somehow exposed to the reality of Christ. Perhaps, he had heard about Him, but if he had, he would surely have heard of the miracles that followed Him. Clearly, Paul did not grow up in our technological time where news can travel throughout the whole world in a matter of seconds. But, in each age they had their own means of informing people, and no matter how you look at it, news always travels. Obviously, something had kept him from seeing the truth about Jesus Christ.

Paul declared that in the midst of his ignorance and sin, he obtained mercy and found grace. This religious man truly found himself behind the times. It was for this reason that he stated he was born out of season. As an apostle of his times, he did not truly fit the criteria to hold such a position. To be an apostle of the New Church, he had to be with Jesus from the very beginning of His ministry to His crucifixion and His ascension to take his place as an apostle. Clearly, Paul was not with Jesus from the beginning. Nor, was he with Him during His ordeal on the cross or His ascension.[8] However, Jesus intruded into his reality as the risen Lord and Savior, the promised Messiah and called him to fulfill such a position. Paul would be identified with the rest of the apostles. Like the rest of them, he would suffer for the sake of Jesus as he proclaimed the very message he had tried to silence.

Paul went on to state that through him, the Lord in His long-suffering, would show forth a pattern to those who should hereafter believe on Him to life everlasting. Great leaders leave an indelible pattern behind for others to follow. The pattern is what serves as their real mark

---

[8]   Acts 1:21-26; 1 Corinthians 15:8

or contribution. The problem is that people often get caught up with the accomplishments of people, while failing to regard the pattern they have left behind. It is the pattern that will lead a person down a certain path that will eventually reveal the character, quality, and end product of past leadership. I look for certain patterns in people's behavior in order to possibly identify problems, attitudes, and what I discern about the mixed fruits coming from their lives.

Even the despots of the world understand the pattern they are following. The pattern will prove to be the same in each scenario as to the goals, methods, and means they will use to bring a matter about. It is for this reason that the great preacher, Solomon, declared that there is nothing new under the sun.[9] It has always been the patterns that people follow that identify their purpose, goal, and fruits. For the despot, such patterns must be kept in darkness. Once it is distinguished by the chaos it creates, the ignorance it rides on, and the wicked results it produces, those who are wise will resist and flee from it.

True leaders never will waste an opportunity to glean from their past failures in order to identify or establish a pattern that will truly benefit others. Paul was no exception. He could have been easily riddled with guilt, overcome by shame, and rendered ineffective by his actions, but he could see how all of it could be used to bring others into the kingdom of God.

It is also interesting to note how the Apostle Paul viewed his past actions. He used them to remind him that he was a chief or leader in relationship to the offense he had committed against his Lord and those who believed in Him and served Him. He was not being noble in his perspective; rather, he was being quite realistic. In my case, I had to become chief in regard to my sin because there is no one else to compare the degrees of it in relationship to the price of redemption.

The truth is we each stand alone in regard to our sin. Without any contrast other than Jesus, without any other recourse other than the work accomplished on a rugged cross, and without any measure of faith to embrace it, we stand alone in judgment before a holy, righteous Judge. As we stand alone in judgment, we will stand as chief in light of the offences committed towards Him, as a leader in the reality of our rebellion, and as the greatest fool in lieu of our unbelief. There will be no

---

[9]   Ecclesiastes 1:9

one who stands with us, behind us, or in front of us. We alone will hold the spot of preeminence as we face the judge of our souls. Such a reality should strip us of any fake nobility we might adopt towards our moral indiscretions, any false pretense about our spiritual status, and rid us of any cloak of self-righteousness that hides the ways of death and decay. Such knowledge should cause us to tremble in dread of facing our judge without first obtaining His mercy, and knowing that ultimately His grace will meet us in the form of eternal life.

The Apostle Paul also kept his reality as a chief of sinner in check so that he would always have a place of humility to come back to. As Peter had to admit to Jesus, those who have been forgiven much have the greatest love and appreciation towards the one who showed them such underserved favor. In his epistle, Peter reiterated this principle by stating that those who are barren in their knowledge of Jesus are so because they have forgotten that they have been purged from their sin.[10]

In humility we have the necessary premise to remember we have been forgiven of grave offenses. We have been saved from the torment of spiritual bondage, and we are constantly being saved from the entanglements of the "old man", as we are ultimately spared from experiencing in the future the fires of hell and damnation. Not only do we have the justification wrought by salvation, and the sanctification established in salvation, but we look towards the glorification that will be realized because of salvation.

Paul understood in part the great forgiveness and salvation he had received when he believed. His love for Jesus compelled him to constantly walk towards his demise. He stated it was not his life that he lived, but the life of Christ in him. No sacrifice was too great for him to offer to his Lord. After all, he totally consecrated his life to the cause of Christ and Him crucified. Like Enoch, his fervor would lead him to a place where he was no more, and all that remained was the reality of his Lord. No challenge became unbearable when it came to possessing what Paul had in Christ. He simply counted everything associated with his former life as dung as he became more identified with His Lord in His death, burial, and resurrection. There was nothing worth holding onto if it meant that Paul would fail to obtain the excellence of the knowledge of

---

[10] Luke 7:40-47; 2 Peter 1:8-10

Christ that he was striving for. He would simply press forward in greater measure in relationship to his high calling.[11]

This was the essence of Paul. He may have started out a "Saul," who initially proved to be desirable to the Jewish leadership, but became a "Paul," considered small, little, or contemptible as an apostle of Jesus. This small man proved that outward status had no significance. In Christ the small man did great things on behalf of his Lord in the power of the Spirit.[12] Even though he started many local churches and influenced many people in his life of ministry, Paul was not looking for a following for himself. He stood against those who, like even Peter on one occasion, resorted to confusing the issues and integrity of the Christian faith. He would not accept anything less but that which displayed an excellent commitment towards Jesus. However, if people followed him, they were to do so as he followed Christ. They were not to assume that his example or leadership was sure, for he had been wrong in the past. He wanted them to be as the Bereans, who studied the Scriptures and made sure that those who were trying to influence them in religious matters came from God.[13] He had no real concern about the personal mark he left on others, for all he cared about was the eternal mark of Christ's life that had to be present upon the hearts and minds of men before they entered eternity.

Paul was forever decreasing in his life. He had fellowship in Jesus' sufferings and conformed his life to His death in order to know Him and the power of His resurrection.[14] He did not want people to remember him for his preaching or his devotion to the One who was worthy of such dedication. He wanted them to know, love, and serve the One he was proclaiming.

When the Apostle Paul was about to offer the last abyss of his life up on the altar of Caesar, there was one reality he had secured in his relentless soul: that he would be in the presence of His Lord. He knew that he had fought a good fight, finished the course set before him, and kept the faith. As a result, he would receive the crown of righteousness.

---

[11]   Genesis 5:24; 1 Corinthians 15:31; Galatians 2:20; Philippians 3:7-8, 10, 14

[12]   The meaning of the names "Saul" and "Paul" were obtained from the Smith's Bible Dictionary.

[13]   Acts 15:36-41; 17:10-11; 1 Corinthians 2:2; 11:1; 2 Corinthians 10:7-18; Galatians 2:1-8; 1 Thessalonians 1:5

[14]   Philippians 3:10

His love would be realized, his diligence rewarded, and his service completed. He would know that there was nothing else he could offer or do because his relentless soul would not only be satisfied, but it would come to the place of promise: The complete rest, which will only be found in the glory of every believer's immortal, invisible, eternal King and only wise God, the Lord Jesus Christ.[15]

---

[15] 2 Corinthians 5:6-9; 1 Timothy 1:17; 2 Timothy 4:6-8

10

Overcoming Souls

As I have been studying the concept of great leadership, I realize that greatness is often born out of utter defeat. To me one of the greatest feats ever accomplished occurred after what appeared to be the greatest defeat the world had ever witnessed. It was as if evil had triumphed over good, and wickedness over righteousness to drown out all possibilities of hope. It was as though the idea that justice would eventually triumph over great injustices was proven to be a mockery, foolish, and immature. The event I am making reference to is the cross of Jesus.

From all appearances, Christ and all that He advocated, was lost the night He hung on the cross. To His disciples, their devotion to Him must have become a point of mockery and torment in their minds as they wrestled in the darkness of the night. To the women who mourned at the foot of the cross, all appeared lost and hopeless. No doubt the devils danced, His religious opposition congratulated each other for their clever moves, and others may have sighed a breath of relief that it was over with.

However, it was not over with. Jesus' death marked the beginning of the kingdom of God coming forth in greater measure. Three days later He would rise from the grave. He would be the firstfruits of an invisible kingdom and the first-born of a new creation that would rise out of the death and destruction wrought by sin and rebellion. He would become the way for others to be born anew with the very Spirit of God. He would become the truth as to the new creation that would be unveiled, and a new life that would be realized in light of His unfolding glory.[1]

As we consider and follow Jesus in His humanity, we must realize that He had to face the obstacles in front of Him as man. The Bible is clear, He was tempted in every way that we are, except He did not sin. We are told He feared that He might not finish the course because He understood that no matter how great the resolve of man was, the flesh remains weak. We know in His humanity that He had to learn

---

[1]   John 14:6; 1 Corinthians 15:20-24; Colossians 1:15

obedience through suffering in order to be made perfect as a means to become the author of our salvation.[2] In His own example, Jesus reveals that great leaders must first face and overcome their own flaws, fears, and uncertainties to ensure the steadfastness of their devotion, the unwavering passion for honorable principles, and the endurance to see a matter through to the end no matter the price, time, or energy.

Leaders who leave an imprint on man or history do so because of the legacy they leave. Although they may have been known, identified, or associated by their names, they are going to be remembered by the examples, patterns, and fruits that follow them. Even though in certain arenas the very mention of certain individuals is cause for some to spit out their names as they are remembered as utter fools, contemptible as to the legacy they left behind, other individuals will be regarded as being great because of who they were. They left a legacy that remains undisputable as to the way that others must follow to arrive at the place of greatness.

The reality of greatness is that it will be based on is the type of witness it leaves behind. Often such a legacy of greatness is riddled with what appears to be failures. However, it is in times of what appears to be utter failure that immense opportunity presents itself. The opportunity I speak of has to do with the forging of character that comes with adversity. To me, much of what we might deem as success comes from learning what not to do versus what to do. However, a person cannot learn what not to do unless he or she is willing to fail in the process of doing.

People want guarantees in life that they will not fail before they explore uncharted territories. But, all greatness is a matter of gambling according to the opportunities presented in order to obtain what is better or excellent. For those who understand the significance of both failure and success, they will tell you it is not as much about the end results as it is about the journey. Defeat teaches us great lessons, while success allows us to partake of the benefits of what proves to be worthy and excellent.

This is also true for those who are named in the Bible. Their lives and examples leave a witness behind that is to be read, pondered, considered, and tested by those who lay claim to the truths and principles of the Word of God. In many ways, much of what the saints

---

[2]   Matthew 26:41; Hebrews 4:15; 5:7-9

of old encountered made them occasionally appear as if they were utter failures. However, their faith and devotion led them out of the despair of failure to a place of victory.

There were also those examples in Scripture of what to avoid or refrain from doing. Each life left an imprint or mark recorded in the Bible that would serve as a witness or testimony to those who dare to follow in such people's footprints. Whether it is a good witness, a mediocre example, or a wicked testimony, each person recorded in the pages of the Scripture continues to serve as a point of establishing scriptural responsibility (doctrine), as well as reproof (a place of accountability), correction, and instruction in righteousness.[3]

The Bible actually mentions the righteous witness that was clearly established in Scripture. It is referred to as the great cloud of witnesses. Consider what Hebrews 12:1 states, "Wherefore seeing we also are compassed about with so great a cloud of witnesses, let us lay aside every weight, and the sin which doth so easily beset us, and let us run with patience the race that is set before us."

The writer of Hebrews is laying out an important pattern. First, there will be no excuse as to why we, as believers, will fail to possess the promises of heaven. We already know according to Hebrews 6:12 that we must not be slothful in becoming followers of those who through faith and patience inherit the promises of God. In fact, according to Hebrews 12:1, we have been compassed about with a great cloud of witnesses that clearly show us how we can inherit the promises of God. However, we must lay aside all the excess weight of sin and the world, and begin running with patience the course or race that is set before us.

People have a tendency to start a race carrying a big bag of the old, worldly life that amounts to vanity. This was true in my situation. It took me years to rid myself of the baggage that clung to me. However, like many Christians, I had to learn to let go of such baggage. As I look back, I can see how I have left much of the weight of my past in the barren wilderness of the world.

As the race intensifies in their lives, Christian runners will have to make one of two decisions in relationship to the bag of burdens, responsibilities, worldly attachments, and demands they are carrying. They will either have to cast the bag aside to finish the race, or they will

---

[3]   2 Timothy 3:16

end up turning back, with their bag in hand, and altogether cease to run the race.

When you consider the wilderness, the Lord was trying to loosen and shake the bag of slavery and worldly associations off of the backs of the children of Israel. He wanted them free to embrace the new life He had promised them. He knew as long as they carried the old, they would never embrace or appreciate the new.

Most of our journey through this world is about us leaving the old behind to embrace the new. It seems like the old clings to us like grave clothes. It is forever associating us to the ways of sin and death. Even though the wilderness experiences can be related to the grave, our old life still clings to us as grave clothes even in the midst of the stench of death and decay.

In order to study the cloud of witnesses, we must study Hebrews 11. The reality of the cloud of witnesses is that they were able to run the race because of their faith towards the Lord. They lived in light of the abiding confidence they had in their God, walked according to expectation of a future world, and proved diligent in their hope of possessing that which was excellent.

As we study the cloud of witnesses, we will see that genuine faith towards the God of heaven inspired their character, attitude, and devotion. We know it is because of faith that Abel offered a more excellent sacrifice. Due to his faith, Enoch was translated from the present world into the next. It was because of faith that Noah prepared for the flood and became heir of righteousness.

Surely, most religious people know of Abraham. He was truly a man of faith. We see that it was because he believed God that he obeyed Him. Even though he would see the land that his descendants would inherit, his hope, confidence, and expectation rested in the city that awaited him in the world that was yet to come. He ultimately died without even receiving the promises, but his faith allowed him to see the promises from afar off in the form of figures, types, and shadows.

Many of the people of faith blessed others based on promises yet to come. Such individuals believed that all would be fulfilled even when it seem impossible to the naked eye. Like Joseph, in regard to his remains being taken to the Promised Land long after his death, many will commit matters to future generations as a testimony of their confidence in God keeping His promises.

When we consider Moses, we see a man who refused to be called the son of Pharaoh's daughter. Instead, he chose to be identified with the affliction of his own people. He could have enjoyed sin for a season, but he realized there were greater riches awaiting him.

It was a matter of faith when the children of Israel passed through the Red Sea, and a new generation believed that the walls of Jericho would not be able to stand against the advancement of God. It was simple faith that caused Rahab to risk her old life in order to gain a new life. For others it was their faith towards God that allowed them to subdue kingdoms, work righteousness, obtain promises, stop the mouths of lions, quench the violence of fire, escape the edge of the sword, and became valiant in victory. Some even received their dead back to life.

As you study the lives of these people, they were always walking towards their demise in light of gaining that which was eternal. Their vision went beyond the present world to embrace another world. They never thought in terms of what they could lose, but what they might fail to gain. They did not get caught up with the logic of the impossible; rather, they maintained the possibilities of what could be obtained by pursuing the excellent.

These people's vision sustained them as some were tortured, others endured trials of cruel mocking and scourging, while others were stoned, sawn asunder, slain with the sword, and were often found to be imprisoned, destitute, afflicted, and tormented. They were forced to wander as strangers, fugitives, and sojourners in a world that had no tolerance towards their type of devotion.

Clearly, their vision of the next world caused them to walk in indifference to their present age. Abraham was looking for a city made with the actual hands of God. Until then, he would be confident and relentless in his pursuits to possess his heavenly portion. For Moses, he would not bring a reproach to the promise of God for he was aware of the excellence of the future reward that awaited him. These people were aware that something better was being prepared for them. They were conscious of the fact that more excellent things awaited them, but they had to allow themselves to be perfected by some form of affliction in the midst of an imperfect world.

In certain instances, some of these individuals refused to accept deliverance, knowing that they had the possibility of obtaining a greater resurrection. These stout, unwavering giants of faith could not be swayed from the eternal prospects of what had been promised them. It is not that they were after that which would serve their purpose the most; rather, they did not want to possess something of lesser quality. The heavenly realm offered them what was and is excellent, but they had to rise up to the occasion of such excellence if they were going to embrace it for themselves.

When you study the motivation of great, honorable leaders, you realize that they possess a faith towards the providence of an unseen hand. In the minds of these individuals, this unseen hand would hold them accountable for the person they became and the actions they would take in securing what they perceived to be honorable and worthy of all dedication and sacrifice. Such individuals could not allow themselves to betray what they knew to be right. Due to their past experiences, they knew how to count the cost to possess what was excellent, regardless of the sacrifice. As a result, they learned how to overcome personal indiscretions, impossible odds, and failures that seemed to dog every step they took.

Today, the world may consider such individuals as failures. After all, how many lost their lives as their blood was spilled out on the land? In many ways, these people were offered up on the various altars of the world. We see this in the case of many of the followers of God. From all appearances, the lives of Jesus, Peter, and Paul would appear as a waste since they were offered up by the age they lived in. However, heaven does not see it that way. In spite of the humanness they had to overcome, they finished the course set before them. For Jesus, the course included the cross. For Peter, his course on this earth ended with the cross. In the case of the Apostle Paul, he was forever applying the cross. Regardless of where the cross is located in our course, it is something we all must face. We must not try to sidestep the cross of Jesus, veer away from our personal cross, or cast it aside because it is unpleasant. We must become identified with Jesus and His cross, embrace our personal cross, and be quick to apply it when we are being tested to betray what we know is true and right. And, yes we must allow the cross to signal our possible defeat and our inevitable demise in order for us to become victorious souls in the kingdom of God.

One of the challenges that I am often confronted with is found in Hebrews 11:38-40,

(Of whom the world was not worthy:) they wandered in deserts, and in mountains, and in dens and caves of the earth. And these all, having obtained a good report through faith, received not the promise: God having provided some better thing for us, that they without us should not be made perfect.

As you consider these Scriptures, what challenge do they pose to you? To me, the challenge is to possess a faith that even the world is not worthy to witness. In fact, such a faith is lost to the world by the vastness of its own barren deserts, obscured from it by the shadows cast by its various mountains of arrogance, and hidden away from it in the dens and caves of indifference. Even though such individuals possess a good report, it is one the world would shun and mock. Although such individuals cannot be moved from standing in light of the promises of God, the world will call such loyalty insane and foolish. However, what the world intends for evil, God will use to bring forth His saints in perfection. Such perfection will prepare them to embrace that which is better and partake of that which is excellent.

As a believer, have you accepted the real challenge of genuine faith? I do not know about you, but in the end I want to embrace what is better and partake of that which is excellent. Once I have received the best, I want to turn around and offer it all back to the Lord, knowing that He alone is worthy of that which is far better in quality, and will ultimately speak of the excellence that is attached to that which is heavenly and eternal.

11

The Beautiful Soul

We have been considering the qualities of a true leader. A tyrant or a despot can lead men, but not just anyone can be a true leader. True leadership is not equated by how many people follow; rather, it comes down to the impact man's footsteps leave on the hearts and minds of those who follow.

Perhaps only one man has followed in the footsteps of a great leader. However, that one man was so-inspired and impacted by the honorable example of the one he followed that he in turn impacted others in a powerful way. Once again, true leaders can only be inspired by that which is worthy of consideration, greater than they, and honorable and pure in its intentions. For this reason, true leaders will often leave a legacy while remaining unknown and obscure to even those of future generations who become impacted by their lives. But, because of the greatness of one man, his legacy and works will not only follow him, but they will mark his greatness by the quality of fruit that is ultimately produced and left behind.

The Bible talks about those whose works follow them. Such individuals may not be known by name, but the fruits of their leadership continue to benefit and nourish future generations. These individuals may have been unassuming in their life, but the legacy they leave speaks of excellence. They may not have sought recognition or pursued the arrogant ways of self-glory, but by being who they naturally were in every day life, they left a footprint on the lives of others. Such individuals always proved to be true to their character, calling, and vision; and, when challenged, they would never compromise their way or approach.

In many ways, these individuals were unseen because their uniqueness or quality pointed to something that cannot be explained or summarized. Their character spoke of that which was greater than they, their calling inspired by something unseen and unknown by most people, and their vision embraced that which proved to be of another dimension.

For me, there are few people who stand out in my life. There was my fourth grade teacher, Mrs. Rue, who showed me kindness by providing me with new tennis shoes to replace the flopping soul of my tattered old ones, as well as provided me with school materials. To this day I have no idea how she knew I needed such things, but she proved that she was aware and cared. Her acts showed me how far kindness can reach into one's life and character.

There were the Munyon cousins, Joan and Mary Ellen, who led me to Christ and went beyond the extra mile to take me to church. There are those spiritual giants that have influenced me through the stories of their lives and their inspired writings such as Oswald Chambers and A. W. Tozer. When I count the people who have made lasting impressions on my life in such a way, they are few. However, their impressions have so impacted me that they have left an imprint on my heart and soul.

As I consider the impact made by these people, I realize that there was some type of death that occurred. Perhaps the individual has long passed from this world, but their works have followed them. Maybe, the vision or works of these people suffered some type of loss or death where eventually their excellence caused them to rise up out of the ashes of obscurity, producing a tremendous impact on people's lives for generations to come. It is the mark of great loss or death upon such matters that causes inspired works to be prized or valued. Once valued or prized, such lives or works bring appreciation or recognition to those who benefitted from these people's examples, experiences, and lives.

The reality is that such recognition is what truly brings glory to God. What death unveils about such a person is that he or she had a beautiful soul. It reminds me of the story of Dorcus (Tabitha).[1] In life Dorcus quietly served others. She was not seeking recognition for her service; she simply did what was within her heart to do. I am sure she thought nothing about what she did in regard to others. She was a servant at heart who was doing her Christian duty as she lovingly served God. However, after her death, her service was so greatly prized by others that they showed the Apostle Peter all the work she had done. In the power of God, he raised her from the dead so that she could continue to serve. Can you imagine how Dorcus might have felt when Peter called

---

[1]   Acts 9:36-41

her forth from the grave of death to continue service that was so greatly prized by others?

When studying the founding fathers of America, many were called back to serve "their country" either on the federal, state, or local levels. These men were highly prized for their leadership by those they had sacrificially served in the past. They were willing to fade into obscurity after America came forth as a nation, only to be called forth from any type of "retirement," to once again take the forefront. Some even died while in office.

So many people live on what is considered the "mediocre" level. They go from day to day just trying to survive or get by. There is nothing that is greatly prized in their life that would inspire them to excellence. Granted, they may have wondrous goals, but such goals do not mark what others would prize.

Great leaders are always marked by that which others would prize. These individuals do not see what others would value for they are just who they are. It is not just what they did, but the trustworthy, excellent manner in which they did it.

The fact that these types of people possess what others highly value once again points to their beautiful souls. There have been many such souls, some known, others unknown. These individuals in some way managed to accomplish and ensure that which proved to be excellent in the end. Granted, the wicked infidel would attempt to tarnish and do away with that which would expose their own foolish, treacherous ways, but even in such attempts the truth about the debauchery of these people's character and ways will eventually rise out of the ashes to reveal their deadly fruits. The fruits will clearly reveal the foolish ways of those bent on destroying the legacy of that which is decent and honorable. You cannot keep honorable legacies buried for they have been recorded in the hearts and minds of those who were compelled by their greatness.

Once again, it is not the person who will be preserved, but his or her legacy. The person will have gone on from this present world, while his or her legacy continues on.

The most beautiful soul who left the greatest legacy was a man named Jesus Christ. What a stunning soul He possessed. In His time on earth He never led any great army. He invited those who appeared to be base, despised, and foolish to learn about His humble, lowly disposition and meek attitude, in order to follow Him into an incredible life.

Through the centuries men have been instructed to consider the manner in which Jesus responded to even His opposition. Granted, He showed a fervent passion when He turned over the tables in the temple. However, it was in relationship to how men were regarding the matters of men's souls. They were not only using the things of God to make money in His own house that was intended for prayer, but they were making merchandise of men's souls who were vulnerable to the religious environment. We see Him rebuking the religious leaders for putting unbearable burdens on their followers and leading them into a damnable ditch of judgment. He called His disciples to follow the narrow, path His legacy would carve in history. The path His legacy left behind marked the approach by which man would find the means to embark upon the ways eternity.[2]

From the very beginning of His entrance into history, Jesus was marked by death. From all appearances, His work was destroyed as His life was offered up on a cross. Mocked, spit upon, and beaten by those who hated Him or felt threatened by His light, potential, and promise, He was put in the silent, barren grave of obscurity. But, the grave could not hold Him. He rose three days later, proving that great legacies will rise out of ashes and shine through the worst of darkness to once again lead men through the dark trying times of their souls. He indeed left an indelible example that, we who follow it, must not only embrace, but choose to remember such a path and follow in its way when we stand at the crossroads of sacrifice and death.

Once the seeking heart sees the life attached to such a legacy as Jesus, it cannot but embrace it with utter abandonment. The world around those who seek such a legacy will truly grow dim as heaven unfolds before these individuals. Granted, the salve of truth must heal their eyes so they can see, and the sweet voice of the Spirit must penetrate the clanging sounds of the world so they can hear. But, once the healing ways of the excellent legacy of heaven penetrates their hearts and spirits, there is no denying that the prophecy in Isaiah 9:6 was correct when it declared that one of Jesus' names would be, "Wonderful".

The word "wonderful" ascribes to that which is indescribable. His very being and work are too beautiful and magnificent to capture with mere words or even thoughts. His ways are too excellent to not properly

---

[2]   Matthew 11:28-29; 1 John 2:6

pursue Him with all the passion and intent of possessing what the Bible describes as the "Pearl of Great Price."[3] His example is too glorious to forget and will be quickly recalled by the tender heart when everything has settled into a state of mediocrity. His way of living and service can even be called to the forefront to be written on the hearts and minds of those who have truly sought after it in order to possess it.

I do not know about you, but it matters little how long the light of our lives burns in this world, but it does matter what legacy we fan into a burning passion. Some allow the fuse of power and greed to fan their light. It might burn hot, but it will prove to be a flash in the pan.

Some people might seek after the stuff or material means of the world, but eventually they find that it was a worthless pursuit that hid the bitterness of vanity. As soon as their fire encounters the shadowiness and emptiness of it all, it will be quickly snuffed out by the lack of life. It will not even leave a flicker.

As others seek after the false promises of the world to ensure their legacy, they likewise will discover that there is no substance, mark of death, or eternal identification of excellence to their heritage. There is no real wisdom or purpose to what they have pursued. They will discover that there is no legacy at the end to pass on.

At such times, some people who have the wisdom of their wits about them will honestly examine this matter as they face their own mortality. They will realize their main challenge in this world was to leave a legacy that would prove not only to be bigger than their own life, but would result in their lives being consumed by it. Like Enoch, they are "no more" because they have been translated by that which is eternal.

In most cases, those who eventually partake or benefit from an excellent legacy would not even know the names of those who were the inspiration behind it, but it will not matter one way or the other to those who inspire the legacy. What matters to such a beautiful soul is not that his or her name is remembered, but that the integrity of the legacy has been preserved and brought forth through the next generation. Such a legacy will require each new generation to always reach for that which will bring glory to our Creator. It will possess heavenly inspiration to produce beautiful souls, create excellent spirits, inspire impeccable

---

[3]   Matthew 13:45-46

character, develop glorious visions, and the ability to discern and recognize worthy pursuits.

Such legacies are what allow those who are designed, or intended to be great leaders, to emerge and lead others to either pursue, fight for, or make the necessary sacrifice for that which is worthy. Such people's names may not be recorded in history books, but the legacy they leave behind continues to speak volumes about their character, vision, and sacrifice.

As we consider the beautiful soul, it brings us to a personal crossroad. What type of legacy do we want our lives to be consumed by? Perhaps to the reader, like the profane Esau, you have no real regard or concern for what legacy you are leaving behind. It was not until Esau was faced with the harsh reality of what he lost that he showed any regret. However, such remorse proved selfish, worldly, and profane. In the end, he was not able to partake of the blessings associated with the real legacy.[4]

Perhaps your pursuit has been the things of the world, and it is no real concern to you whether your life speaks of any real excellence or purpose after you pass through the corridors of history and time. It will not matter whether any of your works or activities continue on in the hearts and minds of those who knew you best. And, since you really do not care whether or not God concerns Himself with such matters, you have no real concern for your eternal outcome either.

The Bible is clear that only the meek will inherit the earth, and those who are wicked will not only discover they are not in line to inherit anything that is of a heavenly nature, but will find that in the end their very names will be remembered no more. All remembrance of them will be wiped out. It will be as though they never lived. The mark of their footprint on history will be forever swept away by the winds of judgment, and all that they have done will turn to ashes as God's holy fire burns and consumes their works in His wrath.[5]

If you fall into the latter category, my advice to you is to cease from being an utter fool before God. Turn from your hard hearted, unbelieving ways of rebellion in repentance. Run as fast as you can to the mercy seat of God, broken by your arrogance, abhorring your foolishness, and

---

4   Hebrews 12:16-17
5   Matthew 5:5; 1 Thessalonians 5:9; Hebrews 12:27-29; Revelation 20:7-15; 21:4

trembling over your stiff-necked ways, and seek His mercy, and plead for His forgiveness as you acknowledge that you are worthy of tasting every kind of conceivable damnation. Do it now before it is too late or you find yourself being required to pay the penalty for your folly: your very soul.

Perhaps you have already been to the mercy seat of God, but upon examination of your life you find it to have been mediocre. In all honesty, there is no evidence of a lasting legacy that has been clearly established by your life in regard to eternity. Maybe you have even tried to establish one, but there was something lacking. You could be standing at some type of crossroads.

When I come to such a crossroad, I remember Joshua.[6] He presented two distinct choices in regard to who people would serve. They can serve the pagan gods of the Amorites, or Jehovah God. Clearly, there is only one right choice and that is to be part of the legacy clearly established by God. However, such a legacy rests on the other side of the Jordan. It will never be found in this world and it will never be bought forth by combining the things of the world with the things of God. There must be a separation of the holy from the profane, the spiritual from the fleshly, and the heavenly from the earthly. One way will be marked by vanity, wickedness, and death, while the other will be marked by Spirit, life, and promises. One will cease to be remembered, and the other will be part of a spiritual legacy that will forever live in the corridors of eternity. One legacy will be eternally mocked by the damnation of hell, and the other will continue to be unveiled and brought forth by the glorious revelation of heaven. One legacy will reveal the insidious wretchedness of the wicked, and the other the beautiful souls forged by the abiding work of God.

Those who possess the wretched soul, will be consumed by hell, while the beautiful soul will fulfill the purpose that was ordained before the foundation of the world. Granted, the beautiful soul will be marked by death, but it will possess the very resurrection power that will raise it up out of the ashes of obscurity to become the expression of the very glory of God. Such an expression will prove to be too wondrous to imagine and too glorious to describe.

---

[6]   Joshua 24:14-16

Will you not accept the challenge? Who knows, maybe you will be named among those whose leadership led others to greatness. Perhaps it will be said of you that you indeed possessed a beautiful soul; a soul that had been birthed in the Spirit, nurtured by the life of Christ, and developed in the secret places of testing, refinement, and death. It was a soul that clearly had been brought forth from the grave by the very resurrection power of the Spirit, allowing you to take your place among the most lowly in God's kingdom, only to be exalted into the very heavenly places of greatness in Christ Jesus.

BIBLIOGRAPHY

Strong's Exhaustive Concordance of the Bible; Word Bible Publishers

Smith's Bible Dictionary, William Smith, Thomas Nelson Publishers

Other books by Rayola Kelley:

Hidden Manna
Battle for the Soul
Nuggets From Heaven
More Nuggets From Heaven
Volume One: Establishing Our Life in Christ
My Words are Spirit and Life
The Anatomy of Sin
The Principles of the Abundant Life
The Place of Covenant
Unmasking the Cult Mentality
Volume Two: Putting on the Life of Christ
He Actually Thought it Not Robbery
Revelation of the Cross
In Search of Real Faith
Think on These Things
Follow the Pattern
Volume Three: Developing a Godly Environment
Godly Discipline
Prayer and Worship
Don't Touch That Dial
Face of Thankfulness
ABC's of Christianity
Volume Four: Issues of the Heart
Hidden Manna (Revised)
Bring Down the Sacred Cows
The Manual for the Single Christian Life
Parents are People Too
Volume Five: Challenging the Christian Life
The Issues of Life
Presentation of the Gospel
For the Purpose of Edification
Whatever Happened to the Church?
Women's Place in the Kingdom of God
Volume Six: Developing Our Christian Life
The Many Faces of Christianity
Possessing Our Souls

Experiencing the Christian Life
The Power of Our Testimonies
The Victorious Journey
Volume Seven: Discovering True Ministry
From Prisons and Dots to Christianity
So You Want To Be In Ministry?
Devotions
Devotions of the Heart: Book One
Daily Food for the Soul

Gentle Shepherd Ministries Devotion Series:
Being a Child of God
Disciplining the Strength of our Youth
Coming to Full Age
Gentle Shepherd Ministries Series
The Christian Life Series